CONTENTS

T0386087

Focus 3 Workbook walkthrough

UNITS (pp. 4–115)

UNITS 1–8

BACK OF THE BOOK (pp. 116–175)

The VOCABULARY BANK is a topic-based word list including vocabulary from all units. It is followed by exercises which provide more vocabulary practice.

Focus 2 Grammar Review contains grammar explanations and revision of the grammar taught in level 2.

The GRAMMAR: Train and Try Again section provides more grammar activities for self-study.

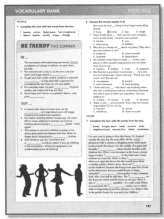

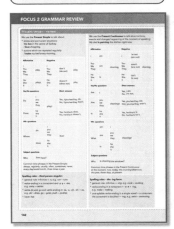

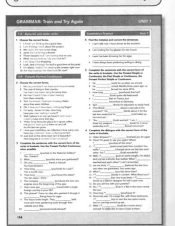

The WRITING BANK provides a list of the useful phrases from the WRITING FOCUS boxes in the Student's Book.

The answer keys to the Focus 2 Grammar Review, Self-check and GRAMMAR: Train and Try Again sections support self-study and promote student autonomy.

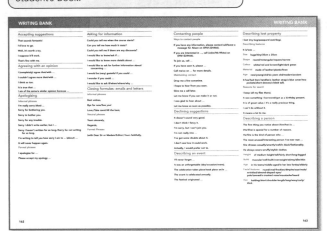

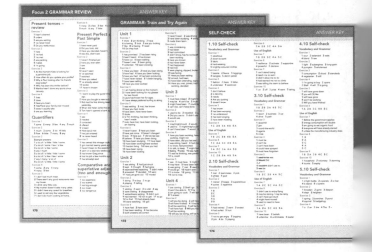

DON'T MISS

The SHOW WHAT YOU KNOW tasks in the Vocabulary and Grammar lessons serve as a warm-up and revise vocabulary or grammar students should already know.

The SHOW WHAT YOU'VE LEARNT tasks in the Vocabulary and Grammar lessons help students to check their progress and be aware of their own learning.

The SHOW THAT YOU'VE CHECKED section in the Writing lessons is a useful checklist that accompanies the final writing task.

SHOW WHAT YOU KNOW

1 Label the forms of transport. The first letters are given.

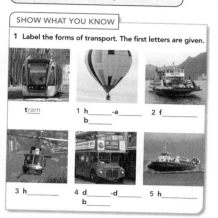

t*ram*

1 h_____-a
b_____

2 f_____

3 h_____

4 d_____-d
b_____

5 h_____

SHOW WHAT YOU'VE LEARNT

5 Find and correct the mistakes.

I played rugby when I broke my arm. *was playing*

1 We went to the Alps in April, but we couldn't ski because the snow already melted. _____
2 I watched the race when Hope won the gold medal and broke the world record. _____
3 Were City beating Arsenal in last night's game? _____
4 The referee didn't concentrate when Burton touched the ball with his hand. _____
5 In yesterday's Brazilian Grand Prix, Lewis was finishing in second place. _____
6 Boxer Joe Foster was fighting over 100 opponents when he retired in 1994. _____

/6

GRAMMAR: Train and Try Again page 155

SHOW THAT YOU'VE CHECKED

Finished? Always check your writing. Can you tick √ everything on this list?

In my 'for and against' essay:

- the first paragraph begins with general or factual comments about the topic. ☐
- the first paragraph ends with a statement that mentions both sides of the issue. ☐
- the second paragraph presents arguments for the topic and supports them with examples. ☐
- the third paragraph presents arguments against the topic and supports them with examples. ☐
- the final paragraph includes a summarising statement and my personal opinion. ☐
- I have not used contractions (e.g. *I'm* / *aren't* / *that's*) or abbreviations (*info* / *CU* / v. *good*). ☐
- I have checked my spelling. ☐
- My text is neat and clear. ☐

The REMEMBER BETTER boxes provide tips on learning, remembering and enriching vocabulary.

The REMEMBER THIS boxes focus on useful language nuances.

The star coding system shows the different levels of difficulty of the activities in the Grammar lessons.

REMEMBER BETTER

Try to learn phrases rather than single words. This will help you in exam tasks where you have to fill in gaps. Often the missing word will form a fixed phrase with other words that appear before and after the gap.

Complete the sentences with the correct form of a phrase in bold from the extract in Exercise 1.

Everybody gets spots sometimes no matter how often they wash their face. *It just happens naturally.*

1 All good things must come to an end. Nothing _____ .
2 A couple should _____ extremely well before they get engaged.
3 _____ to qualify as a lawyer or a doctor.
4 Colin _____ to talk to girls. He gets embarrassed very easily.
5 I'm afraid I can't _____ with anyone who turns out to be untrustworthy.

REMEMBER THIS

Adverbs of manner tell us how we do an action. We form adverbs by adding *-ly* to adjectives, or *-ily* to adjectives ending in *-y*. (*quick – quickly, cheeky – cheekily*). We make online friends very quick + ly.

The adverb from from *good* is *well*.
How *good + ly well* do you know them?

Some irregular adverbs (*early, fast, hard, high, late, long* and *low*) have the same form as the adjective.
It takes a **long** time to become close friends. (adj)
Making online friends … doesn't take **long** at all. (adv)

2 ★ Complete the second sentence with *must*, *might* or *can't*.

1 It's possible that's our taxi.   That *might* be our taxi.
2 I'm sure that's our plane.   That _____ be our plane.
3 I'm sure those aren't our bags.   Those _____ be our bags.
4 It's possible this is the hotel.   This _____ be the hotel.
5 I'm sure this is our room.   This _____ be our room.
6 We're sure that isn't our bill.   That _____ be our bill.

3 ★ Match the sentences in Exercise 2 with the evidence below.

A I ordered it for ten o'clock and it's five to ten now. ☐1
B It was definitely number 321. ☐
C I think I recognise it from the picture on the website. ☐
D We are flying with Lufthansa, aren't we? ☐
E We certainly didn't order room service 5 times. ☐
F Our suitcases are blue, not black. ☐

4 ★ ★ Choose the correct forms.

At the aquarium …
Nick: Look! An octopus.
Anne: Where? I can't see anything.
Nick: Er … well, the sign says there's an octopus, so it ¹*must* / *couldn't* be there somewhere.
Anne: I suppose it ²*can't* / *might* be hiding under that rock.
Nick: Yeah, or it ³*could* / *couldn't* be away on holiday …
Anne: On holiday? You ⁴*might* / *can't* be serious. Honestly, I worry about you, Nick.
Nick: It says here that octopuses can change the colour of their skin and totally disappear. Cool. I'd love to be able to do that.
Anne: Nick, sometimes I think that would be a good idea.

The SPEAKING BANK lists the key phrases from the Speaking lesson.

Speaking tasks in the exam format help students to prepare for their exams.

SPEAKING BANK

Treatment

You need to take antibiotics. _____

You need to put a fresh bandage / a plaster on it. _____

You need a few stitches. _____

I need to check your blood pressure / pulse, etc. _____

I don't think you need an X-ray / operation, etc. _____

I'm not going to give you an injection. _____

We need to bring the swelling down. _____

You need to take painkillers to ease the pain. _____

You need to put ice / ointment, etc. on your ankle. _____

1 A new look

VOCABULARY

1.1

Clothes and accessories
• fashion and style • personality

SHOW WHAT YOU KNOW

1 Match the words from the box with the people in the photos. Some words can go with more than one photo. There is one extra word.

> a pair of jeans belt boots curly cheerful
> earring glasses hoodie jacket long
> outgoing relaxed ring serious shirt short
> sociable straight top trainers watch

1 Emma

2 Meg

3 Ryan

1 _____
_____

2 _a pair of jeans_
_____

3 _a pair of jeans_
_____

2 Write the opposites. The first and last letters are given.

tall	≠	s h o r t
1 caring	≠	s _ _ _ _ _ h
2 hard-working	≠	l _ _ y
3 outgoing	≠	s _ y
4 mean	≠	g _ _ _ _ _ _ s
5 cheerful	≠	m _ _ _ _ _ _ _ e
6 silly	≠	s _ _ _ _ _ e
7 curly	≠	s _ _ _ _ _ t
8 fair	≠	d _ _ k
9 ugly	≠	h _ _ _ _ _ e

WORD STORE 1A | Clothes and accessories

3 Read the definitions. Write the names of clothes and accessories.

This round and often tight-fitting hat covers your head and ears. _beanie_

1 Some women wear these shoes in order to look taller and more elegant. _____

2 A formal piece of clothing which is worn over a shirt and under a jacket. _____

3 These have a classic design from the past and protect your eyes from the sun. _____

4 A casual top which is made of very warm synthetic material, has long sleeves and is excellent in cold weather. _____

5 A piece of jewellery which men or women wear around their necks. _____

6 This is a kind of loose sporty jumper often made from cotton and can be worn for exercising. _____

7 These trousers are made from denim and they look like they have been worn a lot because of the light colour of the material. _____

8 This narrow piece of material, usually animal skin, has a metal piece at one end to help hold your trousers around your waist. _____

4 Choose the correct words.

Fashion in Focus — *Red Carpet Report*

The Prince and Princess attended the premiere of the new James Bond film on Saturday. Prince Nicholas looked very smart in an elegant and stylish ¹*dark suit / denim jacket* and an eye-catching purple ²*leather belt / silk tie* around his neck. Princess Abigail wore a dark knee-length skirt and a gorgeous blue ³*shirt / blouse* from her favourite Paris boutique. The Princess always mixes casual and smart clothes to good effect and for this event she chose to wear large gold ⁴*beanies / bangles* around her wrist and unusual ⁵*ankle boots / leggings* – which helped make sure she wasn't taller than her husband.

REMEMBER BETTER

To help you learn words for clothes and accessories, make a list of some of the things that you own. Include some details about colours, materials, etc. Check any new words in a dictionary.

Write a list of the items from exercises 1, 3 and 4 that you own. Add extra details. Look at the examples below for help.

I own a warm grey fleece, a pair of black leather ankle boots, a pair of blue faded jeans and a green beanie.

WORD STORE 1B | Fashion and style

5 Complete the sentences with the words from the box. There are two extra words.

> across appearance attention casual
> dressed fashion flow look skin ~~trendy~~

I'd say I am quite *trendy* because I enjoy wearing the latest designs.

1 Some clothes never seem to go out of _____ – like jeans, for example.
2 Andrew loves being the centre of _____ and that's why he wears such expensive clothes.
3 It's unusual to see Ronny looking so smart – he usually goes for a _____ look.
4 Ian never looks like he is comfortable in his own _____ . Maybe some fashion advice would help him feel more confident?
5 You don't have to spend a lot of money on caring about your _____ . There are plenty of fashionable clothes in second-hand stores nowadays.
6 Sandy comes _____ as very serious because she wears suits but in fact she's very relaxed most of the time.
7 We never follow the latest trends – we simply go with the _____ and wear what we want.

WORD STORE 1C | Personality

6 Complete the sentences with the correct words. The first letters are given.

Leonard is **e**_*asy-going*_. He never seems to get worried or annoyed.

1 Mark never does anything stupid or has unrealistic ideas. He's incredibly **d**_____-_____-_____ .
2 People who are **c**_____ tend not to worry too much about the results of their actions.
3 Jake's always been **r**_____ and has given his parents a lot of problems over the years.
4 You can tell if somebody is **v**_____ by how often they look in shop windows at their own image.
5 I asked Boris to donate to charity but he said he'd rather spend money on a nice meal or buy something for himself. Is he always so selfish and **s**_____ ?

7 Complete the descriptions of the people with some of the words from Exercise 6.

CHANNEL ①

'Housemates' contestants enter house for new series

Last night the contestants for the latest series of hit TV show 'Housemates' entered their new home for the first time. Here's what we think of them:

- **Phillip** – he seems to be a natural, sensible person. We think he's the *down-to-earth* one in the house.
- **Holly** – she's always happy and never seems to worry about how her behaviour affects the others. She's 22 and a very [1]_____ young woman.
- **Simon** – he really doesn't like authority or doing what people tell him to do. We think he is very [2]_____ and will be a difficult person who will create trouble with everybody.
- **Stephanie** – she is a young lady who doesn't think in a deep or interesting way. She's a very [3]_____ person and only cares about becoming famous and winning the prize money.
- **Tina** – when she's not looking in the mirror at herself, she's probably planning what to wear the next day. She's an incredibly [4]_____ contestant.

SHOW WHAT YOU'VE LEARNT

8 Choose the correct answers A–C.

1 These __ jeans are actually new but they look like they have been worn a lot.
   A faded   B vintage   C antique
2 There's nothing more elegant than wearing a __ tie with an Italian designer suit.
   A straight   B silk   C denim
3 Don't wear a suit if you prefer to go for a more casual __ .
   A flow   B attention   C look
4 Yvette is so __ she spends hours every day just putting on her make-up.
   A trendy   B vain   C down-to-earth
5 I'm surprised Billy was angry. He always comes __ as very calm.
   A over   B through   C across
6 I could never be famous because I hate being the __ of attention.
   A middle   B centre   C point
7 Luke is such a __ person. I've never seen him stressed or worried.
   A carefree   B careful   C casual
8 It can get quite chilly at night, so take your __ with you just in case.
   A sweatshirt   B waistcoat   C blouse
9 My trousers are too large. Where did I put my brown leather __ I wonder?
   A boots   B fleece   C belt
10 Tyler should learn to go with the __ and relax more often.
   A appearance   B flow   C skin

/10

GRAMMAR

1.2

Dynamic and state verbs

SHOW WHAT YOU KNOW

1 Mark the sentences as **H** for habits/routines or **N** for things happening now.

Journalists are waiting outside the hospital for a first look at the new royal baby. `[N]`

1 The doctor doesn't usually arrive until 9 a.m. `[ ]`

2 My cousin is a fashion journalist. She always looks stylish. `[ ]`

3 In this programme, we're reporting from Paris, the fashion capital of the world. `[ ]`

4 'Faraway Travel' is currently selling weekend trips to Berlin at bargain prices. `[ ]`

5 We give free cinema tickets to all customers who spend more than £100 on clothes. `[ ]`

2 ★ Choose the correct forms.

1 **Jill:** What do you think of these shoes, Kate?
  Kate: To be honest, I *prefer / 'm preferring* the ones you tried on first.

2 **Tim:** Are you going to wear that cap, Danny?
  Danny: *Do you ask / Are you asking* if you can borrow it, Tim?

3 **Vicky:** Shall I cook some salmon for lunch, Max?
  Max: Vicky, you know I *don't like / 'm not liking* fish.

4 **Ellie:** *Do you wear / Are you wearing* thermal underwear today, Jo?
  Jo: No, I'm not. I only wear it when it's really cold.

5 **Fran:** I *like / 'm liking* your new suit, Jon. Was it expensive?
  Jon: Yes, Fran. Actually, it was very expensive.

6 **Lewis:** What do you think of the film so far, Grandma?
  Grandma: To be honest, Lewis I *don't enjoy / 'm not enjoying* it at all!

3 ★ ★ Complete the pairs of sentences or questions with the correct present forms of the verbs in capitals. Use short forms where possible.

THINK
a What <u>do you think</u> (you) of my new sweatshirt? Cool, huh?
b You look sad. What <u>are you thinking</u> (you) about?

1 **HAVE**
a I'm sorry but I can't come and meet you right now. I _____ lunch with Becky.
b Kristy _____ four different pairs of trainers.

2 **NOT SEE**
a Dave _____ his girlfriend a lot this month because he's revising for his exams.
b I _____ any difference between this woollen hat and the one you bought last week.

3 **TASTE**
a This coffee _____ strange. Did you clean the cup properly?
b Jeremy _____ the curry to see how spicy it is.

4 ★ ★ ★ Find and correct the mistakes. Use short forms where possible. One sentence is correct.

I ~~am not believing~~ Zoe lost my favourite jacket. <u>don't believe</u>

1 Is she really needing another new handbag? _____

2 Are these flowers for me? Oh, Jack! I'm not knowing what to say! _____

3 What is happening over there? What are all those people looking at? _____

4 I'm not wanting to wear a suit. I hate formal clothes. _____

5 Laura isn't hating Maths, she just finds it difficult. _____

6 Are you seeing the necklace with the three diamonds? That's the one I want. _____

SHOW WHAT YOU'VE LEARNT

5 Complete the blog with the correct forms of the verbs in brackets. Use short forms where possible.

Italian Style

Welcome to my fashion blog. I'm Vittoria from Rome and I <u>love</u> (love) fashion. I ¹_____ (have) my own clothes shop called 'Italian Style' in Via del Corso. Today is Thursday, and that means my business partner ²_____ (work) in our shop, so I ³_____ (not/need) to go to work. Lucky me! The weather is beautiful, so I ⁴_____ (wear) my favourite vintage sunglasses and a simple white cotton blouse. Personally, I ⁵_____ (not/like) clothes with big designer logos all over them – my business partner and I ⁶_____ (believe) that simple, stylish clothes are always the best choice. Come and visit us at 'Italian Style' and see for yourself.

/6

GRAMMAR: Train and Try Again page 154

1.3

Expressions • adverbs
• relationship phrases

1 Read the interview with Jenny. Complete expressions 1–5 with verbs from the box. Change the forms of the verbs if necessary. There are two extra verbs.

> continue   find   ~~get~~   happen
> last   lose   stop   take

Extract from Student's Book recording 🔊 **1.8**

P: It's so easy to make new online friends, isn't it? They ask to be your friend, and you accept. It's not as easy to make real life friends, is it?

J: That's right. Making friends online takes a few minutes. But a real friend is somebody you […] know over a long period of time. You meet, you spend time together and you *get* to know one another – ¹it _____ **a long time** to become close friends.

P: That's right. But some friendships don't ² _____ **forever**. […] when you don't want to ³ _____ **a friendship**, you can simply de-friend people, can't you?

J: I'm not sure I agree with that actually. I ⁴ _____ **it really hard** to de-friend online friends. It seems really mean. I suppose that's why I've got over 300 online friends. In real life, if you fall out with a friend, you don't see them any more. Or sometimes you decide that you no longer have much in common. Then you lose touch. You don't have to make the decision – ⁵**it just** _____ **naturally**.

REMEMBER BETTER

Try to learn phrases rather than single words. This will help you in exam tasks where you have to fill in gaps. Often the missing word will form a fixed phrase with other words that appear before and after the gap.

Complete the sentences with the correct form of a phrase in bold from the extract in Exercise 1.

> Everybody gets spots sometimes no matter how often they wash their face. *It just happens naturally*.

1 All good things must come to an end. Nothing _____ .

2 A couple should _____ extremely well before they get engaged.

3 _____ to qualify as a lawyer or a doctor.

4 Colin _____ to talk to girls. He gets embarrassed very easily.

5 I'm afraid I can't _____ with anyone who turns out to be untrustworthy.

REMEMBER THIS

Adverbs of manner tell us how we do an action. We form adverbs by adding *-ly* to adjectives, or *-ily* to adjectives ending in *-y*. (*quick – quickly, cheeky – cheekily*).
We make online friends very quick + ly.

The adverb from *good* is *well*.
How ~~good + ly~~ well do you know them?

Some irregular adverbs (*early, fast, hard, high, late, long* and *low*) have the same form as the adjective.
*It takes a **long** time to become close friends. (adj)*
*Making online friends … doesn't take **long** at all. (adv)*

2 Read REMEMBER THIS. Complete each pair of sentences with the adverb and the adjective forms of a word in the box. Show which form it is: *adv* or *adj*.

> ~~good~~   happy   late   long

Ryan didn't do very ᵃ*well* in the race, but at least he tried.   **adv**/ adj
Not everyone can be intelligent or attractive, but we can all be ᵇ*good*.   adv /**adj**

1 Will we have to wait ᵃ_____ for the results of the English test?   adv / adj
If you want a lift, be nice to me.
It is a ᵇ_____ walk home from here.   adv / adj

2 Nina and Eliza arrived ᵃ_____ and missed the start of the fashion show.   adv / adj
I can hardly keep my eyes open.
Last night was a ᵇ_____ night.   adv / adj

3 We are ᵃ_____ to announce that school will be closed this Friday.   adv / adj
I will ᵇ_____ wait for you if we can go for ice cream afterwards.   adv / adj

WORD STORE 1D | Relationship phrases

3 Choose the correct answers A–C.

1 Scott is a reliable friend. He's always there __ me when I need someone to talk to.
   A by   B with   C for

2 Have you fallen __ with your sister again, James? Why can't you two just be friends?
   A over   B out   C off

3 Matt and I used to be best friends, but since we left school, we've lost touch __ each other.
   A about   B with   C to

4 Dylan thinks his cousin is arrogant. They don't get __ with each other very well.
   A along   B over   C out

5 Leah and Sophie got to __ each other on a long bus journey. They had hours to talk about everything together.
   A learn   B discover   C know

6 Dan doesn't hang out __ John because he doesn't like him very much.
   A with   B by   C to

1 Read the texts. Match pictures A–C with texts 1–3.

A ☐
B ☐
C ☐

1

NEWS

35-year-old Herbert Chavez from the Philippines has transformed* himself from an ordinary dress-maker into a real-life Superman. After nineteen <u>surgeries</u> that copy the comic book hero's look, Chavez has become a real-life Clarke Kent.

Herbert first fell in love with the superhero when he was five years old. Since then he has spent around 300,000 pesos (£4,400) on his obsession – a <u>huge</u> amount of money compared to the average wage in the Philippines.

When he's not making dresses, Herbert can often be seen in the streets around his home dressed as Superman. He aims to teach children good morals and have some fun at the same time.

Herbert says he feels like a superhero whenever he puts on the costume,* but his mission is not to save the world but to help in his own small way and bring a smile to the faces of local children.

2

Sleepily, Fiona switched off the alarm clock and tried to wake up fully. It was Monday again and she had another busy week ahead. With only four weeks until her final exams, there was lots of hard work to do and no time for her social life. She really wanted to be older, already finished with school, already earning. Perhaps because winter was coming and it was still cold and dark outside, she found it especially difficult to get out of bed this morning. Her legs felt heavy and she seemed to have less energy than usual. Maybe she had slept <u>badly</u>. Finally, she made it to the bathroom, switched on the light and stood by the washbasin. When she saw her reflection* in the mirror, she screamed. Looking back at her was the face of a <u>terrified</u> old woman – herself, but wrinkled,* pale and grey-haired …

3

At **Oddfaces** we like our models to be fabulously fat or superbly skinny, ten feet tall or shockingly short. We love <u>odd</u> models with tattoos, piercings and memorable faces.

We have over 1,000 unique character models between the ages of 18 and 98 and sizes 7 and 27. Our models can bring a truly eye-catching look to music videos, TV shows and films, and of course print and film advertising. For over <u>a decade</u>, we have successfully provided the most unusual faces and bodies for top fashion designers, photographers and film directors.

If you need beautifully strange and strangely beautiful people, then look no further.

Pretty faces are everywhere these days – choose something different. Choose Oddfaces.

A

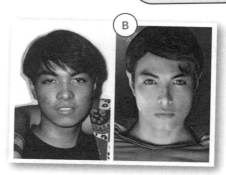

B

C

GLOSSARY

transform (v) – change completely
costume (n) – clothes that make you look like something, e.g. an animal or a famous person

reflection (n) – an image you can see in a mirror, glass or water
wrinkled (adj) – skin or cloth that is wrinkled has small lines or folds in it

2 Read the texts again. Choose the correct answer A–D.

1 According to the article, Herbert Chavez uses his new appearance
   A to earn money.
   B to educate and entertain.
   C to promote his business.
   D to remind him of his childhood.

2 The story describes a change in Fiona's
   A appearance and mood.   B daily routine.
   C behaviour.   D social life.

3 The author of text 3 wants to
   A announce a competition.   B offer advice.
   C advertise a company.   D tell a story.

3 Read the three texts again. Complete the sentences with one or two words from the texts.

1 When Herbert Chavez isn't dressed as Superman, he's a simple _____ .

2 As Superman, Herbert wants local kids to learn _____ and hopes they enjoy themselves.

3 Fiona had one month before taking her _____ and meeting friends wasn't possible.

4 She dreamed of being an adult and then when she looked in the mirror, she saw an _____ and was shocked.

5 The Oddfaces company has existed _____ than ten years.

6 The company doesn't employ models with just _____ , but strange-looking people.

4 Complete the gaps with the underlined synonyms from the texts.

   extremely frightened = _terrified_

1 operations   = _____
2 ten years   = _____
3 strange   = _____
4 poorly   = _____
5 massive   = _____

REMEMBER BETTER

When you learn a new word, look in a dictionary and see if you can also learn a synonym or a phrase with a similar meaning. In this way you will expand your vocabulary. To help you remember the words, write a sentence in which both items fit and add it to your vocabulary notes.

Complete the sentences with one of the pairs of words 1–5 in Exercise 4.

   Polly was _extremely frightened/terrified_ of thunder and lightning.

1 The first time I saw a Batman film was over _____ ago.

2 Since her skiing accident, poor Marta has had three _____ on her leg.

3 Lewis has a _____ tattoo that covers both arms, his chest and the whole of his back.

4 Lola's facial piercing looks very _____ . At first, I thought it was a big spot!

5 Both Claire and Emily think they did very _____ in the Physics exam.

VOCABULARY PRACTICE | Clothing

5 Look at the vocabulary in lesson 1.4 in the Student's Book. Complete the sentences with the correct words. The first letters are given.

Tammy wants to open a shop that sells original **g**_arments_ from the 1960s. Dresses, boots, jewellery – any items of clothing and accessories from that era really.

1 Hoodies may be **i**_____ clothes for today's graffiti artists and skaters but they were first worn in the 1930s in America for sports training.

2 Yes, madam. This jacket is **u**_____ , so it's fine for either your son or your daughter to wear.

3 These trousers are too long, so I need to take them to a **t**_____ before I can wear them.

4 Don't you think it's crazy that people buy designer **u**_____ just to wear beneath their clothes?

5 Cotton is a good **f**_____ for shirts because it's light and easy to dye different colours.

WORD STORE 1E | Compound adjectives

6 Match the halves of the compound adjectives in boxes A and B and complete the sentences.

   A brightly- cutting- hard-
      fast- multi- short-

   B coloured drying edge
      purpose sleeved wearing

The latest in _cutting-edge_ fashion are clothes that don't get wet or dirty.

1 This sports shirt is _____ , so I can wash it tonight and wear it again tomorrow morning.

2 Jacob never wears _____ shirts to work because he has a big tattoo on his arm.

3 Jeans became popular for workmen because they are _____ and last a long time.

4 I love clothes which are _____ . My electric-blue and sunflower-yellow Jimmi Hendrix T-shirt is my favourite piece of clothing!

5 Clothes which are _____ might not be the most fashionable but they are the most practical. You can wear them on any occasion.

SHOW WHAT YOU KNOW

1 Complete the sentences and questions with the Present Perfect Simple forms of the verbs in brackets. Use short forms.

Claire _has disliked_ (dislike) Danny since they first met at Julia's party.

1 _____ (you/know) Megan for a long time?

2 I _____ (never/understand) why people pay so much for brand name clothing.

3 How long _____ (Chloe/want) to be a fashion designer?

4 _____ (they/see) all the paintings in the gallery yet?

5 Grandma _____ (not/need) glasses since she had the eye operation.

2 ★ Complete the tour guide's speech with the Present Perfect Continuous forms of the verbs in brackets. Use short forms.

Welcome to our kilt factory. We hope you enjoy the tour. _Have you been waiting_ (you/wait) long? I hope not. Our company ¹_____ (produce) kilts for over 150 years. Today we are going to see how a traditional Scottish kilt is made. We ²_____ (make) our famous Highlander model since the 1920s. Originally kilts were designed for everyday use, but later they were worn only on more formal occasions. We ³_____ (sell) more and more of them as fashion items in recent years. We also make trousers here at the factory but we ⁴_____ (not/do) that for as long. Now sir, I see that you are wearing one of our kilts. You look wonderful! ⁵_____ (you/buy) our brand for a long time?

3 ★ ★ Charlie and Mary are at an art gallery. Choose the correct forms to complete the dialogue.

M: Can we rest for a minute, Charlie? We ¹_haven't stopped / haven't been stopping_ since we got here. I'm exhausted!

C: Sure, Mary. We ²_'ve walked / 've been walking_ around since 9. Let's get a coffee.

M: Great. I ³_haven't had / haven't been having_ a drink since this morning.

In the café …

C: There are some lovely paintings here, don't you think?

M: Yeah, lovely. It ⁴_'s been / 's been being_ a great morning, Charlie.

C: Listen Mary, I ⁵_'ve waited / 've been waiting_ for the right moment to talk to you.

M: Really, Charlie? What is it?

C: Well, we are good friends, and we ⁶_'ve liked / 've been liking_ each other for a long time, right?

M: Yes, Charlie. We ⁷_'ve spent / 've been spending_ more and more time together recently. What do you want to say?

C: Well, do you think you and I could maybe study for our exams together?

M: Yes, Charlie, I suppose we could.

4 ★ ★ ★ Complete one sentence with the Present Perfect Simple and one with the Present Perfect Continuous form of each verb in capitals.

READ

a Rebecca _has been reading_ that novel all day.

b Rebecca _has read_ five books this year.

1 **LOOK**

a James and Kirsty _____ at photos all morning.

b James and Kirsty _____ at most of the photos from the school trip.

2 **SAVE** (you)

a How long _____ money for a new phone?

b How much money _____ this year?

3 **COLLECT**

a Dan _____ over 200 different Spiderman comics.

b Dan _____ comics for seven years.

4 **NOT PLAY**

a Karen _____ football since she broke her leg last year.

b Karen _____ chess for very long, so she still forgets the rules sometimes.

SHOW WHAT YOU'VE LEARNT

5 Complete the text with the Present Perfect Simple and Present Perfect Continuous forms of the verbs from the box. Use short forms. There are two extra verbs.

buy/you   change   contact   have   help
not read   watch   wear   work

Emma Brady Stylists ⊗

Have you bought any new clothes this year? How long ¹_____ the same old shoes? How many times ²_____ your hairstyle this year? If you ³_____ fashion magazines recently because you've been too busy, but want to know what is stylish right now, then maybe I can help. My name is Emma Brady and I'm a personal stylist and shopping consultant. For the last four years, my colleagues and I ⁴_____ men and women to choose clothes, shoes and hairstyles that really suit them. Since I started my business, I ⁵_____ with over 200 customers. We ⁶_____ some very famous people as extremely satisfied clients. Contact us now at em@ebstyle.net

/6

GRAMMAR: Train and Try Again page 154

1 ★ **Complete the sentences with the correct form of the words in brackets.**

Janice *hopes* (HOPE) you can come to the barbecue party on Sunday.

1 Where was James _____ (EDUCATE)? Did he go to a private school?
2 My grandpa always said: 'If you want to _____ (SUCCESS) in life, work hard and play fair.'
3 I'm so happy! I've been _____ (ACCEPT) into my first choice of university!
4 Getting into the best university in the country was Jane's great _____ (ACHIEVE).
5 Mark's _____ (CREATE) helps him write amazing stories for children.

2 ★ **Choose the correct answers A–C.**

1 **Harry:** I'm sorry but I don't think this style is ___ with your hair.
  Yosef: Seriously? So, should I choose something else?
  A achievement **B** achievable **C** unachievable
2 **Charlie:** Mum says I can't go out today because I was late home last night.
  Adam: What? That doesn't sound like very fair ___ .
  A punishing **B** punishment **C** punish
3 **Mindy:** I told my teacher I lost my homework, but really I didn't do it.
  Claire: That wasn't very ___ , was it?
  A respectful **B** disrespectful **C** respected
4 **Hannah:** You look great in that hat. You should buy it.
  Landen: It's too expensive and buying clothes isn't a ___ for me at the moment.
  A prioritise **B** priorities **C** priority
5 **Dan:** Are you sure you didn't wear my hoodie without asking?
  Nigel: No, I ___ didn't. It doesn't even fit me.
  A honest **B** dishonest **C** honestly
6 **June:** I'm sorry, but can you ___ how this design program works again?
  Karl: Sure, no problem.
  A clarity **B** clarify **C** clarification

3 ★★ **Complete the sentences using the prompts in brackets. Do not change the order of the words. Change the forms or add new words where necessary. Use between two and three words in each gap.**

I have to admit that I *cried pathetically* (cry / pathetic) when I saw just how bad my new tattoo was.

1 I have never _____ (speak / dishonest) to you but have only ever told you the truth.
2 This handbag _____ (be / ridiculous) expensive – who on earth would buy this?
3 Amanda _____ (go / absolute) crazy when she found out she was the Model of the Year.
4 Truman apologised for _____ (behave / bad) when he lost the match.
5 Janice has never _____ (shout / angry) at her naughty little sister.

4 ★★ **Complete the second sentence so that it has a similar meaning to the first. Use between two and five words.**

She has totally no education.
She is *totally uneducated*.

1 My aunt Josie is very creative when she dresses.
  My aunt Josie dresses _____ .
2 If you want to achieve success in the fashion industry, work hard.
  If you want to be _____ , work hard.
3 It surprised a lot of people when Blake accepted the Worst-Dressed Man of 2019 award.
  _____ of the award for the worst-dressed man of 2019 surprised a lot of people.
4 Our sponsors are not obliged to visit the exhibition.
  There is _____ for our sponsors to visit the exhibition.
5 Harvey gave me an angry look when he saw me in his leather jacket.
  Harvey looked _____ when he saw me in his leather jacket.

5 ★★★ **Complete the text with the correct form of the words in the box. There are two extra words.**

create educate honest leader
priority ~~profession~~ regulate respect

Working with stars

Anyone who works in media must look their best at all times. How do they achieve this? Most use the services of a *professional* make-up artist – or cosmetologist. Is this a job you might fancy doing? Well, here's what you need to do.

Firstly, a make-up specialist will need a formal [1]_____ in cosmetology. This is usually a mix of a practical and a theoretical course. One particular skill that is needed at this early stage is [2]_____ because during these studies, trainees should start building a portfolio of their best work.

In some countries, official [3]_____ say that cosmetologists then have to complete an exam in health and safety before they can get a licence to work.

Good [4]_____ skills are not needed because most cosmetologists are their own boss and often run their own business. And, whether they choose to work in a salon, in a theatre, or work in TV or film studios, good make-up artists are always [5]_____ of their clients as good customer service is essential in this job.

1 Match the beginnings with the correct endings to form sentences.

He's in his — (g) — a blue eyes.

1 She's the sort of person who — b hard-working.

2 She's got long — c forgets his manners.

3 He sometimes — d loves kids.

4 The first thing you notice about her is her large — e fashionable clothes.

5 He usually wears — f blonde hair.

6 She's not always — g mid-twenties.

2 Put the words in order to complete the sentences.

in / early / thirties / her / is
Becky _is in her early thirties_.

1 interested / is / not / fashion / in / really
Peter _____ .

2 a / make / would / doctor / great
Lucy _____ .

3 beautiful / hair / long / blonde / got
Marta's _____ .

4 bit / is / too / a / slim
Liam _____ .

5 a / would / great / make / model
Roxanne _____ .

6 who / kind / person / always / your / remembers / birthday / of / is / the
Lucas _____ .

3 Complete Adam's description with the words from the box. There are two extra words.

built   casual   dark   dresses   easy-going
friendly   height   into   ~~our~~   type

Hi Jake

I'm meeting Josh later. U coming out?

U know Josh, don't you? Emily's cousin.

He's _our_ age with long ¹_____ hair.

He's got a ²_____ face.

Oh come on Adam. He's about medium ³_____
and fairly well-⁴_____ . You know him!

He always ⁵_____ in black and he's ⁶_____
Goth music.

Hi Adam

Josh?????

Not sure. What does he look like?

?

What?

Do I?

Oh! U mean 'Goth Josh.' Yeah, he's
an ⁷_____ guy. What time are we meeting?

4 Find and correct the mistakes.

Mrs Baldwin is kinds of easy-going as a teacher if you ask me. _kind of_

1 My baby sister, who is three, tends cry a lot. _____

2 I'm not particular lazy, but I like to do nothing sometimes. _____

3 Andrew always isn't very polite with new people. _____

4 Eva sorts of shy, but she's different when you get to know her. _____

5 Diana can a little tired in the evenings because she wakes up at 6 a.m. every day. _____

6 Paulo could be a bit little smarter, but he has made an effort to dress nicely. _____

7 Dad's exactly not a genius, but he is very clever. _____

5 Complete the text with the words and phrases from the box. Sometimes more than one answer is possible.

a little bit   bit   could be   kind   little
not exactly   particularly   ~~sort of~~

I saw an interesting picture in a _sort of_ gallery or café the other day. It's a portrait of a man. There's a lot of blue in the picture and the man, who is wearing a dark blue jacket, looks ¹_____ of cool, almost like he doesn't care about anything in the world. But he's also ²_____ mysterious in my opinion. He's ³_____ strange-looking, but he has got big blue eyes which look straight at you. His hair ⁴_____ blue too, but because the picture is so dark, it's a ⁵_____ hard to tell for sure. And his coat, which doesn't ⁶_____ fit him very well — it's far too big — makes the man look a ⁷_____ uncomfortable. It was only after looking at the picture for some time that I read the short text below it and learned that it was a self-portrait by one of the most famous painters of the 20th century!

6 Read the task below. Then read the email and complete gaps A–E with the correct form of the words from the box.

> Your friend is going to visit the English city where you stayed as an exchange student last year. The family you stayed with have agreed that your friend can stay with them during his/her visit. They have never met before. Write an email to the family's teenage son/daughter. Include and develop these points:
> - Say briefly how you met your friend.
> - Describe your friend's appearance and personality.
> - Mention some of the things your friend wants to do during his/her stay.
> - Thank the family for agreeing to let your friend stay with them.

(bit   can   particular   sort   tend)

Hi Amy,

I hope you're fine. I'd like to tell you a few things about Imogen – the girl who's going to stay with you this summer.

Imogen and I met in the playground when we were children. First, I wasn't ᴬ_____ nice to her, but later we became great friends.

When you get to the airport, look for a tall and a ᴮ_____ too slim girl with long dark hair and big blue eyes. A girl who looks ᶜ_____ of casual but fashionable at the same time – that's Imogen ☺.

She is a cool, easy-going girl, and the kind of person who ¹*looks / feels* good in her own skin. But sometimes she ᴰ_____ be a bit shy and reserved, especially in new situations.

Imogen's always ²*enjoyed / been enjoying* fashion, so she's coming to the UK to visit some design schools and check the trendiest places. So maybe you could show her what's ³*in / at* fashion in London now?

Thank you again for letting Imogen stay with you. I know how great it is to stay with a British family, and I'm sure you'll have a great time. Just be careful – she ᴱ_____ to talk a lot ☺.

Write soon, so we don't ⁴*lose / drop* touch.

Love,

Ella

7 Read the email again. Choose the correct answers in 1–4.

SHOW WHAT YOU'VE LEARNT

8 You and your friend have decided to stay with your English-speaking cousin in the countryside for a week's holiday abroad. Write an email to your cousin. Include and develop these points:
- Tell him/her about your friend and how you met.
- Describe your friend's appearance, personality and why you like him/her.
- Say what you would like to do when you visit your cousin.
- Thank your cousin and his family for agreeing to let you both stay for a week.

SHOW THAT YOU'VE CHECKED

Finished? Always check your writing. Can you tick √ everything on this list?

In my email:

• I have started with a friendly greeting, e.g. *Dear James* or *Hi Gemma*.	☐
• I have said why I am writing.	☐
• I have described how I met my friend.	☐
• I have described my friend's appearance, personality and interests.	☐
• I have thanked the family and the addressee.	☐
• I have used contractions (e.g. *I'm / aren't / that's*).	☐
• I have perhaps used some emoticons ☺ and abbreviations (*info / CU / gr8*) – but not too many!	☐
• I have finished with a friendly ending, e.g. *Bye 4 now, All the best, Lots of love*, etc.	☐
• I have checked my spelling and punctuation.	☐
• My text is neat and clear.	☐

1 Translate the phrases into your own language.

SPEAKING BANK

Beginning a description

The photo shows ... _____

In this photo, I can see .../ _____
there is .../there are ... _____

Saying where
(in the photo)

in the background/in the _____
middle/in the foreground _____
_____
on the left/on the right _____
_____
in front of/behind/next to _____

Showing uncertainty

It's hard to say/make out _____
what ..., but ... _____
I'm not sure ..., but ... _____
_____

Speculating

He/She/It looks (tired) ... _____
_____
He/She/It looks as if/ _____
as though/like ... _____
It seems to be .../Perhaps _____
it's .../Maybe it's ... _____
I imagine they're .../They're _____
probably ... _____

Giving your opinion

I (don't) think ... _____
I prefer ... _____
Personally, ... In my opinion ... _____

2 Put the adjectives in brackets in the correct order to complete the message.

Hi Kat – just back from the sales. Got some real bargains! First thing I bought was a (grey / woollen / cute) _cute_ [1]_____ [2]_____ hat and a (silver-grey / long / lovely) [3]_____ [4]_____ [5]_____ scarf. They only had (leather / old-fashioned) [6]_____ [7]_____ gloves in the sale, so I'll have to keep looking for those. I also found a coat finally! It's a (black / mid-length / smart) [8]_____ [9]_____ [10]_____ raincoat and it was reduced by 50%! See you at 7 – fingers crossed it stays cold and wet – I want to wear my new stuff ;)
Tina x

Sent 16:41

3 Complete the description with phrases from the Speaking Bank. The first letters are given.

This photo shows a woman and a little boy shopping together. They are **p**_robably_ mother and son. It's [1]**h**_____ **t**_____ say exactly how old the little boy is, but he [2]**s**_____ to be about 7 or 8. The woman is wearing casual clothes and comfortable shoes and the little boy is dressed like a superhero! He looks very unhappy though, in fact it [3]**l**_____ as though he is crying. I think they are in a children's clothes shop because the clothes on sale look very small, and in the background there are several other adults with young children. The woman is showing the boy a little white shirt and a tie – [4]**I i**_____ they are shopping for a school uniform, but I don't [5]**t**_____ he likes it. I'm not [6]**s**_____ , **b**_____ maybe the little boy is upset because he'd prefer to wear his superhero clothes for school.

4 Find and correct the mistakes. Two sentences are correct.

I think he doesn't look very happy.
I _don't think he looks_ very happy.
1 I think she hasn't bought anything.
   I _____ bought anything.
2 I think they're very elegant.
   I _____ elegant.
3 I think those trousers won't fit her.
   I _____ fit her.
4 I think they don't agree on which one to buy.
   I _____ agree on which one to buy.
5 I think green doesn't suit him.
   I _____ him.
6 I don't think she's attractive.
   I _____ attractive.

5 Choose the correct words.

In this photo, I can [1]_show / see_ three young women. They are [2]_probably / as though_ in a hairdressing salon, because the woman on the left [3]_has cut / is cutting_ the blonde girl's hair. The hairdresser looks quite young and a bit nervous, or [4]_perhaps / probably_ she is just concentrating on what she is doing. It's [5]_hard / sure_ to say, but I think the woman [6]_in / on_ the right is checking what the hairdresser is doing. She's dressed quite smartly and [7]_seems / imagines_ to be an instructor or the boss, so maybe the hairdresser is still in training. Personally, I would never go to a trainee hairdresser, but I [8]_think the blonde girl isn't / don't think the blonde girl is_ too worried. She's smiling and looks very relaxed. Maybe she's happy because she is getting a free haircut!

Student A, look below. Student B, go to page 134.

1 In pairs, ask and answer the questions.

Talk about different topics.

1 What's your favourite TV series of all time? Why?
2 Tell me about the type of house and the area where you live.
3 What kind of technological device couldn't you live without? Why?

4 Tell me about a summer job you would like to do using your skills and abilities.
5 When was the last time you felt unwell? What happened?

2 Look at the photo of the young people wearing fashionable clothes. Take turns to talk about what you can see in your photos. Talk about the people, the clothes and the other things in the photo.

3 You and your friend want to buy a birthday present for a fashionable female friend. Here are some of the presents you could choose. Talk together about the different presents and say which would be best.

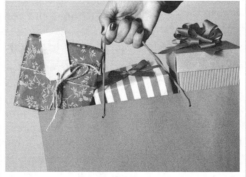

4 Talk about buying presents.

- Do you enjoy buying presents for people? Why?/Why not?
- Where do you usually go to buy presents?
- What sort of presents do you like receiving? Why?

- Do you think it's easy or hard to buy fashionable presents for friends? Why?
- Who is the hardest person you know to buy a present for? Why?

VOCABULARY AND GRAMMAR

1 Choose the correct words.

A black leather jacket with a white T-shirt has been *trendy* / *iconic* since James Dean and Marlon Brando wore them in the 1950s.

1 Why do you have to be so *rebellious* / *shallow* all the time? Can't you do what I ask you to do just once?

2 I wish I could be as *down-to-earth* / *carefree* as Harry. I'm always trying to do stupid and impractical things.

3 What kind of *garment* / *fabric* is that dress made from? It's so soft to the touch.

4 These boots are really *multi-purpose* / *hard-wearing*. I've had them for two years and they're still in excellent condition.

5 Sarah likes to stand out – that's why she usually goes for *a casual look* / *brightly-coloured clothes*.

/5

2 Complete the sentences with the words from the box. There are two extra words.

bangles   beanie   dark suit   denim jacket
fleece   high heels   ~~necklace~~   leggings

Stella bought a very cheap <u>necklace</u> and after a few days the chain broke from around her neck and she lost it.

1 Most heat is lost through the head, so wear a _____ to stay really warm.

2 Put on a thermal T-shirt with a _____ over the top and then a jacket. You can put the jacket in your backpack if you get too hot up the mountain.

3 Tracy likes wearing _____ because they are comfortable and keep her legs nice and warm.

4 I don't like wearing _____ because they're too loose and move around when I use my arms.

5 David, we are going to a funeral! Of course you can't wear a _____ and jeans.

/5

3 Complete the sentences with the correct words. The first letters are given

You look very **t**<u>rendy</u>. Even your shoes are fashionable and up-to-date.

1 What are you wearing!? Sunglasses like those have been out of **f**_____ for years! I suggest you buy a new pair.

2 Whenever I've had problems or been upset, my mum has always been **t**_____ for me.

3 Have you **f**_____ out with Suzie again? Why are you two always arguing?

4 I'm almost ready, Dad. I just need to pack clean **u**_____ and another pair of socks and then I've got everything I need for our weekend trip.

5 That's a lovely **w**_____ , Adam. Is it part of a three-piece suit or a separate item?

/5

4 Complete the sentences with the correct form of the words in brackets. Sometimes more than one answer is possible.

Every time I see you, you <u>look</u> (look) completely different. I love your new hairstyle!

1 I _____ (not/believe) you, Hannah. You've lied about this so many times.

2 Ian _____ (dance) with Kelly at the moment, but he really wants to dance with Alison.

3 Beverly _____ (need) to see a doctor about her headaches.

4 _____ (you/put) raisins in Dad's birthday cake again this year? Please don't. I hate them!

5 Becky _____ (not/know) how to use her new camera – probably because she hasn't read the instructions.

/5

5 Choose the correct forms.

Jessica *has eaten* / *has been eating* the same kind of frozen meal five times this week.

1 Amanda *has known* / *has been knowing* Natalie for about three years now.

2 Lucy *has worried* / *has been worrying* about her hair constantly since we arrived at the party. I've told her she looks great, but she doesn't believe me.

3 Actually, I can speak Italian, so I *'ve understood* / *'ve been understanding* everything you've been saying about me.

4 Nathan *has sung* / *has been singing* the same song all morning. It's driving me crazy!

5 George and Inge *have met* / *have been meeting* in secret since their parents told them to stop seeing each other.

/5

6 Choose the correct answers A–C.

New Uniform for City Hospital Nurses

The nurses of Hallamshire Hospital <u>B</u> the same old uniform for the last 10 years. Recently the hospital decided it was time for a change and today pictures of the nurses' new look are finally up on the hospital website. The old-fashioned white and grey uniforms have gone and been replaced by a much more modern and [1]___ outfit for both male and female nurses. Sophie Baxter, the head nurse on the children's ward, said: 'I [2]___ the new look is great. We [3]___ a very long time for a change. The new dark blue trousers and dark green T-shirts look great together and we [4]___ that the colours and style are much more practical.' Of course, nobody wants to go to hospital, but if you are there, you will now be looked after by some very [5]___ nurses.

	A wore	B have been wearing	C are wearing
1	A vintage	B vain	C unisex
2	A 'm thinking	B think	C have been thinking
3	A 've been waiting	B 're waiting	C wait
4	A are all agreeing	B all agree	C have all been agreeing
5	A well-dressed	B hard-wearing	C short-sleeved

/5

Total   /30

7 Complete each pair of sentences with the same answer A–C.

Oh no, my favourite ___ jeans have got a hole in the knee.

The pages in this book are ___ and I can't read the text very well.

A shallow (B) faded C worn

1 Are ankle-length trousers really back ___ fashion?
Abe's really not that interested ___ going shopping for clothes.

A on B in C out

2 I love your ___-purpose boots. Where did you buy them?
Google is a ___-national company that employs people worldwide.

A many B uni C multi

3 I wish these shorts were ___-drying. I want to wear them now.
I think ___ fashion is a waste of money.

A speed B fast C quick

4 Those ___ boots look cool. Just like what the Beatles used to wear!
I was playing football and got kicked on the ___ – it really hurts.

A leg B ankle C foot

5 I don't know how you can walk in ___ heels.
The prices in this second-hand store are quite ___ .

A high B tall C big

/5

8 Choose the correct answers A–C.

You could wear your new ____ if that skirt is too big.
A silk tie
(B) leather belt
C vintage sunglasses

1 Paddy ____ for weeks now if Martha has a new job.
A is wanting to know
B wants to know
C has wanted to know

2 Have you ____ your old friend Sebastian? Does he still live here?
A lost touch with
B fallen out with
C come across

3 If you ____ , you'd feel better. Looks really matter.
A appeared to be more careful
B looked a lot more carefully
C cared more about your appearance

4 Which of your friends ____ ? Where do you usually go together?
A are you the most comfortable with
B do you hang out with the most
C are the friendliest

5 I ____ myself really well when I went travelling alone.
A got to know
B knew
C have known

/5

9 Choose the correct answers A–C to replace the underlined part of the sentence.

Ursula has always <u>been incredibly vain</u>.
(A) been too proud of the way she looks
B always looked incredible
C dressed very elegantly

1 Do <u>shallow people</u> usually care too much about what they look like?
A people who don't think about serious things
B people who don't care about others
C people who like to be trendy

2 This shop <u>has had cutting-edge</u> fashions from around the world for years.
A has sold the most stylish
B has been offering the most expensive
C has been selling the most modern

3 Why didn't you like Thomas? He <u>came across as</u> very friendly.
A seemed to be B tried to be C pretended to be

4 <u>I'm going to wear this blouse</u> to the open air concert tonight. Does it look OK?
A I intend to have this blouse on
B I'd rather wear this blouse
C I prefer to wear this blouse

5 Ollie thinks he looks really <u>trendy since he changed</u> his hairstyle.
A iconic now he's changed
B fashionable after changing
C rebellious since he's been changing

/5

10 Choose the correct answers A–C.

Just Like Friends

It's an interesting fact that those of us who <u>B</u> friends don't only have certain things in common, but actually sometimes look alike too. Take my best friend Joe, for example. We get [1]___ with each other really well and both like many of the same things. We enjoy [2]___ time in the park, for instance.

But that's not all. We both [3]___ to wear denim jackets. I think it's because we both want to look like [4]___ – although of course, it's one thing to look this way and another to act like it! Still, the jacket's a really practical thing to wear too as it's a particularly strong [5]___ but is still quite light.

I read somewhere that people who wear glasses are more likely to be friends with people that wear glasses too. Maybe it's the same with styles of shirts and jackets? Oh, and there's one thing I forgot to mention – Joe is my dog :-)

A make (B) become C have
1 A through B by C along
2 A to spend B spending C spend
3 A prefer B have preferred C are preferring
4 A rebellion B rebels C rebellious
5 A garment B tailor C suit

/5

Total /20

2 It's just a game

VOCABULARY

2.1

Sport • phrasal verbs
• collocations • people in sport

SHOW WHAT YOU KNOW

1 Complete the dialogues with the correct form of the words in brackets.

John: Quick! Catch the ball!
Roger: Ouch! Sorry, I'm a hopeless basketball _player_ (PLAY).

1 Graham: It's a beautiful day. Let's go to the pool.
Harry: I'm not a very good _____ (SWIM), I'm afraid.

2 Claire: Did I see your brother riding a bike on TV yesterday, Sam?
Sam: Possibly. He's a professional _____ (CYCLE) doing the Tour de France.

3 Paulo: Wow. You've got a lot of medals. Running, jumping, throwing the javelin …
Tess: Yes, I used to be a good _____ (ATHLETICS) when I was younger.

4 Karl: Who's that guy in the picture?
Jan: You are joking! That's Lionel Messi – the best _____ (FOOTBALL) in the world!

5 Aman: Look! It's snowing! Let's go skiing this weekend!
Rafaele: Oh, no – you're not a _____ (SKI), are you? I hate all winter sports.

2 Choose the correct words.

 SPORTS FOR ALL!

At Abbeydale sports club we offer a wide range of sports and activities. In the main sports hall, club members can ¹*do / play* basketball or volleyball on our indoor ²*courts / pitches*. Outdoors, you can ³*do / play* hockey, cricket, football and rugby on full-size ⁴*pitches / courses*. In our fantastic new building we offer the chance to ⁵*do / go* judo, karate and aerobics as well as ⁶*do / play* tennis or table tennis. Plus, we have a brand new badminton ⁷*court / course* and indoor ⁸*ring / rink* for ice-skating too! In the summer, you can ⁹*do / go* athletics on the main field or run around our running ¹⁰*ring / track* and members can also ¹¹*do / go* canoeing and sailing on our beautiful lake. We are currently building a pool, so very soon you will be able to ¹²*do / go* swimming at the club too.

Contact us at abbeydale_sc@hitmail.com

REMEMBER BETTER

To help you remember sets of words, categorise them in different ways. Write the words on individual pieces of paper and then group and regroup them according to different categories. Examples of categories for sports include: team vs individual sports, indoor vs outdoor sports, everyday vs extreme sports, sports which use a ball, etc.

WORD STORE 2A | Phrasal verbs

3 Complete the sentences with the correct prepositions.

How could Jane let us _down_ like that? She's the best player on the team and she didn't arrive for the match.

1 Adam's hurt his arm, so he has to drop _____ of the tennis competition this weekend.
2 Williams has to take _____ last year's champion in the final game of the season.
3 Uma is an excellent sailor. She got _____ it when her dad first took her sailing at the age of six.
4 My mum's running in the marathon this Sunday. Do you want to come and cheer her _____ with me?
5 I've decided to go _____ for a karate tournament. Do you think I can win it?
6 How many calories do you think 45 minutes of yoga burns _____ ?

WORD STORE 2B | Collocations

4 Choose the correct words.

'Welcome to "Sports Thoughts" on Radio Sport. This week we will ask marathon runner, Jeremy Bradshaw, what it was like to ¹*come / win / score* first in the London Marathon. We'll talk to Pat Goodhill who ²*kept / beat / lost* the national speed-climbing champion and ³*scored / won / broke* a world record at last week's UK climbing championships. Skier Daisy Leader will tell us how she ⁴*loses / scores / keeps* in shape during the summer and give us some expert advice on ⁵*beating / keeping / coming* fit during the winter season. We'll also ask footballer, Alastair Madson, what he feels is more important for his career: ⁶*scoring / breaking / winning* goals or ⁷*beating / winning / breaking* matches. Finally, you'll have the chance to ⁸*win / score / keep* a prize in our weekly phone-in competition.

Now, this news has just come in – US basketball player Dick Boyd amazed fans and teammates earlier this evening when he ⁹*scored / kept / won* more than 100 points in a single game. And we have heard that AFC Woolwich's Donny Wellard says he might quit professional football after he managed to ¹⁰*miss / lost / broke* a goal in Saturday's World Cup final from just one metre …'

18

5 Look at the sports results and complete the gaps with the correct names.

FOOTBALL: United 2 - City 1

United won the game.
1 ᵃ_____ defeated ᵇ_____ .
2 _____ scored one goal.
3 _____ lost the match.

TENNIS: WILLIAMS 3 – WOZNIACKI 6

4 _____ won the game.
5 ᵃ_____ beat ᵇ_____ .
6 _____ lost the match.

WORD STORE 2C | People in sport

6 Use the words in the box to label people in sport. There are two extra words.

> opponent   referee   supporter
> spectator   teammate

1 _____ **me**   2 _____   3 _____

7 Complete the dialogue with the names of people in sport. The first letters are given.

Reporter: Here we are live from the National Stadium with Zoe Striker of Team UK, the new women's 100m sprint **c**_champion_. Zoe, you are finally the **c**_hampion_ of the world. How does it feel?

Zoe: Wonderful! I've been training hard with the help of my ¹**c**_____ , and the other athletes in the UK team – my fantastic ²**t**_____ . I couldn't have done it without them or all of the ³**s**_____ that were watching and cheering me on here in the stadium. I've got the best ⁴**f**_____ in the world!

Reporter: And how about the ⁵**r**_____ ? For a moment I thought he was going to stop the race.

Zoe: That was a little worrying, yes. But I've been practising all week with my ⁶**t**_____ and I was prepared for any of my ⁷**o**_____ trying to stop me winning.

Reporter: Thank you Zoe. The UK is proud of you and your thousands of ⁸**s**_____ around the world can't wait for your next competition.

8 Complete each pair of sentences with the same word A–C.

1 How old were you when you first ___ into rowing?
 Don't worry – I've ___ a pair of skates I can lend you.
 A been   **B** got   **C** had
2 I feel that my team really ___ me down after they failed to win the cup.
 James ___ me borrow his tennis racket, so we can play tomorrow.
 A put   **B** took   **C** let
3 Swimmer Simon Davies said his main aim this year is to ___ his own world record.
 You look exhausted, Mike. Let's have a ___ at this café.
 A break   **B** rest   **C** keep
4 The best way to lose weight is to keep ___ and watch what you eat.
 The jacket really suited Rachel, but unfortunately it was the wrong size and didn't ___ her.
 A shape   **B** fit   **C** healthy
5 My sports ___ told me I need to lose some weight if I want to win the trophy.
 I think we'll take the ___ to the stadium. There shouldn't be too much traffic.
 A trainer   **B** fan   **C** coach

9 Complete the sentences with the correct form of the words from the box. There are two extra words.

> beat   come   goal   point   referee
> spectator   ~~teammate~~   win

My _teammates_ threw me into the river after we won the boat race.
1 I know I can't run very fast but I didn't think I'd _____ last in the race.
2 With two minutes of the match left, the fans were screaming at the _____ to blow the whistle.
3 The _____ had paid £275 each for tickets to watch the game from the VIP area.
4 Mai Lee _____ the favourite Jinjing Ho to become this year's women's table tennis champion in our county.
5 If Barlow scores the next _____ , he'll win the match and be the new table tennis champion.

/10

19

1 Put the story in the correct order.

Ray didn't finish the race.

☐ She tried to help him get up.

☐ When the ambulance arrived, Lisa and Ray were chatting and laughing.

① He had only run three miles when he fell over and hurt his foot.

☐ When Ray's leg was better, he asked Lisa on a date.

☐ But he couldn't stand because he had hurt his ankle.

☐ Lisa was watching the race when Ray fell over.
Six months later they got married.

2 ★ Complete the sentences with the correct form of the verbs in brackets.

The official fired the gun and the race *began* (begin).

1 It was raining heavily when Ferguson _____ (crash) his Ferrari.

2 When I reached the 10 km sign, the fastest runners _____ (already/cross) the finishing line.

3 The race began at 16:00 and the last cyclist _____ (finish) at exactly 17:08.

4 Diane was already at the gym when she realised she _____ (forget) her towel.

5 Fyfe and Scott _____ (climb) Everest when the accident happened.

3 ★ ★ Choose the correct verb forms.

1 R: Right, Jones! It's a yellow card for you.

   J: Oh Ref! What ªdid I do / had I done / was I doing?

   R: I ᵇalready blew / had already blown / was already blowing the whistle three times Jones, but you carried on playing!

2 F: Did you see the ice hockey last night, Ben? Great goal by Grabic, huh?

   B: Well, I ªwatched / had watched / was watching the game when the doorbell rang. I went to answer it; it was some sales person, and when I got back I ᵇmissed / had missed / was missing the goal!

3 TV J: Arthur, at 76 years of age you're the oldest competitor to finish the marathon today. Why ªdid you decide / had you decided / were you deciding to run?

   A: Oh, well, last year my grandson and I were watching the race on TV when he ᵇasked / had asked / was asking: 'Grandad, have you ever done that?' I told him that I hadn't run a marathon and he said: 'Maybe you should try'. So, I ᶜdid / have done / have been doing it for my grandson, Timmy.

4 ★ ★ ★ Look at the signs and complete the sentences and questions with the correct form of the verbs in brackets.

BIKE RACE
9 a.m. – 10 a.m.

At 8 a.m. the race *hadn't started* (start).

1 It _____ (begin) at 9 a.m.

2 At 9:30 a.m. the competitors _____ (cycle).

3 A: _____ the race _____ (finish) at 10:30 a.m.?
   B: Yes, it had.

SKI JUMPING
COMPETITION
11 a.m. – 1 p.m.

4 When I arrived at 11:30 a.m., the competition _____ (begin).

5 A: _____ it _____ (snow) when you got there?
   B: Yes, it was.

6 At exactly 12:45 the last competitor _____ (jump).

7 By 2 p.m. the crowd _____ (leave).

5 Find and correct the mistakes.

I played rugby when I broke my arm. *was playing*

1 We went to the Alps in April, but we couldn't ski because the snow already melted. _____

2 I watched the race when Hope won the gold medal and broke the world record. _____

3 Were City beating Arsenal in last night's game? _____

4 The referee didn't concentrate when Burton touched the ball with his hand. _____

5 In yesterday's Brazilian Grand Prix, Lewis was finishing in second place. _____

6 Boxer Joe Foster was fighting over 100 opponents when he retired in 1994. _____

/6

GRAMMAR: Train and Try Again page 155

1 Look at the recording extract. Put questions 1–4 in gaps A–D.

So, why did you take up windsurfing?

1 What other water sports did you do?
2 Are your mum and your cousin still your role models?
3 Was your cousin a good windsurfer?
4 Who inspired you?

Extract from Student's Book recording 🔊 **1.24**

P: First of all, congratulations Jackie. Last month you *became* the world under eighteen windsurfing champion!

J: Yes, that's right. Thank you.

P: *So, why did you take up windsurfing?* **A____**

J: Two people really: my mum and my cousin, Rachel. I first **¹_____** windsurfing with my mum. We lived near the sea, and we spent every summer on the beach. My mum had entered windsurfing competitions when she was a teenager. She **²_____** anything, but she really enjoyed it. She started to **³_____** me how to windsurf as soon as I could swim […]. I was only about 7 years old. My cousin Rachel was there too. She and her family lived near us. My mum gave us both lessons together. Rachel's two years older than me and I've always looked up to her. I still do.

P: **B____**

J: Yes, but she was good at a wide range of sports. […] She was a really good example for me – I wanted to be sporty like her. […]

P: So you grew up near the sea. **C____**

J: All sorts. At first, windsurfing wasn't my favourite thing. I liked other water sports like swimming and sailing. Rachel talked me into **⁴_____** the children's sailing club. We **⁵_____** all our weekends there, even in winter. We did lots of sailing, and then Rachel thought we should try out rowing. I wasn't sure about rowing at first, […] but my mum thought it was a good idea. Now I'm glad I did it because it made my arms strong, and that helped my windsurfing. […]

P: **D____**

J: Yes, definitely. I think I take after my mum – I hope I have some of the same qualities anyway. And Rachel is like a big sister to me.

---

2 Complete gaps 1–5 in the interview with Jackie in Exercise 1 with the verbs from the box. Change the forms if necessary. There are two extra verbs.

> ~~become~~ do go join
> not win play spend teach

3 Choose the combination which is <u>not</u> possible in each group.

1	spend	*sports … / hours … / the weekend …*
2	win	*a competition / a goal / a race*
3	teach	*a subject / someone the rules / first place*
4	go	*surfing / aerobics / running*
5	join	*the gym / a club / athletics*

4 Complete the sentences with verbs from Exercise 3. Change the verb forms if necessary.

If you want a body like a fitness instructor, you'll have to *spend* hours in the gym every week.

1 After Greg finishes studying Sports Science at university, he wants to _____ Physical Education at a secondary school.
2 Sarah didn't buy that snowboard. She _____ a competition and that was the first prize.
3 Hey, can I play too? Will you _____ me the rules?
4 Now that you've spent so much money on trainers and equipment, don't you think you should actually _____ running?
5 Most students _____ several clubs during their first few weeks at university. It's a good way to meet new people.
6 Finally it has snowed and we are going to _____ the weekend in the mountains. I can't wait!

REMEMBER BETTER

When you learn a new verb or review one you already know, use a dictionary and find nouns that often go with it. Write sentences about yourself or people you know to help you remember these collocations.

Write sentences with the verbs and nouns from Exercise 3.

SPEND hours

My brother spends hours playing online games.

WORD STORE 2D | Phrasal verbs

5 Choose the correct words.

1 I really look *up / over / across* to Ronaldo. He's a true professional athlete.
2 My sister takes *up / on / after* my mum – they're both excellent skiers.
3 How did you ever talk me *in / into / to* climbing? I'm terrified of heights.
4 Karen was put *off / on / out* snowboarding after I told her how I broke my leg last winter.
5 A true champion would never give *over / down / up* after losing one match.
6 Rob's always wanted to try *out / on / in* canoeing, so let's invite him too.
7 Sarah had trouble picking *on / up / at* how to play badminton at first, but she's good now.

2.4 READING

A high school hero • collocations
• rituals and routines
• word families

1 Read the text quickly and choose the best title for it.

1 Autistic boy's dream job as school basketball team manager
2 Autistic boy joins national basketball team
3 Autistic boy's basketball dream becomes a reality

It sounds like fantasy: an autistic schoolboy is brought onto the basketball court as a last minute substitute*, scores 20 points in four minutes and becomes a national hero. However, in February 2006 that is exactly what happened to 17-year-old Jason McElwain, from Rochester, New York.

Jason has autism, a condition that makes communicating, socialising and reading other people's feelings difficult. ¹_____. Before that, apart from a couple of minutes in a junior game in 2004, Jason's autism had always stopped him from actually playing for the team. But on the evening of the annual 'Senior Night' game, which was held in the students' final year of high school, the team's coach gave J-Mac, as he is called, a shirt with the number 52 on the back, and told him he would let him play in the all-important game at some point.

In the final few minutes, Jason was sent onto the court. When his teammates passed him the ball, Jason calmly aimed* and scored seven baskets* from 13 shots, scoring five points a minute and breaking school records. Athena beat their opponents Spencerport 79-43. ²_____. His teammate Rickey Wallace said: 'I knew he could shoot, but I didn't know he could score 20 points.'

Jason's father, David McElwain, 51, said: 'He was really happy on the way home. He didn't sleep a lot that night.' Jason's sporting achievement was filmed, and by the evening, a video of him in action had already gone viral*. Eventually, the video reached the television sports channel ESPN and Jason quickly became famous around the country. ³_____. Jason even met the American President at the time, George W Bush, who presented him with a special award.

Since 2006, Jason has graduated from high school and found part-time work with a well-known food store. ⁴_____. He is also involved in public speaking, and is a talented runner. In September 2012, he completed his first marathon in 15th place, in only 3 hours, 1 minute and 41 seconds. With all the activity that is going on in his life, Jason admits that he hasn't been playing as much basketball, but says: 'Occasionally, I'll go and shoot baskets.'

GLOSSARY

substitute (n) – in team sports: a player who is sent onto the pitch/court to replace another player who is tired, injured or playing poorly

aim (v) – in sports: to look carefully and choose the place you want to throw or kick a ball, or shoot a weapon

basket (n) – in basketball: the rings at either end of the court; also, the point which is scored when you throw the ball successfully into one of those rings

go viral – if a picture, video, joke, etc. goes viral, it spreads widely, especially on the Internet

2 **Read the text. Complete gaps 1–4 with sentences A–F. There are two extra sentences.**

A When that happened the coach couldn't believe the team's good luck.

B He wrote a book, *The Game of My Life*, which was published in 2008 and now travels across the United States raising money for autism charities.

C However, that did not prevent coach Jim Johnson from making him 'manager' of Greece Athena High School's basketball team.

D What is more, because of this condition, he often found it difficult to do any sports activities.

E He received offers from celebrities, such as basketball hero Earvin 'Magic' Johnson and TV star Oprah Winfrey, as well as film companies and publishers keen to tell his story.

F At the end of the game, spectators carried Jason off the court on their shoulders.

3 **Read the text again and answer the questions.**

1 What is autism?
_____

2 Who gave Jason the opportunity to play in the 'Senior Night' game?
_____

3 At what point did Jason join the game?
_____

4 Which team won the game?
_____

5 Who described Jason's feelings after the game?
_____

6 What did certain celebrities, film companies and publishers want to do?
_____

7 Where does Jason do his charity work?
_____

8 Which of Jason's other sporting achievements is mentioned in the text?
_____

4 **Complete the collocations with the verbs from the box. Use the text to help you. There are two extra verbs.**

beat   bring   complete   go   pass
~~play~~   present   raise   score

play for a team

1 _____ someone on as a substitute
2 _____ the ball
3 _____ a basket
4 _____ someone with an award
5 _____ money for charity
6 _____ a marathon (or any other race)

REMEMBER BETTER

When you learn a new verb-noun collocation, you can extend your vocabulary knowledge by looking up alternative verbs that go with that noun in a dictionary. Write them as a word web in your notebook with the noun in the centre.

VOCABULARY PRACTICE | Rituals and routines

5 **Look at the vocabulary in lesson 2.4 in the Student's Book. Complete the sentences with a phrase from the box. You may need to change part of the phrase.**

a decisive moment   break from sb's routine
do the same thing over   give sb peace of mind
repeat a sequence   the first step
the last phase   ~~the point of no return~~

As soon as we go around the next bend, we will go past *the point of no return*. The water moves so fast that we will only be able to move in one direction – down the river towards the sea!

1 As a _____ I chose to run around the hill rather than over it. It's good to do something different once in a while.

2 The referee sent off our best player for cheating. That was _____ in the game. What a joke!

3 The _____ in becoming a professional athlete is to decide which specialisation to focus on.

4 You can beat this boxer. He always _____ of punches after he moves back two steps. Watch! Left, left, right, left, right. It's the same every time!

5 It might be boring _____ but every successful tennis player knows it's the only way to hit the ball perfectly with your racket.

6 The fact that winning or losing isn't important can really _____ and help you see the bigger picture. It's simply a game and we're playing for fun – so just enjoy it!

7 This is _____ of our yoga class this morning and then you can all go home. Take a deep breath, touch your toes and hold the position for three minutes.

WORD STORE 2E | Word families

6 **Complete the sentences with the correct form of the words in brackets.**

I'm quite lazy, so I prefer less *active* (ACT) sports like darts or snooker.

1 Plenty of sportspeople are _____ (SUPER). For example, Michael Jordan used to wear his college shorts under his official NBA sports kit.

2 Why can't I be more _____ (DECIDE)? I just don't know which team I want to play for the most.

3 You need pretty _____ (POWER) legs to be a professional long jumper.

4 Don't you find playing chess rather _____ (REPEAT)? You do the same moves over and over again.

5 Athletes need a lot of _____ (RESILIENT) if they are to return after a serious injury and compete at the highest level again.

SHOW WHAT YOU KNOW

1 Match verb patterns A–E to the sentences.

A verb + *to* infinitive
B verb + object + *to* infinitive
C verb + *-ing*
D modal verb + infinitive without *to*
E verb + object + infinitive without *to*

I <u>want to drive</u> a Formula 1 car one day.   (A)

1 We <u>might go</u> for a swim later. ◯
2 The coach <u>makes us run</u> 3 kilometres before the training starts. ◯
3 Please <u>remind me to put</u> a clean towel in my gym bag. ◯
4 Karen <u>fancies watching</u> basketball on TV at home. ◯
5 We <u>arranged to meet</u> at the top of the ski lift at 4 o'clock. ◯

2 ★ Cross out *to* where it is not necessary.

> **Welcome to the Singapore F1 Grand Prix, where today's race should ~~to~~ be very exciting.**
>
> 1 We'd like to remind to our viewers that this is a very important race for Sebastian Vettel.
>
> 2 Vettel is attempting to win his third race in a row here in Singapore.
>
> 3 If the other drivers let him to win again, he'll almost certainly become this year's champion.
>
> 4 It is raining, so the teams have all decided to start the race with wet-weather tyres.
>
> 5 Remember, Vettel only just avoided to crashing during this year's wet Monaco Grand Prix.
>
> 6 Vettel's manager has warned him not to drive too fast in these difficult conditions.
>
> 7 Keep to watching after the race for more exciting motor racing action here on Turbo Channel.

3 ★★ Complete the texts with the correct form of the verb in capitals.

1 **RUN**
Shelly tries *to run* every day. She doesn't mind
ᵃ_____ when the weather is good but she
refuses ᵇ_____ when it's cold and wet.

2 **EAT**
Nick's mum makes him ᵃ_____ cabbage
even though he hates it. She forces him ᵇ_____
bananas, which he doesn't like, and even though
he can't stand ᶜ_____ seafood, she cooks fish
every Friday.

3 **BUY**
Irene could ᵃ_____ the trainers if she had more
money, but she can't afford ᵇ_____ them at
the moment. The sales assistant in the shop advised
her ᶜ_____ them next month because they will
probably be cheaper then.

4 ★★★ Use the words in capitals to complete sentences with a similar meaning.

Would you like to play one more game?
FANCY
Do you *fancy playing* one more game?

1 Our PE teacher forces us to run round the hockey field three times before the game.
MAKE
Our PE teacher _____ round the hockey field three times before the game.

2 Gavin said he would pick us up after the game tomorrow.
OFFER
Gavin _____ after the game tomorrow.

3 We don't go to judo classes anymore.
STOP
We've _____ to judo classes.

4 Alan really doesn't like losing at badminton.
CAN'T STAND
Alan _____ at badminton.

SHOW WHAT YOU'VE LEARNT

5 Complete the sentences with the correct forms of the verbs in brackets.

Sunny Gym Personal Trainers

Are you attempting <u>to get</u> (get) fit but not
having much success? Are you wasting time
¹_____ (do) exercises that don't work? You
could ²_____ (benefit) from the help of
a personal trainer. Our trainers will teach you
³_____ (exercise) efficiently and effectively, and
help you to avoid ⁴_____ (injure) yourself when
you work out. Training should ⁵_____ (be) fun,
not frustrating. Let our trainers ⁶_____ (show)
you the fastest route to success.
**Contact Becky in Reception for details
and bookings.**

/6

GRAMMAR: Train and Try Again page 155

USE OF ENGLISH

2.6

so, too, neither/nor, not either

1 ★ **Choose the correct answers A–C.**

1 Chiara: Luther and Alex are training for the mini-marathon.
   Jules: Really, ___ !
   A so do I   B so am I   C so are they

2 Lior: I hope we can win the game today.
   Felicia: Yeah, ___ , but I'm feeling a little nervous, I have to say.
   A so we can   B so have I   C so do I

3 Laurie: Eddy can run 100 metres in under 14 seconds!
   Harriet: Well, ___ !
   A Mark can too   B so does Mark too   C so does Mark

4 Aileen: Lucy is going to do a course in judo.
   Sherrie: ___ Judith. Maybe they'll be in the same class.
   A So does   B So is   C So will

5 Eddie: I want to meet United in the next round of the cup.
   Ryan: Yeah, ___ .
   A us too   B you too   C me too

2 ★ **Choose the correct answers A–C.**

1 Sammy had never visited such a big stadium before and ___ .
   A neither have I   B neither had I   C nor me

2 None of the other runners want to re-start the race and ___ .
   A nor us   B nor we   C nor do we

3 James says he shouldn't have to take a blood test, so ___ .
   A neither should I   B nor should he
   C neither should he

4 Lewis can't play tennis this Sunday and ___ .
   A I can't either   B either can I   C neither can't I

5 We hadn't seen the results immediately after the game and ___ .
   A neither they too   B neither had they
   C nor them

3 ★★ **Choose the correct forms.**

1 Agnes: Alberto would never go climbing. It's too dangerous for him.
   Mel: Really? *He would / I would / We are!* It looks like such fun, don't you think?

2 Sheila: My parents haven't been jogging for weeks.
   Freddy: Ha, *nor do they / nor have mine / so have yours.* And we're lazy teenagers!?

3 Jasmin: I can't say I like playing basketball very much.
   Tanya: Oh, *I can / I like / I did.* In fact, I think it's the best sport ever!

4 Fran: I'm planning to go swimming this afternoon.
   Liza: Really? *So am I / So do I / So will I.* We can go together if you like.

5 Lexie: Marcelle had never been ice-skating before yesterday.
   Denise: And *nor has / so hadn't / neither had* Jane. They were quite good though, weren't they?

4 ★★ **Choose the correct answers A–C.**

MyBlog.com

I've just ¹___ a conversation with my sports coach and I have to say I'm a bit disappointed. He thinks I'm not ready to run in the mini-marathon next month. Really? Well, ²___ . I wouldn't say I wanted to do it if I didn't feel ready. What does he know? But maybe he doesn't understand – I don't actually care about winning and neither ³___ he. What I really care about is getting more racing experience. I believe that's more important – and my parents ⁴___ . Which is why I'm going to enter the marathon with or without the support of my running coach. What do you think? Do you think I'm making a big mistake? I ⁵___ . I'm sure it is a good idea! And ⁶___ my friend Sophie, who thinks I might even come in the top 100.

1 A have   B had   C done
2 A I do   B I don't   C he doesn't
3 A should   B would   C could
4 A are too   B do too   C have too
5 A don't   B haven't   C didn't
6 A either does   B too does   C so is

5 ★★★ **Complete the sentences with phrases showing similarities (+) or differences (−) in situations. Sometimes more than one answer is possible.**

   Rico: I can't swim very well, I'm afraid.
   Noah: Really, *neither / nor can I* (+)

1 Pauline: I'm going to the cup final on Sunday.
   Lucas: Oh, _____ (+) actually. We can go together.

2 Alba: I have never played volleyball.
   Rosie: Don't worry, Jamie and George _____ (+).

3 Krysta: Oh, no. I didn't bring any tennis balls with me.
   Johanna: What? _____ (+). Can we buy some here?

4 Ayleen: Heather loves watching Kyle play football.
   Lynn: _____ (+). I think he's wonderful.

5 Keren: I'll never win a sports competition.
   Ossie: Really? _____ (−). I'm quite sporty, I think.

6 ★★★ **Complete the sentences with the words in brackets. You may need to add words. Use at least three words.**

   James is going on an adventure holiday in June and *so are we* (we).

1 I've had my hair cut short for the race and _____ (Angelica).

2 Stacy's parents didn't go horse racing and _____ (my).

3 Those little children are running very fast and our _____ (too).

4 Evelyn won't wear the new uniform and _____ (I).

5 My school doesn't have a football pitch and _____ (your).

4 Complete the story in Exercise 3 with the correct form of the verbs in brackets. Where possible, use the Past Perfect or the Past Continuous.

5 Read the story *A Mistake on the Mountain*. Choose the correct linkers.

1 Match the opening sentences 1–3 with techniques a–c.

1 My dream of going on safari finally came true last year, but it almost turned into a nightmare! ☐
2 How high is a mountain? ☐
3 What's the worst thing your best friend has ever said to you? ☐

a Asking a rhetorical question
b Referring to personal experience
c Speaking directly to the reader

2 Complete the advice for writing a story with the words from the box. There are two extra words.

adjectives   character   conclusion
ending   opening   problem   scene
speech   tenses   ~~title~~

1 Give your story a catchy *title*.
2 Use direct _____ to make the story come alive.
3 Give your story a memorable _____ .
4 Set the _____ by saying where and when the story is set and who is involved.
5 Include a _____ or introduce an exciting situation.
6 Use a range of narrative _____ to tell your story.
7 Write a strong _____ sentence to engage the reader.
8 Include a variety of adverbs and _____ to make the language interesting.

3 Read the story *An African Thriller* and match the underlined sentences and phrases with the advice in Exercise 2.

1 ⓐ   2 ☐   3 ☐   4 ☐   5 ☐   6 ☐   7 ☐   8 ☐

A Mistake on the Mountain

How high is a mountain? I've reached many peaks, but on this trip everything possible went wrong.

My best friend Joe and I arranged to meet early one morning in summer. We both know mountains are dangerous, but it was also really **ªhot** / _____ so **¹**after that / before we left we had agreed to pack a map, some water and just a few snacks.

²After a couple of hours / By the end of the journey, the path started to get very difficult. We had intended to reach a small lake **³**by lunch time / the following afternoon but we couldn't find it. We kept looking at the map but we didn't want to waste time arguing, so we just kept walking. **⁴**Later / At first, we saw it. But strangely, it looked different to what we had expected.

⁵By the end of the afternoon / On the first morning we had finished all our food and water and were feeling extremely **ᵇtired** / _____ . We weren't walking anymore either, we were climbing. I was quite **ᶜscared** / _____ .

Suddenly Joe shouted excitedly. 'I can see the top'. **⁶**Finally / Later, we had arrived. We felt really **ᵈgood** /_____ . While we were looking at the view, we clearly saw the mountain we had planned to climb. We were on the wrong mountain! Luckily, we found an easier path down.

⁷ After that / Eventually we got back home. Everyone was very impressed with our amazing achievement, so we decided not to mention our big mistake!

6 Replace the adjectives in bold in the story in Exercise 5 with stronger adjectives from the box. There are two extra words.

angry   awesome   awful
boiling   exhausted   terrified

ªAn African Thriller

ᵇMy dream of an African safari finally came true last year, but it almost turned into a nightmare! ᶜIt was our third night in Africa and my sister Jenny and I were getting ready for bed in our log cabin. It *had been* (be) an amazing day and we were completely exhausted but we couldn't stop talking about the incredible animals we ¹_____ (see) that morning. ᵈTen minutes later we had just put out the light when Jenny screamed.

Earlier that day, our guide ²_____ (tell) us stories about dangerous African animals. One man ³_____ (work) outside when a rhinoceros ⁴_____ (begin) to run after him. ᵉAnd two girls spent the night in a tree after a crocodile had tried to eat them. The guide warned us to check under our beds before going to sleep. Of course we thought he ⁵_____ (joke).

I ⁶_____ (look) where Jenny ⁷_____ point) and then I saw it. A huge snake was lying under the table right next to the door. I was ᶠabsolutely terrified. ᵍ'Quick! Get in the cupboard' I shouted. As we were running for safety, I grabbed my phone. After we ⁸_____ (shut) the cupboard door, I ⁹_____ (ring) our guide.

He quickly arrived to help. While he ¹⁰_____ (shine) his torch under the table, Jenny and I ¹¹_____ (realise) our mistake. ʰIt wasn't a snake after all, just some rolled up clothes. I ¹²_____ (never/be) so embarrassed in all my life.

7 Read the task below. Then read the story *The Extra Special Surprise* and write the verbs in the correct form.

> Your school is holding a competition for the best short story about a surprising turn of events. Write your story and include and develop these points:
> - Begin your story by setting the scene and introducing a problem or interesting situation.
> - Describe what happened using a range of tenses.
> - Use direct speech and different words and phrases to make the story interesting for the reader.
> - Give your story an exciting, funny or unexpected ending.

The Extra Special Surprise

What's the worst thing your best friend can ᵃ*say / to say / saying* to you? 'I won a volleyball scholarship in Australia and I'm moving away'. Zara ¹_____ (always / be) sporty. While she ²_____ (win) prizes, I was cheering her on or coming last! I was very upset but I intended ᵇ*do / to do / doing* something special before she left.

Zara loves surprises, so I wanted ᶜ*organise / organising / to organise* a surprise leaving party. I told a few friends but warned ᵈ*them not to tell / not to tell them / them not telling* anyone.

First I arranged the food. Zara's favourite café promised to deliver cakes on the day. Next I spent time ᵉ*to make / make / making* a playlist with our favourite songs. By that evening I ³_____ (make) decorations too – photos of Zara scoring goals and beating opponents. While I ⁴_____ (look) at the photos, I ⁵_____ (feel) sad again.

Finally, after I ⁶_____ (prepare) everything, I couldn't avoid ᶠ*tell / telling / to tell* people any longer. Everyone ⁷_____ (be) excited.

We ⁸_____ (hide) when Zara ⁹_____ (arrive). 'Surprise!' we shouted. 'We're so sad you're leaving that we decided ᵍ*to have / have / having* a party', I ¹⁰_____ (say), to explain. Zara looked shocked, then gave a huge smile.

'I have a surprise for you, too' she said. 'I'm not leaving after all! I got into our national team, so I can ʰ*to train / training / train* at home!'

8 Read the story again and choose the correct verb forms a–h.

SHOW WHAT YOU'VE LEARNT

9 You have decided to write a short story for your class magazine. The theme of the next edition is 'Pushing your limits.' Include and develop these points:
- Begin your story by setting the scene and introducing a problem or interesting situation.
- Describe what happened using a range of tenses.
- Use direct speech and different words and phrases to make the story interesting for the reader.
- Give your story an exciting, funny or unexpected ending.

SHOW THAT YOU'VE CHECKED

Finished? Always check your writing. Can you tick √ everything on this list?

In my story:

• I have given my story an interesting title.	☐
• I have started my story by setting the scene and introducing a problem or interesting situation, e.g. *It was the last thing we were expecting*, *Just when we thought we were safe, Jack and I realised our mistake.*	☐
• I have described what happened using a range of tenses, e.g. *We were both feeling quite nervous, We'd booked lessons before we arrived.*	☐
• I have used different words and phrases to make the story interesting for the reader, e.g. *We were completely exhausted, Eventually …*	☐
• I have included direct speech to make the story come alive, e.g. *'What are you doing?'*	☐
• I have given my story an exciting, funny or unexpected ending.	☐
• I have divided my story into paragraphs.	☐
• I have checked my spelling and punctuation.	☐
• My text is neat and clear.	☐

SPEAKING

Asking for and giving an opinion
• agreeing and disagreeing

1 Translate the phrases into your own language.

SPEAKING BANK

Asking for someone's opinion

What do you think about ...? _____

Giving an opinion

I think ... _____

I (just) don't think ... _____

If you ask me ... _____

The thing is ... _____

To be honest ... _____

Agreeing with an opinion

I agree. _____

That's true. _____

Absolutely! _____

Half agreeing with an opinion

I'm not so sure about that. _____

I'm not convinced. _____

Disagreeing

That's not true. _____

I'm sorry, I don't agree with you. _____

Disagreeing strongly

No way! (informal) _____

Are you kidding? (informal) _____

I'm afraid I completely disagree. _____

Not having strong opinions

Personally, I don't feel strongly one way or the other. _____

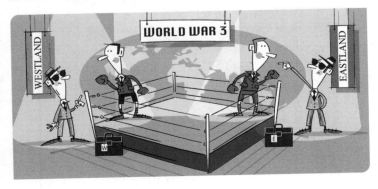

2 Choose the appropriate response.

1 **Tim:** What do you think about the fact that professional footballers are paid so much money?

Tom: *To be honest / No way*, I think it's ridiculous.

2 **Jane:** Do you think we will win the next World Cup?

Jean: *Are you kidding? / That's true*. With our current team we don't have a chance.

3 **Paul:** Aerobics is only for women.

Paula: *That's not true / I agree*. There are several men in my class.

4 **Sarah:** Oh come on, referee! That was clearly a foul. Don't you think, Sam?

Sam: *I'm not convinced / Absolutely*. It looked OK to me.

5 **Matt:** I just don't think we do enough sport at school.

Mary: *The thing is / I agree* I don't really enjoy sport, so I don't mind.

6 **Neil:** Helen thinks motor-racing is too dangerous and should be banned.

Noel: Well, *I agree / If you ask me* the drivers have a choice, don't they? They don't have to take part.

7 **Jack:** I'm glad they have decided to let girls play in the school football team, aren't you?

Jackie: *Personally, I don't feel strongly one way or the other / Absolutely*. I suppose it's good for the girls who are into football. I'd prefer to go to the gym.

3 Complete the dialogue between Scott and Owen. The first letters are given.

Scott: Did you see that there's going to be a big boxing match at the new stadium next month? Do you fancy going?

Owen: Boxing? No thanks. In my opinion, boxing isn't even a sport. I t*hink* it's horrible.

Scott: Really? Well, I'm ¹s_____ , I don't a_____ w_____ y_____ . I think it's really exciting to watch. Boxers are skilled athletes.

Owen: ²A_____ you k_____ ? Watching grown men try and kill each other is not what I call exciting. Personally, I don't find violence entertaining.

Scott: I'm ³n_____ c_____ . People have been playing and watching violent sports for thousands of years.

Owen: ⁴T_____ t_____ , but that doesn't make it right. People have been fighting wars for thousands of years. Do you think war is exciting too?

Scott: Of course not, but ⁵I d_____ t_____ you can compare boxing to war. For a start, the boxers have a choice. They don't have to fight.

Owen: Well, if you ⁶a_____ m_____ , there's always a choice whether it's boxing or war.

Scott: Well, perhaps. Hey, how about this – maybe instead of fighting wars, we could put world leaders in the boxing ring. I bet you'd watch that.

Student A, look below. Student B, go to page 135.

1 In pairs, ask and answer the questions.

Talk about looks and personality.

1 How do you find out about clothes that are in fashion and out of fashion?

2 Do you think it's important to have a break from your routine sometimes? Why?/Why not?

3 Do you think you come across as friendly when you first meet someone? Why?/Why not?

4 Have you ever lost touch with a friend? What happened?

5 When was the last time you wore brightly-coloured clothes? Why?

2 Discuss this question together. 'Is winning more important than taking part in a sport?' What do you think?

> **For taking part:**
>
> **Taking part in a sport ...**
> * is fun and thrilling! It doesn't matter who wins!
> * is a great experience that helps you learn about yourself and other people.
> * is great exercise for your body and mind (without the pressure to win!).
> * is good preparation for life. You don't always win but you can learn a lot by fighting hard along the way!

3 Look at the two photos showing people at sporting events. What can you see in the photos? Which activity would you prefer to do? Why?

4 Read the instructions on your card and role-play the conversation.

> **Student A:**
>
> **You and your friend (Student B) are discussing a suggestion that sports should be removed from the curriculum.**
> * Greet Student B and ask his/her opinion on the subject.
> * Half agree with Student B's opinion, but give your own opinion too: say that doing a sport is important for general health and fitness.
> * Disagree with Student B's opinion. Explain that students don't have a lot of free time, so it's hard to organise sports.
> * Say that you'll have to agree/disagree on the subject.

VOCABULARY AND GRAMMAR

1 Complete the sentences with the words from the box. Change the form if necessary. There are two extra words.

> fan goal lose pick phase
> power teammate win

The team's _fans_ ran onto the basketball court to celebrate with the players at the end of the game.

1 I think we've _____ this game. I haven't got any good cards to play. And you?
2 I hurt my arm when my _____ dropped me on the court while we were celebrating. How embarrassing, eh?
3 Badminton isn't too hard to play if you play tennis and I'm sure you'll _____ it up quickly.
4 Congratulations on a good result, but this is only the first _____ of the competition. There's still a long way to go!
5 Ryan scored the fastest _____ ever by a player in our team – 12 seconds after the match had started!

/5

2 Complete the sentences. The first and last letters are given.

My brother's a r**efere**e for the local football league and he loves giving players yellow cards.

1 My athletics t_____r says I'm good enough to be a professional one day.
2 My great grandad is 78 but he still k_____s in shape by going Nordic walking.
3 Celia is s_____s and always wears the same socks when she's competing in a race.
4 Sebastian isn't a very a_____e person. In fact, I don't think I've ever seen him do any sports or other physical exercise.
5 To get a body like Arnold Schwarzenegger you have to do lots of r_____e lifting of heavy weights. It must be quite boring, really.

/5

3 Choose the correct option.

I didn't know your little brother played chess. When did he ____ into that?

(A) get B came C broke

1 What a terrible match! Our team ___ and I injured my foot.
A defeated B lost C beat
2 We are all hoping that the Austrian ski jumper won't ___ up because of his bad performance at the Winter Olympics.
A break B hang C give
3 LeBron James ___ 34 points for Los Angeles in last night's big game against Miami.
A won B scored C threw
4 Of course, the most important thing is taking part in a sports event, but I really like to beat my ___ too.
A opponent B teammate C supporter
5 We decided to have a break from our ___ of waking up early to go jogging. Instead we slept late and had a lazy breakfast in a local café.
A custom B routine C practice

/5

4 Choose the correct words.

Unfortunately, we weren't watching when Bolt (won)/ had won / was winning the 200-metre race.

1 Chloe finally beat her personal best time because she trained / had trained / was training so hard.
2 Dan tried snowboarding when he went / had gone / was going to the French Alps.
3 The marathon finally ended / had ended / was ending when the last runner crossed the finishing line after almost 6 hours.
4 Andrew was prepared for the freezing temperatures because he surfed / had surfed / was surfing in winter before.
5 Naomi wasn't actually skating when she hurt / had hurt / was hurting her foot. She was trying to take her skate off!

/5

5 Complete the sentences with the correct forms of the verbs in brackets.

If our team manages _to win_ (win) the European Championships, I will buy everyone dinner.

1 I remind my players _____ (not/get angry) with the referee. Shouting and complaining doesn't help.
2 Do you really enjoy _____ (jog) when the temperatures are so high?
3 I think I might _____ (join) the gym again. I've put on so much weight recently.
4 Our PE teacher made the boys _____ (do) aerobics after they said it was easy and only for girls. They were exhausted afterwards.
5 Jenny misses _____ (play) badminton with her sister now that she's gone to university.

/5

6 Choose the correct answers A–C.

Adzo Kpossi from Togo, Africa, _B_ the youngest athlete at the Olympic Games in 2012. When she ¹____ into the water in London to compete in the women's 50 metres freestyle event, she was just 13 years old. In the qualifying race, she ²____ second to Nafissatou Moussa Adamou, a 14-year-old from Niger, but beat her own personal best time. Before she arrived in London to represent her country, she ³____ lots of training at a hotel in Sarakawa, which was the only place in her part of the country with a swimming pool. Although she failed ⁴____ any medals, Kpossi was later asked ⁵____ the flag for Togo at both the opening and closing ceremony of the 2016 summer Olympics and hopes to be present at the 2020 games in Tokyo.

	A	B	C
	A had been	(B) was	C was being
1	A dived	B was diving	C had dived
2	A got	B came	C lost
3	A was doing	B has done	C had done
4	A to win	B win	C winning
5	A to carry	B carry	C carrying

/5

Total /30

7 Complete each pair of sentences with the same answer A–C.

Would you __ if I closed the window? It's pretty cold in here.

Regular yoga and meditation can give you real peace of __ .

Ⓐ mind   **B** like   **C** think

1 When you reach the __ of no return, you can never go back!

We need one more __ to win the match. Come on The Blues!

A score   **B** point   **C** goal

2 How did you __ Antonio into going jogging with you at 6 a.m.?

Mr Brown wants to __ to me about missing too many training sessions.

A speak   **B** talk   **C** chat

3 My grandfather was a great athlete and I really __ up to him and his achievements in sport.

Oh, __ ! Isn't that Boris Becker, the ex-Wimbledon champion?

A see   **B** watch   **C** look

4 Barry has always wanted to __ out bowling, so he's looking forward to tonight's game.

Where can I __ on this tracksuit to see if it fits me?

A try   **B** go   **C** put

5 Henrikson has had to __ out of the race after pulling a muscle in his leg.

Please, be careful with that expensive trophy. Don't __ it!

A fall   **B** break   **C** drop

/5

8 Complete the sentences with the correct form of the words in brackets.

Footballers Lionel Messi and Christiano Ronaldo share the same _superstition_ (SUPER) – they must both be the last players onto the pitch.

1 Boxers need a lot of _____ (RESILIENT), because they have to pick themselves up every time they get knocked down.

2 I find the best way to _____ (ACTION) myself in the mornings is to do fifteen minutes of yoga.

3 My manager has been very _____ (SUPPORT) of my decision to quit the national team.

4 King Kong and Godzilla are probably some of the most _____ (POWER) creatures created by the film industry before the dinosaurs in _Jurrasic Park_.

5 At the last minute, I noticed that my passport was out-of-date. That was a _____ (DECIDE) moment.

/5

9 Complete the sentences using the prompts in brackets. Change the forms or add new words where necessary. Use up to six words in each gap.

The manager _forced us to train_ (force / we / train) despite the bad weather.

1 Javier _____ (not / stand / lose) and gets very upset whenever he doesn't win.

2 Janice, could you _____ (teach / swim)? I really trust you and you're always patient with me.

3 When I was a kid, my parents _____ (not / allow / do) karate, but I've always wanted to try it.

4 Mum _____ (warn / not / climb) the tree in our garden – but then, of course, I did and I fell out and broke my arm.

5 While the coach _____ (tell / the team / believe) that they really could get to the final, one of the footballers started to laugh.

/5

10 Complete the text with one word in each gap.

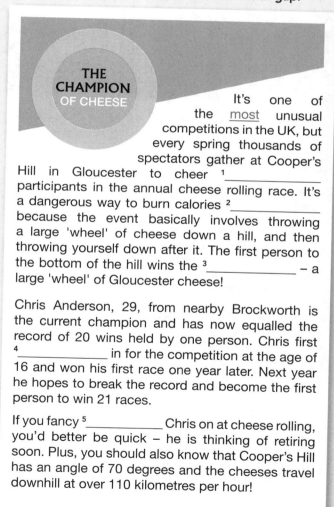

THE CHAMPION OF CHEESE

It's one of the <u>most</u> unusual competitions in the UK, but every spring thousands of spectators gather at Cooper's Hill in Gloucester to cheer ¹_____ participants in the annual cheese rolling race. It's a dangerous way to burn calories ²_____ because the event basically involves throwing a large 'wheel' of cheese down a hill, and then throwing yourself down after it. The first person to the bottom of the hill wins the ³_____ – a large 'wheel' of Gloucester cheese!

Chris Anderson, 29, from nearby Brockworth is the current champion and has now equalled the record of 20 wins held by one person. Chris first ⁴_____ in for the competition at the age of 16 and won his first race one year later. Next year he hopes to break the record and become the first person to win 21 races.

If you fancy ⁵_____ Chris on at cheese rolling, you'd better be quick – he is thinking of retiring soon. Plus, you should also know that Cooper's Hill has an angle of 70 degrees and the cheeses travel downhill at over 110 kilometres per hour!

/5

Total   /20

3 On the go

VOCABULARY

3.1

Means of transport • noun phrases
• collocations • synonyms for *trip*

SHOW WHAT YOU KNOW

1 Label the forms of transport. The first letters are given.

t<u>ram</u>

1 h_____-a_____
b_____

2 f_____

3 h_____

4 d_____-d_____
b_____

5 h_____

WORD STORE 3A | Noun phrases

2 Match the halves of the compound nouns in boxes A and B and complete the sentences.

A [cable dirt public rush ~~short~~
suspension traffic winding]

B [bridge car ~~cut~~ hour
jams path track transport]

We can save ten minutes on our walk to the centre if we take the <u>shortcut</u> across the field.

1 There's no road to get to my aunt's house but we can use the _____ if you drive slowly and don't mind getting the car muddy.

2 The Tibetan saint Thangtong Gyalpo built a _____ with iron chains as early as 1433 in Bhutan. However, earlier designs using rope and wood were also used to cross rivers and valleys.

3 The longest journey made by a _____ is 7,455 metres. It's in China and goes from Zhangjiajie city centre to the top of Heaven's Gate Mountain.

4 If more people used _____ like buses and trams, there'd be less traffic on the roads and less pollution in the air.

5 Sorry we're late. It's ª_____ and there are always awful ᵇ_____ at this time of day.

6 There's a wonderful _____ through the forest. It turns left and right and then left and right again – all the way to the lake at the end.

WORD STORE 3B | Collocations

3 Choose the correct verbs.

Last night I had a very strange dream. I decided to ¹*miss/catch* the bus to school because I was feeling too lazy to cycle ²*uphill/downhill* like I usually did for my regular morning exercise. But because it was raining really heavily, a boat came along instead. I got on the boat, in fact, I was the only passenger, and it began to ³*cross/swim* the river. But the journey was very rough and the captain ordered me to sit down and ⁴*close/fasten* my seatbelt. Then suddenly there were lots of other boats and we were ⁵*stuck/caught* in traffic. It took ages for the boat to make any progress, and all the time it was raining. When I finally arrived at school, I noticed I was ⁶*walking/going* barefoot. And I was completely wet and shaking from the cold. The teacher looked confused and asked me why I was late. I simply told her I'd ⁷*missed/lost* the bus. Very strange.

4 Complete the sentences with the verbs *catch*, *cross*, *get* or *miss* in the correct form. Sometimes more than one answer is possible.

I <u>caught</u> the train from Waterloo and got here as soon as I could.

1 Marco Polo was the first westerner to _____ the continent of Asia. In total, he travelled through the area for 24 years.

2 We _____ stuck in traffic and that's why we're a little late.

3 My school bag was so heavy this morning that I _____ a lift in the car from my mum.

4 Janet _____ the train and there isn't another one until tomorrow morning. She'll have to stay the night in a hotel.

5 Before bridges existed, the only way to _____ a valley was to climb down one side and then climb up the other.

WORD STORE 3C | Synonyms for *trip*

5 Read the definitions and choose the correct word.

1 a trip on a plane = *a drive / a flight / a ride*
2 a trip by sea or in space = *a ride / a drive / a voyage*
3 a long trip overland = *a flight / a cruise / a journey*
4 a trip by boat from one
   piece of land to another = *a tour / a crossing / a ride*

6 Complete the sentences with the correct words. The first letter is given.

The first time my mum went on a plane was to Australia! The **f**<u>light</u> took over twenty-two hours with a stopover in Hong Kong.

1 My sister and her husband are going on a **c**_____ in the Mediterranean. Their ship leaves from Liverpool and the first stop is Monaco!

2 The **d**_____ from London to Paris by car is six and a half hours. The high speed train takes just over two hours!

3 The ferry **c**_____ in the Baltic Sea from Poland to Sweden takes up to 19 hours.

4 Paloma is going on a 15-day cycling trip this summer. Her **j**_____ will take her from Berlin all the way to Malaga in the south of Spain. She must be mad!

5 I went on a camel **r**_____ when I was in Egypt but I wouldn't recommend it. I don't think the animals are treated very kindly.

6 Our guided **t**_____ around Toledo took us to the cathedral and then to the El Greco Museum.

7 When Columbus discovered America, he was actually on a **v**_____ to find a new route to Asia.

REMEMBER THIS

travel (v) *I'd love to <u>travel</u> to the United States.*
travel (n, uncountable) *Jo's job involves a lot of <u>travel</u>.*
travels (n, pl) *My <u>travels</u> took me through Europe and Asia.*
~~My travel across Guatemala was awesome!~~
My journey across Guatemala was awesome!

---

7 Read REMEMBER THIS. Complete each sentence with the correct form of the word *travel*. Then label each word with *V* (verb) or *N* (noun).

<u>Travel</u> broadens the mind. Ⓝ

1 This picture shows the _____ of the planets around the sun. ☐

2 The book *Uncommon Traveller* describes Mary Kingsley's solo _____ through Africa in the 1890s.

3 Some food doesn't _____ well. ☐

4 Before the train was invented, _____ between cities used to take days. ☐

5 Sound _____ through water. ☐

6 Joseph _____ to experience different cultures. ☐

7 Tell us all about your _____ in Central and South America. ☐

8 We _____ 200 kilometres on the second day – it was exhausting! ☐

---

8 Choose the correct answers A–C.

My 'Dream' Holiday

After studying hard and passing my exams I decided to ¹__ a holiday. I had been really stressed, so I wanted the kind of holiday where you lie in the sun and do nothing for a week. This, I was sure, would help me relax. So, I opted for a short ²__ on the ship 'The Ocean Dream.' This would be perfect, I thought. But unfortunately, my holiday wasn't the 'dream' I had hoped for. To begin with, I ³__ the train to Southampton. That meant I had to get a lift from my dad at the last minute, which was quite stressful for both of us. And, of course, we also got ⁴__ in traffic, so I was really stressed the whole way thinking that I wouldn't be able to get on the ship before it left.

Well, I made it just in time. But as soon as we left land, the weather turned bad and it stayed wet and cloudy the whole ⁵__ . For four whole days the ship was bouncing up and down on the large waves. I got seasick and began to worry that the ship might sink and go under water like the Titanic. When the ship finally made it back to Southampton, I was more stressed and nervous than when I had left. What a nightmare! I now wish I had just booked a cheap ⁶__ to Egypt instead and spent a week lying on the beach doing nothing!

1	A make	B take	C do
2	A voyage	B journey	C cruise
3	A lost	B missed	C crossed
4	A held	B stuck	C fastened
5	A journey	B tour	C ride
6	A drive	B crossing	C flight

9 Find and correct the mistakes.

I know a shorter cut through the park. <u>shortcut</u>

1 The suspending bridge is moving in the wind.
   _____

2 Traffic is always bad during the hurry hour. _____

3 Let's take the dirty track – it'll be quicker. _____

4 Always fast your seatbelt when in a moving car.
   _____

/10

33

SHOW WHAT YOU KNOW

1 Match the speakers' words to the explanations.

1 Awful club. Don't go. Terrible music and no atmosphere. ☐

2 It was OK, we danced for a while, then we sat and chatted. Not bad, but not great. ☐

3 The music was absolutely fantastic. How come I didn't know about this place earlier? ☐

a I'm sure this person liked the club.

b It's possible this person liked the club.

c I'm sure this person didn't like the club.

2 ★ Complete the second sentence with *must*, *might* or *can't*.

1 It's possible that's our taxi. That *might* be our taxi.
2 I'm sure that's our plane. That _____ be our plane.
3 I'm sure those aren't our bags. Those _____ be our bags.
4 It's possible this is the hotel. This _____ be the hotel.
5 I'm sure this is our room. This _____ be our room.
6 We're sure that isn't our bill. That _____ be our bill.

3 ★ Match the sentences in Exercise 2 with the evidence below.

A I ordered it for ten o'clock and it's five to ten now. [1]
B It was definitely number 321. ☐
C I think I recognise it from the picture on the website. ☐
D We are flying with Lufthansa, aren't we? ☐
E We certainly didn't order room service 5 times. ☐
F Our suitcases are blue, not black. ☐

4 ★ ★ Choose the correct forms.

At the aquarium …

Nick: Look! An octopus.
Anne: Where? I can't see anything.
Nick: Er … well, the sign says there's an octopus, so it ¹*must* / *couldn't* be there somewhere.
Anne: I suppose it ²*can't* / *might* be hiding under that rock.
Nick: Yeah, or it ³*could* / *couldn't* be away on holiday …
Anne: On holiday? You ⁴*might* / *can't* be serious. Honestly, I worry about you, Nick.
Nick: It says here that octopuses can change the colour of their skin and totally disappear. Cool. I'd love to be able to do that.
Anne: Nick, sometimes I think that would be a good idea.

5 ★ ★ ★ Choose the correct forms to complete the dialogue. Sometimes more than one answer is possible.

> ~~can't have~~   could have   couldn't have
> may have   must have

Out for a walk …

Violet: Look at that! A turtle on a fence post. How did that happen?

Daisy: Woah! That's weird. It *can't have* got there on its own. Its legs are so short it ¹_____ climbed up so high.

Violet: There's only one possibility. Someone ²_____ put it there. What a cruel thing to do.

Daisy: Well, it ³_____ been a person, or I suppose a bird, like an eagle or something ⁴_____ left it there … as a snack for later.

Violet: Urgh, Daisy! That's horrible.

Daisy: Violet my dear, we all have to eat.

SHOW WHAT YOU'VE LEARNT

6 Choose the correct answers A–C to replace the underlined part of the sentence.

1 It is possible we are too late to catch the bus. Are there still people at the stop?
   A We can't be
   B We might be
   C We must be

2 They only left half an hour ago. I'm sure it's not true that they have arrived already.
   A They can't have
   B They may have
   C They mustn't have

3 It is possible that Alice brought some sun cream. She's so pale-skinned.
   A Alice must have
   B Alice can't have
   C Alice could have

4 I'm sure it's true that you are tired. We've been walking and sightseeing all day.
   A You can't be
   B You must be
   C You might be

5 She can't find her passport! I'm sure it's true that she left it in the hotel room.
   A She might have
   B She must have
   C She can't have

6 It is possible that the plane was delayed because of bad weather.
   A The plane may have been
   B The plane must have been
   C The plane can't have been

_____ /6

GRAMMAR: Train and Try Again page 156

Functional language • prepositions • collocations • compound nouns

1 **Put the words in order and then mark the phrases as R for *something a hotel receptionist would say* or G for *something a hotel guest would say*.**

help / I / you / can
Can I help you ?   (R)

1   book / you / online / did
    _____ ?   ◯

2   was / thought / I / included / it
    _____   ◯

3   room / two / booked / a / I've / for / nights / single
    _____   ◯

4   have / at / special online offer / we / moment / the / a
    _____   ◯

5   this / fill / can / in / form / please / you
    _____ ?   ◯

6   you / would / breakfast / like
    _____ ?   ◯

2 **Complete the dialogue with the phrases from Exercise 1.**

Extract from Student's Book recording 🔊 **1.42**

R: Yes, *can I help you* ?
G: Er, yes ¹ _____ . My name's Baker. James Baker.
R: Baker. Yes, here you are. Two nights. [...] ² _____ ?
G: Oh, yes please.
R: That will be an extra £16.
G: Oh, ³ _____ .
R: ⁴ _____ ?
G: Yes, I did.
R: Oh, right. ⁵ _____ . Your first breakfast is free, so you just need to pay for the second day.
        ⁶ _____ ?

3 **Choose the correct prepositions A–C.**

Extract from Student's Book recording 🔊 **1.42**

A: So, how was your family cruise?
B: Oh, it was OK. Pretty good really. [...] We all got on well most ¹__ the time. We didn't have any arguments. Well, not ²__ the last day, and then I had a really big argument ³__ my sister. It was stupid really. I wanted to get ⁴__ the ship and visit Naples. But my sister was tired and wanted to stay ⁵__ the ship ⁶__ the pool. [...] She always does what she wants, and she doesn't think ⁷__ other people. I had to go ⁸__ Naples ⁹__ my own with our parents. It was really boring.

1	**A** in	**B** of	**C** with
2	**A** after	**B** by	**C** until
3	**A** with	**B** to	**C** against
4	**A** on	**B** from	**C** off
5	**A** until	**B** on	**C** in
6	**A** by	**B** against	**C** to
7	**A** on	**B** to	**C** of
8	**A** to	**B** at	**C** in
9	**A** by	**B** on	**C** with

4 **Look at the text below. Complete the expressions in bold with a word from the box. There are two extra words.**

(all   part   real   rest   spend   sure   ~~time~~   trip)

Extract from Student's Book recording 🔊 **1.42**

It's *time* **to** leave package holidays behind and **take a ¹ ____** that you will remember **for the ² ____ of your life**. With 'Overland Tours' you will **see the ³ ____ world**. 'Overland Tours' believe that travelling is not only about the destination. The bus journey is **an important ⁴ ____ of the experience**. Come with us on one of our Overland buses and travel to places other travel companies don't reach. [...] Our tour leaders will take care of you and **make ⁵ ____** you have everything you need.

REMEMBER BETTER

To help you remember the phrases and expressions you learn, use them in sentences about your own important personal experiences, e.g. your exams.

Write sentences with the remaining expressions.

   It's time to start saving money for a holiday after I finish my exams.

WORD STORE 3D | Compound nouns

5 **Choose the correct words.**

1   If it's four hours one way, that's an eight-hour *double / return* journey. Do we have to go so far?

2   Dad's away on a *round-the-world / business* trip in Japan for the next two months.

3   Many travel *agents / leaders* have closed their shops because people prefer booking online these days.

4   'Teentour' is looking for teenage tour *guides / companies* to show young visitors around the city this summer. Full training given.

5   Ellen always chooses a *package / budget* holiday because she doesn't have to plan anything by herself.

6   Because of its glacier, snow is guaranteed almost all year in the *ski / skiing* resort of Kaprun, Austria.

7   Are you sure this is a *three-star / double* hotel? The rooms aren't even clean.

8   I'm sure a *twin / single* room should have two beds. I'll call the hotel reception.

READING

3.4

Travelling on my own • colloquial expressions • negative adjectives • verb phrases

1 Read blogs 1–3 and match them with photos A–C.

1 ☐　　2 ☐　　3 ☐

A

B

C

www.travelblogging.com

Sign in ▾　　Search 🔍

1

Around the world in 6 months

Blogger: **Jo**

Well, my journey didn't <u>get off to a very good start</u> as I lost my passport in Manchester Airport. I panicked, then found it where I was sitting earlier. How stupid! I hope this is not a bad sign for the rest of the trip. The plane was one of those new two-level ones and was really <u>posh</u> inside. It wasn't even half full, so I lay across several seats and managed to get plenty of sleep.

Arrived in Bangkok at 7:00 and feeling fresh but immediately had problems. My card didn't work in any of the ATMs, so I panicked again until I realised that I was using the wrong pin number. Again, pretty stupid. Got a taxi to the hostel, which is great and full of young people like me. I'm writing this in the lounge area. Feeling excited, but also a bit nervous – not really sure how anything works here in Thailand. Please keep reading – hopefully, my travelling (and blogging) skills will improve soon …

2

Summer in Austria

Blogger: **Alex**

Yesterday I said bye to Mum and Dad and took the plane from Liverpool to Vienna. My cousin Gretel lives here (my English uncle is married to Anna, my Austrian aunt) and I was very glad to see them waiting for me at the airport. I've been to lots of places including Austria before with my parents, but this is my first trip alone and I don't speak any German except 'Guten Tag' and 'Danke'. As you can see, that's not really much! Gretel is really cool and she speaks brilliant English (thank goodness). It's school holidays here too, so we've got lots of time to enjoy ourselves. My uncle and aunt are <u>totally chilled</u>, I've got my own room at their house and the tram stop is just outside. Freedom! Tonight we're going to a party at Gretel's friend's house. I'll blog again tomorrow and tell you all about it … if I don't sleep all day ;)

3

Old York

Blogger: **Adél**

After a fantastic <u>fortnight</u> studying English in beautiful York, it's almost time to head back home to Budapest. Although it was sometimes difficult to find time each day, I <u>reckon</u> that writing this blog has really helped me improve my English.

Tonight is the farewell party organised by the school, and all the students in my group will be there. I <u>can't get over</u> how many people I've met from all over the world. Especially cool are Sonata from Lithuania, Marta from Poland and Nico from Italy. We're definitely going to stay in touch and Marta even said she will come and visit me in Budapest. Despite a few problems with accommodation, which we eventually solved, it has been a great experience. I'll miss everyone and I'll even miss writing to you, my patient readers.

2 Read the three blogs. For questions 1–3, choose the correct answer A–C.

1 Jo experienced two problems which
  A created difficulties for the rest of his trip.
  B he managed to solve quite quickly.
  C added to the initial excitement of travelling.

2 Alex's trip to Austria was different because
  A she had never met her Austrian relatives before.
  B she was going there to study the language.
  C she was travelling on her own for the first time.

3 Which of the following does Adél not talk about positively?
  A The English city of York.
  B The people that she met.
  C The place where she stayed.

3 Match statements A–D with blogs 1–3. One blog has two matching statements.

In this blog …

A the blogger suggests that he/she won't be updating the blog again. ☐

B it is clear that the blogger is not an experienced traveller. ☐

C the blogger describes two potentially big problems which are solved quickly. ☐

D the blogger mentions that this is not his/her first visit to the country he/she is currently in. ☐

4 Match the definitions with underlined words in the blogs.

completely relaxed	*totally chilled*
1 two weeks (from fourteen nights)	_____
2 begin well	_____
3 think	_____
4 luxurious or expensive	_____
5 find it difficult to believe	_____

5 Complete the sentences with words and expressions from Exercise 4. Change any verb forms as necessary.

Katrina *reckons* we'll be in Prague by midday, but in this weather, I think it'll take a bit longer.

1 Jenna's uncle and aunt are really rich, so they always stay in _____ hotels when they go on holiday.

2 Simon and his friends have gone camping for a _____ , so he won't be back until the end of the month.

3 Amy's birthday party _____ when her favourite cousins from Italy turned up unexpectedly.

4 We _____ how much you've grown! How tall are you now?

5 Mum had a massage in the hotel spa. She loved it and was _____ afterwards.

REMEMBER BETTER

Go to a travel blogs section of a site dedicated to travel. Read some of the blogs and make a note of any useful vocabulary. Don't worry if you don't understand everything. Check new words in a dictionary.

6 Complete the sentences with the correct negative adjective form of the verbs in brackets.

Now that there's the Internet, there's very little excuse for being _uninformed_ (INFORM) about how to behave when you are abroad.

1 There's no real reason why mobile devices should be _____ (CONNECT) from the Internet during a flight. It's not at all dangerous.

2 I always think that having problems while travelling is _____ (AVOID) – that way I don't get too upset when they actually happen.

3 If you are completely _____ (FAMILIARISE) with a country's culture, you need to aim to be polite at all times.

4 For me, the idea of going backpacking around Europe is completely _____ (THINK). I like my comfort, so I prefer to stay in hotels.

5 When we arrived in Athens, the weather was particularly _____ (PLEASE) but fortunately it got better after a few days.

6 Kyle believes that people who find travelling _____ (REWARD) should probably just stay at home. That's a bit hard, don't you think?

VOCABULARY PRACTICE | Verb phrases

7 Look at the vocabulary in lesson 3.4 in the Student's Book. Complete the travel advice with words from the box.

(challenge   cut   immerse   retrieve   ~~take~~)

Gap year

Young people choose to _take_ a gap year for different reasons. Some want to ¹_____ themselves off from their family and home for a while in order to develop a greater sense of independence. Some view it as an opportunity to ²_____ beliefs that may have become too familiar. Still others see it as a chance to ³_____ oneself in a foreign culture and experience a different way of life. Whatever your reasons, don't feel like you should give up your modern day comforts. Your smartphone is an invaluable gadget wherever you go, both for contacting people when you feel lonely or if needed in an emergency. And always carry your bank card with you – you never know when you might need to ⁴_____ cash from an ATM in order to get hold of some local currency.

GRAMMAR

3.5

Used to and would

SHOW WHAT YOU KNOW

1 Mark the sentences as either *A* for describing an *action* or *S* for describing a *state*.

When my dad was young, he <u>went</u> to the seaside in Cornwall every summer. [A]

1 My grandad <u>had</u> an old Mini Morris he called 'Kiddo'. ☐
2 Grandma, Grandad, my dad and my uncle all <u>squeezed</u> into the tiny car. ☐
3 They <u>drove</u> all the way from Edinburgh to St. Ives. ☐
4 It <u>took</u> them all night and most of the next day. ☐
5 Despite the long drive, Dad <u>loved</u> going on holiday in the 'Kiddo'. ☐

2 ★ Rewrite the sentences with *used to* and the correct form of the verbs.

In the 1990s, people chose bright colours.
In the 1990s, people *used to choose* bright colours.

1 Many women wore tight jeans and cowboy boots.
Many women _____ tight jeans and cowboy boots.
2 Tattoos and body piercings weren't as popular as now.
Tattoos and body piercings _____ as popular as now.
3 Supermodels such as Cindy Crawford and Claudia Schiffer were very famous.
Supermodels such as Cindy Crawford and Claudia Schiffer _____ very famous.
4 Was short hair fashionable?
_____ fashionable?

3 ★ ★ Change the underlined words with *used to* or *would*. Use *would* whenever possible.

DOWNTHELINE.COM
Advice for teens from twenty-somethings

● Tired of advice from mums, dads and teachers three times your age?
● Check out our advice from young people just a few years ahead of you on life's long journey.

'Reality Check' by Simon Foster (23 yrs old)

Five years ago, I <u>thought</u> / *used to think* I was going to make lots of money when I left school. I <u>told</u> / ¹_____ my parents I'd be the president of a company with a fancy car and a big house by the time I was 21. I <u>believed</u> / ²_____ that companies were going to fight to offer me a job because I was going to be a great innovator like Bill Gates or Steve Jobs. I <u>didn't feel</u> / ³_____ that further study was necessary and I wanted to get a job and start my 'amazing' career as soon as possible. I <u>said</u> / ⁴_____ that I'd be able to 'do whatever' and 'go wherever' because I'd be so rich and successful. I <u>didn't know</u> / ⁵_____ much about real life back then.
What would I say to my teenage self now? WAKE UP, MATE! The real world is tough and competitive, and success requires hard work. Take a reality check, work hard, and if you are very lucky, success might follow.

---

4 ★ ★ ★ Tick the correct sentences. Sometimes both sentences are correct.

When we went on family summer holidays …
1 a We used to leave very early in the car. ☑
  b We would leave very early in the car. ☑
2 a One summer, we drove all the way from Germany to Spain. ☐
  b One summer, we would drive all the way from Germany to Spain. ☐
3 a I used to think it was amazing that Mum and Dad could find the way. ☐
  b I would think it was amazing that Mum and Dad could find the way. ☐
4 a We wouldn't have GPS in those days. ☐
  b We didn't use to have GPS in those days. ☐

SHOW WHAT YOU'VE LEARNT

5 Complete the second sentence so that it has a similar meaning to the first. Use the word in capitals.

When she was young, Helen didn't get on very well with her cousin, Madeline.
USE
When she was young, Helen *didn't use to get on* very well with her cousin, Madeline.

1 I wasn't fair-haired as a baby.
DIDN'T
I _____ fair-haired as a baby.
2 Tina and her brother fell out every night when they shared a bedroom as teenagers.
WOULD
Tina and her brother shared a bedroom as teenagers and they_____ every night.
3 Kim looked up to her teammate Ellie, until she discovered that Ellie was a cheat.
USED
Kim _____ her teammate Ellie until she discovered that Ellie was a cheat.
4 We hated playing football on cold, rainy Sunday afternoons.
HATE
We _____ playing football on cold, rainy Sunday afternoons.
5 At every match, the fans started singing at the beginning of the match.
WOULD
At every match, the fans _____ singing at the beginning of the match.
6 You thought you'd always be skinny, but now you're sixteen you're very well-built.
THINK
You _____ you'd always be skinny, but now you're sixteen you're very well-built.

/6

GRAMMAR: Train and Try Again page 156

1 ★ **Choose the correct answers A–C.**

1 **Evie:** How do you think you __ the air conditioner?
  Kirsten: I don't know. Try pushing that red button again.
  A get off **B** make off **C** turn off

2 **Julio:** Come on! Come on! I don't want to be late.
  Miles: Please, slow down. I can't __ you.
  A keep up with **B** go out with **C** look out for

3 **Brenda:** Look. It's starting to rain.
  Nolan: I know! Quick! Help me __ the tent.
  A build up **B** open up **C** put up

4 **Rodrick:** Stephen's on the phone. His hotel is fully booked for tonight.
  Jo: No problem. We can __ for one night.
  A give him up **B** put him up **C** take him up

5 **Daria:** Oh, no. Ferne can't drive us to the airport tomorrow.
  Irina: Really? She always __ at the last minute, doesn't she?
  A puts us down **B** lets us down **C** gets us down

6 **Bethal:** What time were Jon and Nicol going to __ at the pool?
  Ethan: Almost an hour ago. I wonder what happened to them.
  A turn up **B** get up **C** make up

2 ★ **Complete each pair of sentences with the same answer A–C.**

1 Aleisha's plane takes __ in an hour, so we'd better hurry up.
  Please turn your music __ and listen to me, will you?
  A out **B** off **C** up

2 I'm afraid to say Colene has dropped __ of the trip because she's got flu.
  Karl has run __ of money and wants to borrow some from me again.
  A out **B** off **C** up

3 Jerry, please put a hoodie __ – it's cold outside.
  One of our lights was broken but we carried __ driving to the hotel.
  A in **B** by **C** on

4 We weren't expecting very much but it turned __ a fascinating tour.
  I'm going __ the sea. It's too hot here on the sand.
  A in **B** out **C** into

5 Abdul will be here soon. The heavy traffic is holding him __ .
  This hat was cheaper yesterday. They've put the price __ by over 20 per cent.
  A up **B** down **C** off

6 Aimi speaks perfect Japanese because she was brought __ there.
  There's a lovely café __ on the top of the hill. Let's go there for a drink.
  A up **B** out **C** over

3 ★ ★ **Complete the text with one word in each gap.**

Last week me and some friends decided to go camping. Before we _set_ off on our drive, we had arranged to go to the train station to ¹_____ up our friend, Hugh. But on the way to collect him, we saw somebody by the side of the road looking for a lift. So, we pulled ²_____ to see where he was going. He said he was going to the train station and, as we were going there ourselves, we offered to drop him ³_____ there. In the car he told us he'd been standing there for nearly an hour and was about to give ⁴_____ waiting, so he was happy we had stopped: he was on his way to meet his cousin Hugh to go camping! Unbelievable! The chance of running ⁵_____ him like that must be a million-to-one. And the look on Hugh's face when he saw us all in the car together was the funniest thing I've ever seen!

4 ★ ★ ★ **Complete the sentences with the correct forms of the words in brackets and any other words needed. Use phrasal verbs.**

On our last holiday we _hung out with a couple_ (hang / a couple) from France.

1 Gareth _____ (fall / brother) again. They're always fighting.

2 I've always _____ (want / try / badminton). I'd love to play with you tomorrow.

3 Mark's entered a TV travel quiz. Let's go and _____ (cheer / he) in the studio.

4 I _____ (take / dad) – we're both really into long motorbike rides.

5 ★ ★ ★ **Complete the second sentence so that it has a similar meaning to the first one. Use between two and five words, including the word in capitals.**

The car stopped working on the way to the airport.
DOWN
The car _broke down_ on the way to the airport.

1 Why does Frankie admire Thomas so highly?
  LOOK
  Why does Frankie _____ so much?

2 I'm hoping to learn some Spanish when I'm in Barcelona next month.
  PICK
  I hope _____ when I'm in Barcelona next month.

3 Claire wasn't interested in camping holidays before last summer.
  GOT
  Claire _____ camping holidays only last summer.

4 Trudy persuaded Lizzy to give her a lift to the station.
  TALKED
  Trudy _____ giving her a lift to the station.

1 Put the words in order to make informal sentences.

the / hours / every / spending / on / beach / day
Spending hours on the beach every day.

1 in / super / Bordeaux / time / here

_____

2 like / only / seems / we / yesterday / arrived

_____

3 want / don't / come / home / to / really

_____

4 to / visit / tomorrow / hope / the / pyramids

_____

5 wait / can't / try / diving / scuba / to

_____

2 Rewrite the sentences using ellipsis where you can.

I'm going to Paris in July – I can't wait!
Going to Paris in July – can't wait!

1 It feels like I've been here forever.

_____

2 It's amazing to be here all on my own.

_____

3 We're dreaming of a holiday but we always are dreaming of one.

_____

4 It's 32 degrees here in the shade. It's wonderful!

_____

5 We're loving it in Australia. We wish you were here.

_____

3 Complete Zara's email with useful phrases. The first letters are given.

Dear Shaun,

How are things? ¹**T**hanks **f**or **y**our **m**essage. The pictures from your holiday were great and Maria is very pretty ;)

²I **c**_____ **s**_____ why you are **w**_____ about the situation though. Long distance friendships aren't easy – especially when they start on holiday. If I ³**w**_____ **y**_____ , I'd try to keep things casual – don't make any promises you can't keep. Wait a while and see how you feel. ⁴**H**_____ you **t**_____ **a**_____ asking Maria to visit you in England?

⁵**B**_____ **t**_____ way , did **y**_____ **h**_____ that James broke his ankle? He fell off his skateboard outside school. Everyone was laughing at him until they realised he was really hurt. Eight weeks with his leg in plaster. Poor thing! Whatever you decide with Maria, I'm ⁶**s**_____ **t**_____ will **w**_____ **o**_____ fine. Try not to worry.

Love
Zara x

4 Read Zara's email again and match sentences 1–6 to the parts below.

A general news or a reference to the email/message you received ☐1

B expressing sympathy for your friend's situation ☐

C offering advice by asking a question ☐

D offering advice by making a statement ☐

E reassuring your friend ☐

F changing the subject ☐

5 Put the useful phrases in order, then match them to parts A–F in Exercise 4.

don't / you … / Why ☐C
Why don't you …

1 sure / OK / will / everything / be / I'm ☐

_____

2 hear / you / did / remember, / While / I / that … ☐

_____

3 is / it / understand / situation / what / difficult / a / I ☐

_____

4 good / It's / idea / a / to … ☐

_____

5 was / lovely / It / hear / to / you / from ☐

_____

6 Read the task below. Then read the email and choose the correct verbs.

You received the following message from a friend.

> Hi Sam,
>
> U OK? I've read that book you lent me. You're right – it's excellent! Unfortunately, however, I'm a bit sad at the moment 🙁. I hurt my back a few days ago and the doctor told me I need to stay in bed. Why is that bad? Because there's a school trip to Marburg Castle this weekend and I planned to take photographs and write about it on my blog. Now I have to lie in bed and do nothing. I can't read all the time – any ideas about what else I can do?
> Speak soon!
>
> Eddie

Write a personal email with a reply. Include and develop these points:

- Express sympathy for your friend's situation.
- Offer some advice based on your own experience.
- Change the subject and share some news about your life.
- Reassure your friend at the end of the email.

Hi,
A <u>Sorry to hear about your bad back</u>. **B**¹<u>*Must / Might* be horrible to be stuck in bed all day</u>. I ²*had / would have* a similar problem last year when I ³*used to break / broke* my ankle. How did you hurt yourself? You ⁴*might have lifted / might lift* something too heavy, perhaps?

Anyway, I ⁵*understand / am understanding* how boring it can be and I remember how active you ⁶*used to be / would be*, so it's even harder to do nothing every day. Why don't you download some audio books? I ⁷*did / had done* this last year. **C** <u>Much better than</u> reading to yourself all the time!

By the way, I'm visiting Hohenzollern Castle near Stuttgart with my parents next month. **D** <u>Want to join us?</u> I'm sure you'll be back on your feet by then and we can ⁸*pick you up / put you up* on our way there and ⁹*hold you up / drop you off* on the way back. No problem. **E** <u>Would be great to have you come along</u>!

P.S. **F** <u>Pleased you liked the book</u>. **G** <u>Will recommend something else next time I write</u> ;-)

7 Look at the underlined parts of the text. Write them in the full form. Sometimes more than one answer is possible.

A _____
B _____
C _____
D _____
E _____
F _____
G _____

8 You received the following message from a friend.

> Hi Peter,
>
> U OK? I've got that book you wanted to borrow. I'll bring it tomorrow. I'm not feeling good today, in fact, I'm super stressed out 🙁. I haven't even started revising for the final exams and I'm totally disorganised! I don't know where to begin. Have you started? Have you got any advice or ideas to make revision easier?

Write a personal email in reply. Include and develop these points:

- Express sympathy for your friend's situation.
- Offer some advice and share a similar experience you have had.
- Change the subject and suggest some other future plans.
- Reassure your friend at the end of the email.

Finished? Always check your writing. Can you tick √ everything on this list?

In my personal email:

• I have used a friendly greeting, e.g *Dear Sam* or *Hi Charlotte*.	☐
• I have started with some general news and/or a reference to what my friend wrote in their last email.	☐
• I have included everything in the bullet points in the question, i.e. expressed sympathy, offered advice, changed the subject and given some positive news, and reassured my friend at the end.	☐
• I have used contractions (e.g. *I'm / aren't / that's*).	☐
• I have perhaps used some emoticons ☺ and abbreviations (*info / CU / gr8*) – but not too many.	☐
• I have checked my spelling and punctuation.	☐
• My text is neat and clear.	☐

1 Translate the phrases into your own language.

SPEAKING BANK

Asking for advice

Can you do me a (big) favour? _____

_____

Can you give me some advice? _____

_____

Do you think I need ...? _____

_____

What do you think I should (do)? _____

_____

Giving advice

The first thing you should do is ... _____

_____

_____

If I were you, I'd (I wouldn't) do ... _____

_____

_____

I (don't) think you should ... _____

_____

You (don't) need to ... _____

You (really) ought to ... _____

_____

You must (mustn't) ... _____

The best thing would be to ... _____

It's a good idea to ... _____

Why don't you (go) ...? _____

_____

Accepting advice

Good idea! _____

Good thinking! _____

That's really helpful. _____

Oh, I didn't think of that! _____

_____

2 Match questions 1–4 with advice A–D.

Do you think I need to get them a gift? (E)
1 What do you think I should wear for the journey? ( )
2 Do you think we need to reserve a table? ( )
3 What sights do you think we should see in Paris? ( )
4 Which train should she catch? ( )

A I think you should. The restaurant is usually very busy on Saturday afternoons.
B Why doesn't she drive? It's much faster than the train.
C I don't know. I've never been. The best thing would be to look online or buy a guidebook.
D It's a good idea to wear something comfortable. We're going to be on the bus for 18 hours.
E Yes, you ought to buy them something. You're staying at their house for free.

3 Put the words in order to complete the dialogues.

1 **Shelly:** Mum, *do / favour / big / can / me / you / a*
can you do me a big favour and help me to decide what to pack for the school trip?

Mum: Of course. Er ... well I'm pretty sure ᵃ*don't / you / to / need*

_____

take those high heels, Shelly. You are going hiking and camping, right?

Shelly: Well, er ... yes. ᵇ*didn't / I / of / think / that*

_____

2 **Dennis:** ᵃ*need / think / you / I / Do / to*

_____

buy medical insurance for the ski trip, Dad? It's expensive.

Dad: Well, can you afford to pay for helicopter rescue and hospital fees?

Dennis: Er ... not really, no.

Dad: Then ᵇ*were / you / I / if / I'd*

_____

get some insurance.

Dennis: OK, ᶜ*thinking / good*

_____

Can I borrow £50, Dad?

4 Complete the dialogue with the correct words. The first letters are given.

A mum, her teenage son and his friend are at the travel agency ...

Mum: Excuse me. C_ould_ y_ou_ g_ive_ u_s_ s_ome_ a_dvice_ ? My son Anthony and his friend Tom want to go on holiday on their own this summer.

TA: I see. Well, boys, ¹t_____ f_____ thing you s_____ d_____ is decide what kind of holiday you would like. ²W_____ d_____ you have a quick look at our special offers?

Anthony: ³G_____ i_____ ! We don't have much money but maybe a beach holiday.

Tom: Mm hm.

TA: We have a week in San Antonio, Ibiza for just £249 per person.

Anthony: Sounds great ...

Mum: Ibiza? I don't think so. Too many parties.

Anthony: Mum!

TA: Er ... OK, maybe the ⁴b_____ t_____ would b_____ to go on an adventure holiday. We have rafting, hiking and climbing in Austria.

Tom: Mm hm.

Mum: Climbing? I don't think so. Too dangerous

Anthony: Mum!

TA: Sightseeing in Rome?

Mum: Italy? No way. Crazy drivers.

Anthony: Mum! Look, thanks for your advice, it was ⁵r_____ h_____ , but I think we need to talk about this at home.

Tom: Mm hm.

Student A, look below. Student B, go to page 136.

1 **In pairs, ask and answer the questions.**

Talk about sport.

1 Have you ever disagreed with a decision from a referee? What happened?
2 What's the hardest sport you've ever tried? Why was it so hard?
3 Have you ever felt that you let your teammates down in a sport? What happened?

4 When was the last time you cheered your team on as a supporter at a sporting event?
5 Why do you think sportspeople try to break world records? Would you like to do this?

2 **Look at the photo of an interesting journey. Take turns to talk about what you can see in your photos. Talk about the people, the place and the other things in the photo.**

3 **You and your friend are planning to take a gap year. Here are some of the places where you could work when you travel. Talk together about the places and say which would be the most interesting.**

4 **Talk about a gap year.**

• What are the advantages of having a gap year before you go to university?
• What are the disadvantages of having a gap year before you go to university?
• What would you like to do most during your gap year and how would you organise this?

• Which places would you include on your itinerary? Why?
• Would you rather take a gap year on your own or with a friend? Why?

VOCABULARY AND GRAMMAR

1 Choose the correct answer A–C.

I paid £30 for a ___ journey on the train to Manchester and back. Pretty cheap, eh?
(A) return   **B** back   **C** single

1 Adam is thinking of ___ a gap year and travelling around Asia.
   A making   **B** taking   **C** doing
2 We have booked a ___ room, so it'll be comfortable enough for us both to get a good night's sleep.
   A package   **B** twin   **C** single
3 You should never cut yourself ___ from your family. Why would you want to do that?
   A off   **B** up   **C** out
4 I think I'd like to work in the tourism industry and help people who want to travel. I find my current job is too ___ .
   A uninformed   **B** unrewarding   **C** disconnected
5 Amelia is studying tourism and when she graduates, she wants to be a tour ___ .
   A holiday   **B** company   **C** guide

/5

2 Complete the sentences with the words from the box. Change the forms if necessary. There are two extra words.

> business   car   ~~cruise~~   drive
> path   resort   ride   transport

The _cruise_ visits three different Caribbean islands before we sail back to Southampton.

1 It's a beautiful seaside _____ at a good price. We go there every summer.
2 I've never been on a _____ trip before. Does the company pay for everything?
3 Dave won't go up in the cable _____ . He's scared of heights.
4 Let's share the _____ – you can sleep in the back of the car for the first part of the journey and we'll swap places when we get to Amsterdam.
5 Just follow this winding _____ until you get to the end. It takes you through the woods down to the sea.

/5

3 Complete the sentences. The first and last letters are given.

Phileas Fogg is a fictional character created by Jules Verne. His name is well known because he took an incredible **v**_oyag_**e** around the world in 80 days. Maybe you've read the book?

1 Most of the cycle ride today is **d**_____**l**, so it's not a very tiring route. But please be careful and check your brakes before we begin.
2 There's a big traffic **j**_____**m** due to an accident on the motorway.
3 Wouldn't you love to go on a **r**_____-_____-_____**d** trip and visit every country on the planet?
4 At 'Faraway Holidays' our travel **a**_____**s** specialise in trips to south-eastern Asia. Contact us for details.
5 How can we **c**_____**s** this river without a boat? It's too dangerous to try and swim to the other side.

/5

4 Choose the correct form in the second sentence so that it means the same as the first.

It's possible that's not the right trail. Do you have a map? We (might be) / must be / can't be lost.

1 Julia is sure that these are her mum's keys. They look exactly the same.
   These _might be / may be / must be_ Julia's mum's keys.
2 Leo is sure that this is not his luggage. His bags are much bigger.
   This _might not be / can't be / must not be_ Leo's luggage.
3 Jess is sure the light in the sky was not a UFO. She doesn't believe in UFOs.
   According to Jess, the light in the sky _must have been / might have been / can't have been_ a UFO.
4 It was possible that Harry sprayed the graffiti on that wall.
   Harry _must have sprayed / could have sprayed / can't have sprayed_ the graffiti on that wall.
5 Cindy is sure that Edward forgot to pay for his lunch.
   Cindy thinks Edward _might have forgotten / can't have forgotten / must have forgotten_ to pay for his lunch.

/5

5 Find and correct the mistakes. One sentence is correct.

Thirty years ago, airports wouldn't be as secure as they are nowadays. _didn't use to be_

1 On October 23, my little brother used to be born.
   _____
2 Would you use to go abroad on holiday when you were little? _____
3 Our family didn't use to go camping in the summer. We always stayed in hostels or hotels.
   _____
4 I wouldn't like travelling on planes when I was younger, but now I really enjoy it. _____
5 Helen used to was a pilot before she retired.
   _____

/5

6 Choose the correct answers A–C.

The Super-jumbo-jet

Let's talk about public _A_ for a moment – in particular, planes. Did you know that the Airbus A380 is the largest passenger plane in the world? It has two levels, or decks and can carry up to 853 people. The Boeing 747 **¹**___ the biggest commercial airliner in the world, but the A380, which has been flying since October 2007, has around 40 per cent more space. The A380 carries enough fuel for it to take off in Dubai and **²**___ passengers off in Los Angeles without stopping. The **³**___ takes an average of 16 hours and 20 minutes. In the past, passengers **⁴**___ have to cope with a lot of noise during journeys like this one, but the A380 is 50 per cent quieter than other similar planes. A380s are currently owned by 9 airlines in Europe, Australia, Asia and the Middle East, so if you have flown from any of these regions, it **⁵**___ on an A380.

	A	B	C
	(A) transport	**B** traffic	**C** travel
1	**A** would be	**B** used to be	**C** used to
2	**A** lift	**B** take	**C** drop
3	**A** travel	**B** journey	**C** ride
4	**A** would	**B** should	**C** could
5	**A** must have been	**B** can't have been	**C** might have been

/5

Total /30

7 Choose the correct answers A–C.

Travelling abroad ___ be so easy in the past, you know.
A wasn't used to
(B) didn't use to
C wouldn't

1 This old sofa actually turns ___ a comfortable bed big enough for two.
A into
B up
C out

2 If you ___ over here, I'll jump out and buy some snacks for the journey.
A put
B turn
C pull

3 For some people doing a little work while on holiday is almost ___ nowadays because of mobile technology.
A disconnected
B uninformed
C unavoidable

4 Tony ___ have been to Egypt before. He only got his first passport a few months ago.
A can't
B might
C must

5 You can't really ___ yourself in a foreign country's culture unless you live there for a few months or more.
A plant
B immerse
C save

/5

8 Complete the sentences using the prompts in brackets. Do not change the order of the words. Change the forms or add new words where necessary. Use up to six words in each gap.

Where's my luggage? Oh, no. The travel company *must have lost* (must / lose) it.

1 Graham _____ (not / use / enjoy / fly) but he loves it now.

2 It _____ (may / rain) in London at the moment but in two hours' time we'll be in sunny Spain!

3 I don't know why Jim's late. He _____ (can / not / get) stuck in traffic because there are hardly any cars on the road today.

4 It's possible that our favourite hotel _____ (might / move) but I'd be very surprised if it closed down. It was always very popular with tourists.

5 Before the EU, you _____ (use to / need / have) a passport to travel from Hungary to Germany.

/5

9 Complete each pair of sentences with the same answer A–C.

Hurry up or we'll ___ the school bus and be late for class.
When are you coming home, Barbara? I really ___ you.
(A) miss
B pass
C lose

1 Jason wants us to ___ him up on the way.
Please don't ___ the fruit from the gardens.
A pick
B take
C drop

2 I hope heavy traffic doesn't ___ Josie up too long. We'll be late for the party.
Could you ___ these flowers for a second. I need to tie my shoe laces.
A hold
B take
C stand

3 Candice doesn't need a hotel. We can put her ___ for a few nights.
Where should I hang this landscape painting ___ ? By the door?
A over
B on
C up

4 The ___ from Dover in England to Calais in France takes only 1.5 hours and there are over 30 boats per day to choose from.
An accident happened this morning on the zebra ___ near our school. The driver claimed he wasn't driving too fast.
A track
B crossing
C path

5 If we stay in a ___ hotel, we'll have more money to spend during our holiday.
I'm afraid I can't join you at the cinema tonight. I've spent my ___ for this month.
A budget
B cheap
C change

/5

10 Complete the text with the correct form of the words in the box and any other words you need. There are two extra words.

accept   be   believe   catch
familiar   lead   pleasant   think

When my first choice of university *accepted* me onto their tourism programme, there can't **¹**_____ a happier person in the world than me. Firstly, I knew I wanted to leave home and challenge the **²**_____ I had about living away from my parents. Would I cope well on my own, I wondered? But there was one thing I knew for sure – I wanted to live in a(n) **³**_____ place, where everything and everybody would be new. And you know what? I love it. I stay in touch with my parents regularly, because I really love them and miss them. But living at home again has become **⁴**_____ for me. In fact, I've already decided that when I finish university, I'm going to apply for a job as a tour **⁵**_____ in another country. That way, I'll get to travel even further, work in my main field of interest, and continue to be independent.

/5

Total   /20

45

4 Eat, drink and be healthy

VOCABULARY

Fruit and vegetables • describing food • collocations

SHOW WHAT YOU KNOW

1 **Choose the odd one out in each group of four words and complete the sentences.**

jam   honey   (rice)   sugar
ᵃ*Rice* is the odd one out because all the others taste ᵇ*sweet*.

1 carrot   onion   potato   lemon
ᵃ_____ is the odd one out because all the others are types of ᵇ_____ .

2 pineapple   cucumber   mango   raspberry
ᵃ_____ is the odd one out because all the others are types of ᵇ_____ .

3 milk   biscuits   crisps   spaghetti
ᵃ_____ is the odd one out because it's the only one that you can ᵇ_____ .

4 pumpkin   pear   leek   grape
ᵃ_____ is the odd one out because all the others are types of ᵇ_____ .

5 chicken   beef   pork   pasta
ᵃ_____ is the odd one out because all the others are types of ᵇ_____ .

WORD STORE 4A | Fruit and vegetables

2 **Complete the menu. Some letters are given.**

WORD STORE 4B | Describing food

3 **Write the opposites. Use the photos to help you.**

bitter	≠	*sweet* (e.g. honey)
1 cooked	≠	_____ (e.g. vegetables)
2 mild	≠	_____ (e.g. chillies)
3 ripe	≠	_____ (e.g. green bananas)
4 fresh	≠	_____ (e.g. bread and cakes)
5 fresh	≠	_____ (e.g. milk)
6 lean	≠	_____ (e.g. meat)
7 tasty	≠	_____ (e.g. rice without spices)
8 sweet	≠	_____ (e.g. lemon)
9 hot	≠	_____ (e.g. sauce)
10 fresh	≠	_____ (e.g. tomatoes)

Vegi Artiano Restaurant

Starters

🍲 Bright orange **pumpkin** soup made with hot red ¹c_____i pe_____s.

🥗 Exotic red and green salad with ²rad_____s, ³ca_____e leaves and slices of ⁴av_____o.

Main Dishes

🍅 Lasagne with ⁵sp_____h and ⁶aub_____s.

🍲 Baked ⁷cau_____r served with baby ⁸ca_____ts and ⁹g_____ic.

Sides: order a side dish of ¹⁰bee_____t or ¹¹sw_____rn to enjoy with your main course.

Desserts

🍨 Fruit salad with ¹²che_____s, ¹³pi_____le, ¹⁴apr_____ts and ¹⁵fi_____s.

🍨 Mousse made from ¹⁶co_____ut or ¹⁷gra_____t served with home-made vanilla ice cream.

All our fruit and vegetables are fresh each day

4 Complete the dialogues with adjectives from Exercise 3. The adjective *sour* is used twice.

1 W: Are you ready to order, madam?
   C: Yes, er … could I ask you about the Thai Red Curry? Is it *hot* ? I'm afraid too much chilli gives me stomachache.
   W: That's no problem, madam. I can ask the chef to make a _____ version for you without the chilli.

2 C: Excuse me, waiter!
   W: Yes, sir. How can I help?
   C: Well, I'm not satisfied with this meal at all. First of all, the rice is cold and worse than that, the fish is completely uncooked – it's _____ ! Are you trying to poison your customers?
   W: Sir, are you aware that this is a sushi restaurant?

3 A: I love travelling, but it's always great to get home. I'm hungry. What have we got?
   K: Er, well … it looks like the electricity went off while we were away. The food in the fridge is not exactly fresh anymore. We've got some ᵃ_____ potatoes, some ᵇ_____ milk and there are a few slices of ᶜ_____ bread.
   A: Hmm … doesn't sound very tasty. Shall we phone for pizza?

4 R: So, what fruit do you eat in Indonesia, Aulia?
   A: Well, we eat a lot of mangoes. At this time of year, most of them are yellow and ᵃ_____ , or in other words ready to eat. Green ones can be quite ᵇ_____ tasting but the yellow ones are exactly the opposite; really ᶜ_____ and delicious.

5 P: Oh, dear. Is this cake old? It breaks into pieces instead of melting in the mouth. And it's ᵃ_____ too – it has almost no flavour.
   M: Really? Let me try. The woman in the baker's said it was ᵇ_____ and baked only today.

6 L: What a wonderful steak this is. Not too much fat, nice and ᵃ_____ , just how I like it. And the pepper sauce on top makes it even more delicious. Mmmm.
   B: Do you think so? It's quite ᵇ_____ if you ask me. There's too much fat on it I'd say.

WORD STORE 4C | Collocations

5 Match adjectives 1–7 to nouns a–g.

stale	*h*	a	pepper
1 sliced	○	b	bread
2 ground	○	c	syrup
3 long-grain	○	d	water
4 side	○	e	salad
5 mushroom	○	f	soup
6 maple	○	g	rice
7 soda	○	h	biscuits

6 Complete the sentences with the nouns A–H from Exercise 5.

I'm not very good at baking. I'm afraid these *biscuits* are too dry and crunchy.
1 I don't like sugar or chocolate _____ – I prefer bitter coffee.
2 Would you like still or sparkling _____ , madam?
3 Would you like white or wholemeal _____ for your toast?
4 Which is spicier – the black or the cayenne _____ ?
5 Would you like a mixed or a green _____ as a starter?
6 Is this home-made or tinned _____ ? It's delicious. Can I have another bowl, please?
7 I'd like white _____ with my curry, please. No, actually make that brown.

SHOW WHAT YOU'VE LEARNT

7 Choose the correct words.

1 Jackie doesn't like spicy food, so don't add too many *figs / chilli peppers / carrots* to the curry.
2 Mum, how do I know if this baked potato is *stale / ripe / cooked*? It's been in the oven for 20 minutes.
3 I prefer chicken to beef because white meat is not as *lean / raw / fatty* as dark meat.
4 Where did you buy these *beetroots / cherries / radishes*? They're really hot!
5 Mmm. Delicious! How does your dad make such wonderful *home-made / tinned / crunchy* soup?
6 Wow! This coffee is extremely *sour / bitter / sweet*. Could you pass the sugar, please?
7 If you eat *cooked / unripe / fresh* fruit, you may get stomachache. Choose softer pieces as they are usually ready to eat.
8 My young brother doesn't eat many vegetables, but he will have *cauliflower / spinach / pumpkin* because he says he loves green!
9 Grandma can't eat *crunchy / stale / sour* food because she doesn't have her own teeth!
10 Jess spilled *beetroot / syrup / grapefruit* all down her white blouse. Her dad washed it three times but the red stains just turned pink.

/10

SHOW WHAT YOU KNOW

1 Match the sentence beginnings with the correct endings. Tick the sentences that refer to the future.

I have to deliver this parcel tomorrow between ☐ g ✓

1 I'm thinking of spending my next holiday ☐☐
2 It might rain in the mountains during ☐☐
3 I'm planning to visit my old friends in Denver at ☐☐
4 Peter and Mary may be out somewhere with ☐☐
5 I intend to keep calm throughout ☐☐
6 I would love to go travelling around ☐☐

a	Christmas this year.	e	the long May weekend.
b	in Portugal.	f	their children.
c	the family dinner.	g	10 and 11 a.m.
d	South Africa one day.		

2 ★ Rearrange the words to make sentences. There is one extra word in each sentence.

~~about~~ / Do / worry / clean / Charlotte / not / because / will
Don't worry because Charlotte will clean the kitchen.

1 top / I / some / put / Shall / on / cherries / will
_____ of the cake?

2 bar / to / a / burger / We / going / eat / are
_____ for dinner tonight.

3 not / shall / Jason / will / until / again / be / hungry
_____ this evening.

3 ★ ★ Choose the correct forms.

1 M: Sally ᵃ*is cooking / will cook* breakfast tomorrow morning, so we should buy some milk and cereal just in case! We don't want to be hungry if it ᵇ*is / will be* a disaster.

K: No problem. I ᶜ*will go / am going* to the shops this afternoon with Jo, so I ᵈ*will buy / am going to buy* some then.

2 F: The restaurant ᵃ*will close / closes* at 9 p.m. tonight because tomorrow's a holiday.

P: That's perfect for me. Tomorrow I ᵇ*wake up / am waking up* early to go on an excursion with some friends.

3 S: Tori ᵃ*won't be / isn't being* able to meet us for lunch but she ᵇ*joins / will join* us later.

O: I hope so. I ᶜ*am going to give / might give* her the birthday present I've just bought her because I ᵈ*am not / won't be* here for her party tomorrow.

4 D: I ᵃ*will make / am making* Joe's favourite dish for dinner tonight and have just finished shopping for all the food.

E: That's very nice of you. ᵇ*Will / Shall* I help you with the preparations? I can help us as soon as I ᶜ*finish / will finish* my homework.

5 L: Polina says she ᵃ*is not going to eat / isn't eating* the fish from yesterday, so we should throw it away.

W: Don't waste good food. I ᵇ*am going to / will* eat it if nobody else wants it.

4 ★ ★ ★ Complete the dialogues. Put the verbs in brackets in the correct form.

1 J: Are you looking forward to your meal? It *is* (be) tonight, right?

M: Yes, Franco ᵃ_____ (cook) my favourite dish – spinach lasagne with rocket salad on the side.

J: When ᵇ_____ (he/come) over?

M: I think he ᶜ_____ (be) here at around 5 p.m. and we ᵈ_____ (plan) to eat at about 7 p.m.

J: OK. I guess I will leave before he ᵉ_____ (get) here, so give him my congratulations on getting the job!

2 I: ᵃ_____ (you/do) anything interesting this weekend, Tim?

T: Not really, I ᵇ_____ (work) in the shop on Saturday till 6 p.m. What about you?

I: Actually, I ᶜ_____ (have) a barbecue in the evening. We ᵈ_____ (begin) cooking at around 7 p.m. That's the idea anyway. Do you want to join us?

T: That sounds great. I ᵉ_____ (definitely/be) there! I'll go home and change clothes before I ᶠ_____ (come) but I can be there just after seven. Thanks, Iza.

SHOW WHAT YOU'VE LEARNT

5 Find and correct the mistakes.

What time ~~will~~ the bus leave the station? *does*

1 I'm exhausted after so much work this week. I think I stay home and go to bed early. _____

2 Am I going to help you? You look like you could use some help. _____

3 We're ready to order food now, right? I am calling the waiter. _____

4 As soon as I am getting on the train, I will call you. _____

5 Where you going to stay when you go to France next week? _____

6 Henry and Martha are to go to the food festival in town. Let's go with them. _____

/6

GRAMMAR: Train and Try Again page 157

1 Read what two speakers said about their diet. Choose the correct verbs 1–8 to complete the collocations.

Extract from Student's Book recording 🔊 2.8

S1: I'm interested in having a natural diet, and so for the last two years, I've only ¹*eaten / cooked / used* raw food. I believe that when you ²*cook / eat / buy* fresh <u>food</u>, you lose <u>the goodness and vitamins in [the food]</u>. I eat raw vegetables [...], but of course I also need protein. [...] So [...] I eat raw eggs. [...] I feel <u>healthy</u> and I ³*feel / have / need* lots of energy, but [...] it's difficult to ⁴*stay / live / eat* with the rest of my family, [and that's a problem].

S4: I'm a vegan. [...] That means that I don't eat or ⁵*like / use / make* any <u>animal</u> products for any purpose. I don't eat meat, fish, dairy or anything that comes from animals. I don't ⁶*wear / make / sell* clothes made from animals either. [...] When I was a child, I ate meat and drank milk like most people. But then when I was 13, I started thinking about where my food came from. I learnt about how animals suffer and I was shocked. I decided to ⁷*eat / become / cook* a vegan. [I ⁸*eat / respect / kill* <u>animals</u> and I don't want them to suffer].

2 Complete gaps 1–4 in the diagrams with the verbs from the box. There are two extra verbs. Then complete gaps a–d with the underlined words from the extract in Exercise 1.

(cook   drink   eat   feel   ~~lose~~   respect   use)

lose ·········· *the goodness and vitamins in the food*
  ···· weight / control / blood
  ···· your appetite / your memory / your job
1 _____ ········ ᵃ_____ / nature / the environment
  ···· somebody's wishes / views / privacy
  ···· the law / a rule
2 _____ ···· spicy / Italian ᵇ_____
  ···· a meal (for two/three/four)
  ···· (somebody) breakfast / lunch / dinner
3 _____ ···· ᶜ_____ products
  ···· a computer / phone / machine
  ···· chopsticks / a knife and fork / your hands to eat
4 _____ ···· ᵈ_____ / happy / fit
  ···· hungry / thirsty
  ···· fear / excitement / relief

Add three more items to the word maps for *eat* and *a drink*.

1 eat
   ································ meat / vegetables
      ····· out / in a restaurant
      ····· *healthily*
      ····· _____
      ····· _____

2 have
   pour (somebody) ·····
   spill ·····
   _____ ····· a drink
   _____ ·····
   _____ ·····

WORD STORE 4D | Collocations

3 Complete the advice with the correct adjectives. The first and last letters are given.

Aceyourexams.com

Eat well, perform well – today Emma Peel tells us about the relationship between diet and study

Are your exams coming up soon? Are you studying hard and feeling stressed? In order to do your best, you need to think carefully about what you eat. A h<u>ealthy</u> diet means a ¹b_____d diet, so living off mostly light snacks or ²c_____d snacks like sandwiches is not recommended. To stay energised, try to eat plenty of ³o_____c food if possible and avoid too much processed or fast food. You don't need to change to a ⁴v_____n diet but it might be a good idea to reduce the amount of meat you eat. Avoid ⁵h_____y meals in the evenings, especially if you are going to sit at your desk and study until late. If you get hungry while revising, choose a ⁶h_____y snack such as fruit, low-fat yoghurt or some nuts rather than crisps or sweets. Eat ⁷f_____g food such as chocolate, chips, pizzas and burgers only occasionally, perhaps as a reward for a hard-working week rather than as part of your daily diet. And remember, just because you don't have time to prepare and enjoy a full ⁸t_____-_____e meal does not mean you can't eat well.

READING

4.4

Feed your mind • collocations

1 Read the two texts quickly and decide which statement 1–3 is false.

1 Both texts offer advice to young people. ○

2 Both texts were written by students. ○

3 Both texts concern the topics of students and food. ○

The Uni Years

year 1, day 86 by Scott Hastings

Although we still argue about who does the washing up, my housemates and I are doing a bit better with cooking than we were. **1___** Tonight we're doing spaghetti bolognese.

Yes, we're doing better now, but the first few months of cooking and eating on our own were pretty terrible. Gavin <u>survived on</u> his mum's frozen meals which she delivered every month in sets of 25. Liam didn't even know how to make toast when he first arrived, but then he learned to open cans and heat up the contents, and so <u>lived off</u> baked beans and soup. At first, Sarah managed to persuade Gavin to share quite a few of his mum's frozen delights, but then she got a boyfriend.

2___

However, there have been a few disastrous* attempts* to feed ourselves. **3___** According to Liam, it was 'absolutely delicious' and 'sure to appear in Jamie Oliver's next cookbook: *One Minute Meals*'.

10 Top Tips For Student Cooks

Chef Sam Stern, who has been writing about cooking since he was just fourteen, shares his cooking tips for students who are leaving their families soon and heading off to university.

1 Try and <u>learn the basics</u> before you leave home: you will know what recipes work for you and what equipment to take. There probably won't be much storage space* in your student kitchen, so <u>only take the essentials</u>.

2 Get someone to cook with you if you haven't cooked before. If you can't find anyone, then follow the recipe very carefully.

3 Don't get stressed out if things go wrong, you will learn from it. I still make mistakes all the time. The skill of a good cook is learning how to correct these mistakes.

4 Give yourself enough time and always read the recipe through before you start. Cooking in a relaxed environment is much easier. I find that listening to music always helps.

5 Look out for good places to shop – butchers' and greengrocers' can often <u>offer better value</u> and taste than supermarkets. They can also give you some great advice for what to do with the cheaper cuts of meat or more unusual vegetables.

6 Remember vegetarian food is cheap and can be just as tasty. Many of the world's finest cuisines use only a little meat and yet are some of the most creative and healthiest.

7 Put your money together with your housemates to create your kitchen store cupboard – herbs, spices, etc. These can be expensive, but not if you share. They <u>make a world of difference</u> to the flavour of your meals, so are <u>well worth the investment</u>.

8 Great eating starts with wise shopping. If you make a plan before you head to the supermarket, you'll avoid making impulse buys. For the same reason, avoid shopping when you are hungry. Shop at the end of the day as you will find the reduced section full, which means great bargains. Supermarket own-brands can be better and cheaper than named brands. Remember to look for the products with the longest sell-by dates* too. You can often find them by checking at the back of the shelves.

9 Plan food that will last for more than one meal if you can. For example, a whole chicken is more expensive than pieces, but can make three or four other meals. A curry or a stew can last for days and is often cheap to make. The freezer is your friend!

10 Cooking with your friends and housemates is not only a great social event but also lets you <u>split the cost</u>. I'm a student, and every Tuesday night, we have a dinner party for 10–15 people with each person paying a few quid.* As a result, we have wonderful huge roast dinners and lots and lots of laughs.

GLOSSARY

disastrous (adj) – very bad or unsuccessful

attempt (n) – the act of trying something

storage space (n) – space in a house or flat where things can be kept until they are needed

sell-by date (n) – the date stamped on a food product after which it should not be sold

quid (n) – *informal* pound (£) *(plural also quid, not* quids)

2 **Read Text 1 again. Complete gaps 1–3 with sentences A–D. There is one extra sentence.**

A Since then he's been less keen to offer her anything from his personal supply.

B Perhaps the worst one was when Liam came home late one night and microwaved a packet of cheese slices, then ate the sticky results with a spoon.

C We've even started shopping and cooking together regularly, which has made our meals cheaper, easier to prepare, and generally less stressful.

D Fortunately, that was the last time Liam tried to cook a meal for seven people.

3 **Read the two texts again and answer the questions.**

1 Who are Sam's cooking tips addressed to?

_____

_____

2 How do some students manage their diet when they start living away from home?

_____

_____

3 What are the advantages of cooking in the company of other people?

_____

_____

4 What should inexperienced cooks do when they start preparing meals on their own?

_____

_____

5 What example of a cooking mistake is given to readers?

_____

_____

6 What advice and explanation is given about choosing where to go for shopping?

_____

_____

7 What is the advantage of shopping for food late in the evening?

_____

_____

8 What do both authors have in common?

_____

_____

4 **Match the definitions with the underlined expressions in the texts.**

divide the bill   *split the cost*

1 ate only one or

   two types of food (x2)   & _____

2 give you more for your money   _____

3 a good use of your money   _____

4 really change the situation   _____

5 take only what you really need   _____

6 learn the most important or
   simplest things about a topic   _____

5 **Complete the sentences with the answers from Exercise 4.**

Shall we share a pizza and salad and *split the cost*?

1 We have to carry everything that we pack for this hiking trip, so please _____ .

2 Before you try skiing on your own, take some lessons and _____ .

3 Check the price online before you buy. Websites often _____ than shops.

4 When they ran out of money, the students _____ rice and soy sauce.

5 If you turn down the heaters in your house, it will _____ to your electricity bills.

6 The juice-maker was quite expensive, but _____ . We drink healthy juice almost every morning.

WORD STORE 4E | Collocations

6 **Complete the quotes with the words from the box.**

agriculture   alarming   catering   ~~energy~~
government   household   human   industrial
international   minimum   voluntary

'Now that everybody has a smartphone and a computer, *energy* consumption is higher than ever. In some areas of the world the ¹_____ statistics are a great cause of worry.'

'Conditions for animals in the ²_____ sector in some cases are very bad. A lot of investment is needed to meet the ³_____ standards demanded by the EU.'

'As well as the problem of ⁴_____ waste from factories, ⁵_____ consumption of packaged items is creating ⁶_____ waste at levels which are quickly becoming uncontrollable.'

'As a result of the new strict ⁷_____ standards in food hygiene, many companies in the ⁸_____ industry had to close down.'

'The number of workers in the ⁹_____ sector has reached a very low, almost ¹⁰_____ level. If the situation continues to worsen, charity organisations will not be able to help so many people.'

GRAMMAR

4.5 Future Continuous and Future Perfect

SHOW WHAT YOU KNOW

1 Mark the underlined verbs as either **P** for in progress or **C** for completed.

This week, Dad's made breakfast for you three times and dinner twice. ☐C

1 I'm phoning from my car. I've run out of petrol! ☐
2 They've been to the same ski resort seven times. ☐
3 Excuse me, we are waiting for our desserts. Are they coming? ☐
4 I'd only eaten Indian food once. ☐

2 ★ Mark the underlined verbs as either **P** for in progress at a certain time in the future or **C** for completed before a certain time in the future.

The dishwasher will have finished in 10 minutes. ☐C

1 We'll be eating seafood on the beach at this time tomorrow. ☐
2 While we are eating the main course, the chef will be preparing dessert. ☐
3 Go to the shop now or it will have closed by the time you get there. ☐
4 They'll be baking bread at 5 a.m. ☐
5 Tomorrow morning at this time we'll have arrived in the mountains. ☐

3 ★ ★ Choose the correct forms.

1 **Ryan:** Can I call you again tomorrow at seven?
   Meg: No way! I won't *be waking up / have woken up* by seven.

2 **Kelly:** Shall I pick you up in half an hour?
   Grace: Yes, I'*ll be waiting / 'll have waited* outside the café.

3 **Amelia:** Let's meet outside the school gates at eight.
   Jacob: I won't make it. I'*ll be cycling / 'll have cycled* to school at eight.

4 **Mum:** Are you at home, Alex?
   Alex: No, I'm leaving school now.
   Mum: Well, the courier has a package to deliver. *Will you be arriving / Will you have arrived* home by five?
   Alex: Yes, the bus stops right outside at half past four.

5 **Dad:** I'm coming to listen to you sing at eight, right Emily?
   Emily: Dad, I *won't be singing / won't have sung* at eight. The concert finishes at seven.

6 **Ethan:** *Will you be leaving at / Will you have left by* nine?
   Paige: Oh definitely. I'm tired and I want to be home by eight at the latest.
   Ethan: So, I won't see you because I can't be there till nine.

4 ★ ★ ★ Complete the sentences with the Future Continuous or the Future Perfect forms of the verbs in bold in the list. Use short forms.

> **Start** dinner @ 11:00
> 11:00 **put** pork in oven
> 12:45 **peel** potatoes and carrots
> 13:00 **wash** brussels sprouts
> 13:30 **boil** vegetables
> 14:00 **serve** dinner
> 15:00 **sleep** in front of the TV ☺

By 11:05 we '*ll have put* the pork in the oven.

1 At 10:30 we _____ dinner yet.
2 We _____ the potatoes and carrots at 12:45.
3 By 13:30 we _____ the brussels sprouts.
4 We _____ the vegetables by 13:55.
5 We _____ dinner at 14:00.
6 At 15:05 we _____ in front of the TV.

SHOW WHAT YOU'VE LEARNT

5 Complete the sentences with the Future Continuous or the Future Perfect forms of the verbs in brackets. Use short forms where possible.

Will you have checked (you/check) the timetable by the time we leave for the concert?

1 I can't meet you at six because I _____ (not/finish) my homework.
2 Dad _____ (wait) for you outside school at 4 o'clock. Don't be late!
3 Will _____ (he/finish) that book by the end of the year?
4 Sorry, but by the time you get home, I _____ (eat) all the chocolates.
5 Will _____ (we/sunbathe) next to the pool at this time next week?
6 By this time next year, she _____ (study) law at Cambridge University.

☐ /6

GRAMMAR: Train and Try Again page 157

1 ★ **Complete the text with the correct words.**

We all love cooking, don't _we_? And one thing which proves this is the current popularity of cooking programmes on TV. You can probably name two or three popular cooking shows, can't ¹_____? And that's because we also enjoy watching other people cook. That, basically, is what this recent trend is all about, isn't ²_____?

Jamie Oliver, Gordon Ramsay, Jordi Cruz – we've all heard of them, haven't ³_____? They all became famous for the same reason – they are celebrity chefs, aren't ⁴_____? If you don't know who they are, then you haven't been spending enough time in the kitchen, have ⁵_____? Or, in fact, in front of the TV.

2 ★★ **Complete the dialogues with the correct answers A–C.**

1 **Laurel:** We can start baking the cake now, ___?
   Adrianne: Not yet. We're waiting for Kyle to bring the eggs.
   A cannot we **B** can we **C** can't we

2 **Lester:** I'll have a slice of mushroom pizza.
   Carlo: But you're allergic to mushrooms, ___?
   A are you **B** aren't you **C** will you

3 **Eva:** It's cold in here, don't you think?
   Megan: Yes, that window's open, ___?
   A isn't it **B** is it **C** doesn't it

4 **Dario:** I don't think I'd like anything to eat, to be honest.
   Rufus: Oh, I'm not the only one of us that's hungry, ___?
   A is it **B** am I **C** are we

5 **Maureen:** Did Martha say she wanted something to eat?
   Hollis: Well, she hasn't had anything to eat since breakfast, ___?
   A has she **B** had she **C** did she

3 ★★ **Complete the sentences with one word in each gap.**

You won't tell anyone I took the last biscuit, _will_ you?

1 That's octopus meat, isn't _____? Yuk.

2 James and Oli absolutely love avocados, _____ they?

3 There's a new burger bar opening in town, isn't _____?

4 We don't have to leave a tip for the waiter, _____ we?

5 We should complain about the service, _____ we?

4 ★★ **Choose the best answer A–C to complete the text.**

Enjoy!

Every nationality has its traditional meals, ¹___ they? Scotland, for example, with their haggis – a meat dish made with a sheep's stomach. You'd just love to try that, ²___ you? Yummy! Well, here are some more strange and delicious dishes from around the world.

We all know the Japanese are famous for eating fish, ³___ we? But did you know that one speciality is tuna eyeballs? These are boiled in hot water and served with soy sauce or garlic.

But you don't really fancy that, ⁴___ you? Then how about some tasty white ant eggs soup? Sounds tasty, ⁵___ it? This speciality comes from Laos, is topped with baby ants and tastes like squid (an animal similar to octopus) apparently. Eating insects is your thing, ⁶___ it? Yes? Then how about some fried tarantula? A popular snack in Cambodia so I hear.

1 **A** do **B** don't **C** haven't
2 **A** wouldn't **B** couldn't **C** won't
3 **A** don't **B** doesn't **C** can't
4 **A** don't **B** aren't **C** do
5 **A** aren't **B** doesn't **C** isn't
6 **A** is **B** are **C** isn't

5 ★★★ **Complete the sentences with the correct question tags.**

Jamal: Can I have another piece of cake?
Bridget: You're on a diet, _aren't you_?

1 **Heidi:** I fancy an ice cream.
   Glenda: Let's walk into town and buy one, _____?

2 **Lara:** They say the café is open but they haven't cleaned it from yesterday.
   Alisia: Well, then they shouldn't let us inside, _____?

3 **Mary:** They will serve us in this expensive restaurant, _____?
   Freddie: I don't see why not. We're both wearing smart clothes.

4 **Jamison:** You haven't got some money you can lend me, _____?
   Clinton: Don't worry. I'll pay for the meal this time.

5 **Leisa:** Margot left her bag in the restaurant, _____?
   Cindi: Oh, no. So we have to go back?

WRITING

Formal/informal style

1 Complete the tips with words from the box.

> clarification   faithfully   informal   politely
> refer   reply   responding   sincerely   why

1 Start the email *politely*.
2 Don't use abbreviations, _____ phrases or contractions.
3 In the first paragraph, ª_____ to the letter/ email/advert you are ᵇ_____ to (if appropriate).
4 Also, in the first paragraph, say _____ you are writing.
5 If something is unclear, ask for _____ .
6 In the final paragraph mention that you would like a _____ .
7 Close the email with Yours ª_____ (if you know the name of the person) or Yours ᵇ_____ (if you do not know the person's name).

2 Match the beginnings and the endings to make phrases. Then match the phrases to the tips from Exercise 1. You do **not** need to use all the tips.

Dear Sir/

1 Could you clarify how much …
2 There are ~~lots of~~ several …
3 I look forward to …
4 I am writing to ask for …
5 I saw your advert …
6 I would like to know …

a … questions ~~I'd~~ I would like to ask.   Tip ◯
b … in the local newspaper.   Tip ◯
c … some information about your offer.   Tip ◯
d … discount you offer to groups?   Tip ◯
e … receiving your reply soon.   Tip ◯
f … which activities the centre offers.   Tip ◯
g Madam,   Tip ①

Dear Sir/ → g

3 Complete the formal email. The first letters of the missing words are given.

Dear Mr Mckinney,
¹**T**_____ **y**_____ for **y**_____ email **r**_____ the training courses offered by your organisation. ²I am **w**_____ to **e**_____ about the level 1 course in food hygiene.

First of all, ³**c**_____ I ask **a**_____ the possibility of studying this course part-time rather than full-time? I am still at school, so I can only study in the evenings or at weekends. If a part-time course is available, ⁴**c**_____ you confirm **w**_____ the price is the same as for a full-time course? I ⁵**w**_____ also like to **a**_____ **i**_____ your organisation runs this course during the summer holidays. This would be an ideal option for students such as myself.

⁶I **h**_____ to **h**_____ from you **s**_____ .

Yours sincerely,
Oliver Thornber

4 Put the words in order to make indirect questions.

I'd / what / to / know / like / have / drinks / you / non-alcoholic
I'd like to know what non-alcoholic drinks you have.

1 Can / there / tell / are / what / desserts / you / me?
_____
2 Could / you / is / us / who / the / chef / tell?
_____
3 I'd / how / to / are / like / many / tables / know / there
_____
4 I'd / who / know / to / like / also / is / the / manager
_____
5 Could / the / restaurant / me / what / time / you / tell / closes?
_____

5 Cross out the unnecessary word in each request. Two requests are correct.

I'd like to know what seafood ~~do~~ you have.

1 Could you tell me what time does the café closes?
2 I'd like to see the dessert menu, please.
3 Can you tell me how long it will it take to prepare the duck?
4 Could you tell me what is the vegetarian special is?
5 I'd like to know if do you have a table for two at 8 o'clock this evening.
6 Can you tell me what flavours of ice cream do you have?
7 Could you tell me where the gentlemen's toilets are, please?
8 I'd like to know if is the chicken curry is very spicy.

6 Read the email to Benjamin's head teacher and re-write the direct questions to make them more polite. Use the beginnings below.

Dear Mr Jones,

Have you thought about my idea for changing the menu in the school canteen? Most students I spoke to understand the value of a balanced diet but would like to have a greater choice from time to time.

¹Is it possible to add just one or two fast food items such as pizzas or burgers one day of the week? Maybe on Fridays? ²Let me know if we can have something other to drink than still or sparkling water. Even some fruit juice would make a nice change.

³Have you spoken about this to the other teachers and the school authorities?

I look forward to receiving your reply.

Yours sincerely,
Benjamin Moody

I am writing *to enquire whether / if you have thought about my idea for changing the menu in the school canteen.*

1 I would like _____
2 Could you tell _____
3 Can you confirm _____

7 Read the task below. Then complete the email with the correct form of the words from the box and any other words you need. There are two extra words.

> You want to organise a family meal to celebrate your birthday and decide to contact the restaurant where your family enjoyed a meal two years ago. Write a formal email to the manager of the restaurant. Include and develop these points:
> - Say why you are writing.
> - Inform the manager about the meal you had in the past and why it was enjoyable.
> - Tell the manager about the number of people attending and ask about arrangements for guests to park their cars.
> - Ask for information about any discounts they may offer.

> arrive   diet   ~~enquire~~   food   healthy
> like   meal   receive   snack

Dear Sir / Madam,

I am writing to _enquire_ about a reservation for a family meal. Two years ago my family and I enjoyed such a meal at your restaurant and I would ¹_____ to organise a similar event to celebrate my 18th birthday. ᴬ<u>Could you tell me</u> ⬭

The last time we celebrated at your restaurant was a great success. There were light ²_____ on the table when the guests arrived, and after this the waiters served a three-course ³_____ with a selection of side salads. I would like to ask whether the same can be arranged this time. One guest, however, is on a vegetarian ⁴_____ . ᴮ<u>Could you clarify</u> ⬭

In total, there will be around fifteen guests. We expect that most of them ⁵_____ by car. ᶜ<u>Could you inform us</u> ⬭ Finally, the last time we organised a family meal at your restaurant we received a discount for the group booking. ᴰ<u>I would like to know</u> ⬭

I look forward to ⁶_____ your reply soon.

Yours faithfully,
Roger Coombes

8 Read the email again. Match the questions below to the missing indirect questions A–D in the text. Then write the indirect questions below. Use the underlined beginnings from the email.

1 What discount can you offer us on this occasion?
_____

2 Will you be able to provide parking spaces for our guests when they arrive?
_____

3 What options will be available for our vegetarian guest?
_____

4 Will this be possible on 3 June?

---

9 You would like to attend a weekend cooking course offered by a local college. Write a formal email to the college. Include and develop these points:

- Say where you saw the course advertised and why you are writing the email.
- Describe your previous cooking and/or training experience.
- Say why you want to attend the weekend cooking course.
- Find out some more information about what the content of the course will be.

SHOW THAT YOU'VE CHECKED

Finished? Always check your writing. Can you tick ✓ everything on this list?

In my formal email:

• I have started the email with a polite greeting appropriate to the gender, age and marital status of the person I am writing to.	⬭
• I have mentioned the advert I saw in the first paragraph.	⬭
• I have given a reason for writing in the same paragraph.	⬭
• I have provided the information required and politely asked for information and clarification (e.g. with indirect questions) in the main body paragraphs.	⬭
• I have made it clear that I would like the person to respond to my email in the final paragraph.	⬭
• I have only used formal language and have avoided abbreviations (e.g. _info / CU / gr8_) emoticons ☺ and contractions (e.g. _I'm / aren't / that's_).	⬭
• I have checked my spelling and punctuation.	⬭
• My text is neat and clear.	⬭

1 Translate the phrases into your own language.

SPEAKING BANK

Ordering food

Can I order, please?
_____
_____

Do you have any vegetarian dishes?
_____
_____

Can I have chips with that?
_____
_____

Could I have the bill, please?
_____
_____

Asking for information

Could you tell me what the soup is?
_____
_____

Can you tell me what the Mario Special Salad is?
_____
_____

Do you know what the pasta sauce is?
_____
_____

I'd like to know if there are onions in it.
_____
_____

2 Complete the restaurant phrases with *Could/Can I* or *Do you*. Then mark them as W for said by the waiter or C for said by the customer.

Could /Can I have the bill, please?   Ⓒ

1 What _____ get for you?   ◯
2 _____ know what the pasta sauce is?   ◯
3 _____ have chips with that?   ◯
4 _____ have any vegetarian dishes?   ◯
5 _____ order, please?   ◯
6 _____ take your order?   ◯

3 Put the words in order to make phrases. Then mark them as S for suggesting or A for asking for information.

you / what / special / know / do / today's / is
Do you know what today's special is ?   Ⓐ

1 about / fish / what   salmon / is / the /delicious
ᵃ_____ ? ᵇ_____   ◯

2 tell / what / can / you / the Chef's Special Lamb / me / is
_____ ?   ◯

3 me / you / the Farmer's Lunch / what / is / tell / could
_____   ◯

4 about / the Diavolo Pizza / how   very / spicy / it's
ᵃ_____ ? ᵇ_____   ◯

5 know / there / olives / I'd / in / the pasta / like / if / to / are
_____   ◯

6 get / can / I / where / the best pizza
_____   ◯

4 Complete the dialogue between the waiter and the customer. The first letters are given.

C: Excuse me, waiter. **C**_an_ I o_rder,_ please?
W: Good evening, sir. Certainly, what can I get for you?
C: ¹**C**_____ you **t**_____ me **w**_____ the special **i**_____ ?
W: Yes, sir. This evening's special is roast beef.
C: Oh no. I don't eat red meat. I'll have chips please. But, ²**c**_____ I **h**_____ them cold?
W: Cold chips? Er … well … certainly, sir. A large portion?
C: Yes, that ³**s**_____ **g**_____ . Large please.
W: Perhaps you'd like some salad with your chips?
C: I'm ⁴**s**_____ , but I'm **a**_____ to salad. It makes me cough.
W: Of course, sir. Is that everything?
C: ⁵**D**_____ you **h**_____ any kiwi fruit?
W: Er … I'll check with the chef. So, that's cold chips followed by kiwi for dessert.
C: No, kiwi with the chips please.
W: With the …? Er, whatever you want, sir. And to drink?
C: Just tap water, please. But I'll have it warm.
W: Warm? Well … er of course, sir.
C: And ⁶**c**_____ I **s**_____ the dessert menu, please?
W Certainly, sir. Perhaps you'd like some hot ice cream or fruit salad with sardines?
C: Don't be ridiculous! What kind of restaurant is this?
W: Sorry, sir. It's just that your order is rather … unusual.
C: Well, I know what I like, and I like what I know and you, young man, will definitely not be getting a tip!

Cold chips, kiwi fruit a glass of warm water, Enjoy your meal.

Student A, look below. Student B, go to page 137.

1 **In pairs, ask and answer the questions.**

Talk about travel.
1 Describe your journey to school.
2 Have you ever got stuck in a long traffic jam? What happened?
3 Would you prefer to work as a travel agent, tour leader or travel guide? Why?
4 What places would you like to visit on a round-the-world trip? Why?
5 When was the last time you missed a bus, train or a plane? What happened?

2 **Discuss this question together. 'Should we all be vegetarian?' What do you think?**

For vegetarians:

Eating a vegetarian diet ...
- is healthier than eating meat.
- is better because we don't have to kill animals to make our food.
- is better for the environment.
- is delicious!

3 **Look at these two meals. What can you see in the photos? Which would you prefer to eat? Why?**

A

B

4 **Read the instructions on your card and role-play the conversation.**

Student A:

You are in a restaurant. Order your food from the waiter (Student B).
- Get the waiter's attention and ask if you can order.
- Ask politely what the soup is.
- Say you're vegetarian and ask if he/she has any vegetarian dishes.
- Ask politely if it's spicy.
- Ask politely if it comes with anything else on the side.
- Say you'll have that.

VOCABULARY AND GRAMMAR

1 Complete the sentences with the opposites of the words in brackets. The first letters are given.

Make sure you choose a **r**_ipe_ (unripe) mango. They aren't good if they are not ready to eat.

1 Eurgh! I've just drunk a big mouthful of **s**_____ (fresh) milk. I think I'm going to be sick!

2 A **b**_____ (fattening) diet can include some sweet or greasy food, just not too much.

3 Did you know that you shouldn't feed **s**_____ (fresh) bread to ducks? Any bread, in fact! It's very bad for their health.

4 This salad dressing is a bit too **b**_____ (tasty). Let's add some more honey and lime juice.

5 I'm afraid this meat is still rather **r**_____ (cooked). It needs to go back in the oven. Sorry everyone.

/5

2 Complete the sentences with words from the box. There are two extra words.

> aubergines food ~~healthy~~ light
> long-grain pumpkin spicy wholemeal

The best way to stay fit is to do plenty of exercise and have a _healthy_ diet.

1 Don't have a big meal if you're not hungry. Have a _____ snack instead.

2 What are those strange purple vegetables called? Are they _____ ?

3 Would you like _____ rice with your chicken curry?

4 Jack-o'-lantern is the name of those big orange heads that people make from a _____ at Halloween.

5 Why don't we start buying _____ bread instead of white? It's healthier and tastier.

/5

3 Complete the sentences with the missing words. The first letters are given.

I've bought some oranges and I'm going to make some **f**_resh_ juice out of them. Would you like a glass?

1 Household **c**_____ of the planet's natural resources is now three times higher than it was 40 years ago. We must do something about it!

2 I prefer not to buy **s**_____ bread so I can make each piece as thick as I like.

3 All packaging for food must meet new government **s**_____ by the end of the year, or companies will face a fine.

4 Devon follows a strict **v**_____ diet. He doesn't eat any meat or fish at all.

5 I'll have a bottle of **s**_____ water. I don't like it when there are too many bubbles.

/5

4 Choose the correct words.

As soon as I (finish) / will finish my homework, I'll start preparing dinner.

1 *I'm buying / I'm going to buy* as many apples as I can when we get to the farm. They're much cheaper and more delicious than apples in the supermarket.

2 This baker's *opens / will open* at 6.30 a.m. and I'm sure there'll be a long queue outside.

3 Do you have plans for tonight? *Will / Shall* we go out somewhere?

4 I think I *will / am going to* invite Nigel and Norma around for lunch one day. Is that OK with you?

5 Milly *will go / is going* to a concert with Thomas tonight. They bought the tickets last weekend.

/5

5 Complete the sentences with the Future Perfect Simple or Future Continuous forms of the verbs in brackets. In one sentence you need to use the Future Simple.

Tomorrow at this time we _will be sitting_ (sit) in the restaurant enjoying my birthday dinner.

1 We predict the price of beetroot _____ (go down) by the end of the year.

2 One day, I think you _____ (like) strong flavours such as blue cheese. Your tastes change as you get older.

3 Tomorrow, Uncle Mark _____ (go) without meat for four years.

4 Mum _____ (not/work) this Saturday morning, so we are going shopping together.

5 _____ (you/finish) that book by the time we go on holiday? I'd like to read it while we're away.

/5

6 Choose the correct answers A–C.

Mum and Dad have been married for nearly 20 years – well, exactly 20 years on Sunday! So, me and my sister _B_ a little surprise for them. We've already arranged for them to be out of the house for a few hours in the afternoon. And then, **¹**___ they get back home, I **²**___ them into the garden where the guests will shout 'SURPRISE' as loudly as possible **³**___ they see my parents. I hope we can keep the secret from them before Sunday. It might be hard because on Saturday I need to prepare the mixed **⁴**___ , and of course there's a big cake arriving in the afternoon which we need to keep **⁵**___ until the next day. I know, maybe we can buy Mum and Dad tickets for the theatre on Saturday and pretend that's their anniversary gift!

	A	B	C
	A are to going to plan	(B) are planning	C will plan
1	A as soon as	B if	C unless
2	A shall take	B am going to take	C am taking
3	A if	B before	C when
4	A bread	B salad	C soup
5	A crunchy	B tinned	C fresh

/5

Total /30

7 Complete the sentences using the prompts in brackets. Do not change the order of the words. Change the forms or add new words where necessary. Use up to six words in each gap.

The new café _doesn't open_ (not / open) until 10:00 a.m. on Saturdays.

1 _____ (before / government / apply) the new regulations, we will need to inform our staff about the changes.

2 Experts predict that_____ (energy consumption / double) between now and 2050. This is based on the current increase of around 2 percent per year.

3 I intend to be healthier, so I _____ (eat / organic food) in the future.

4 We're going to be late. By the time we get to the restaurant, _____ (everyone / already / start) their meals.

5 I believe that _____ (unless / manufacturing industry / do) something soon, the government will close even more factories.

/5

8 Choose the correct answers A–C.

Marine: And what are you going to do with those figs?

Raymonde: I think _A_ them in a fruit salad.
A I'll put   B I'm going to put
C I'll be putting

1 **Karina:** At exactly this time tomorrow ___ lunch with Salman Rushdie at the Ritz Hotel in London!

Dudley: You have such a cool job! I'm really jealous.
A I'm eating   B I'll be eating
C I will have eaten

2 **Daniel:** Hugh and Rebecca haven't got a smoke alarm, ___ ?

Tracy: I'm not sure. Maybe you should ask them before you decide to light a cigarette?
A have they?   B do they?
C haven't they

3 **Laurence:** When are you going to the shops, Agatha?

Agatha: I'll go ___ I finish this pineapple.
A till   B before   C as soon as

4 **Joslyn:** ___ to the same restaurant on Sunday that we went to last year for my birthday?

Marcel: That's the plan. Is that OK with you?
A Are we going   B Will we have gone
C Will we go

5 **Lucas:** I will have baked the ___ cake by the time you arrive.

Meg: Great! I can't wait.
A aubergine   B radish   C apricot

/5

9 Choose the correct answer A–D.

Changing EATING habits

Perhaps it's due to the fact that we're eating more _B_ food? Or perhaps our work routines mean we are eating more ¹___ snacks like sandwiches? Whatever the reasons, our eating habits have changed and some experts now say that the traditional three-course ²___ is dead.

Experts in the ³___ industry report that fewer people now choose to eat the once standard soup, main dish and dessert. Instead, people prefer to order a number of dishes to eat at the same time or even share food freely from each other's plates. Some people think this is because it's cheaper to eat out this way, others say it's because we have less time today. Indeed, in the past we would sit and enjoy eating and talking for around two hours. Now, the average length of a meal is at a record low ⁴___ of only 40 minutes! And with our current obsession of spending even less time enjoying face-to-face contact with friends and family, the situation really doesn't look good, ⁵___ ?

	A spicy	B fast	C healthy	D vegetarian
1	A heavy	B cold	C fast	D balanced
2	A meal	B food	C snack	D diet
3	A eating	B catering	C organic	D home-made
4	A platform	B standard	C level	D limit
5	A is it	B isn't it	C does it	D doesn't it

/5

10 Complete the sentences by using the correct form of the words in brackets.

Apparently meat _consumption_ (CONSUME) is one of the major causes of damage to the ozone layer. Well, it's because of farming animals really, but if people ate less meat …

1 We try to recycle as much as possible at home. But it's impossible not to create some _____ (HOUSE) waste, isn't it?

2 I admire people that work in the _____ (VOLUNTEER) sector. I mean, they work really hard and do it for no money!

3 There are some really _____ (ALARM) statistics about the effects of eating too much sugar.

4 There are lots of career opportunities in the _____ (TOUR) industry. You can be a guide, get into publishing, run a hotel. The list of jobs is endless!

5 This milk tastes awful. When was the _____ (EXPIRE) date? Yuk, last week!!

/5

Total /20

59

5 Planet Earth

VOCABULARY

5.1
Phrasal verbs • collocations
• word families

---

2 Choose the correct particles.

1 We should start walking back to the car. Look, the tide is coming *in / out / up* pretty quickly.

2 The United Kingdom is made *out / up / in* of England, Scotland, Wales and Northern Ireland.

3 Walk slowly across the stream and you won't stir *over / in / up* too much mud from the bottom.

4 This soup is cold. Let's put it on the camp fire to heat it *up / over / out* a little.

5 Did dinosaurs really die *out / over / up* because a giant meteorite hit the planet?

6 We were walking through the forest when we came *over / up / across* some ancient ruins.

7 The sand on the beach goes on for miles when the tide goes *out / in / across* all the way.

3 Complete the extracts from travel guides with words from the box. Make the nouns plural if necessary. There are two extra words.

> calm   coast   ~~ocean~~   range   tide
> tropical   volcano   wave   winding

You can see thousands of interesting marine plants in the Sargasso Sea. Because of the <u>ocean</u> currents, they get trapped and cannot escape back into the open waters. It's an incredible sight to see!

A visit to Camber Sands is recommended for lovers of sandy beaches – and at low ¹_____ it's possible to walk for miles across the golden flat sand before the sea comes back in.

The ²_____ island of Bali is the ideal destination for lovers of sandy beaches and surfing – or, in fact, anyone that wants to relax under clear blue skies.

The Carpathians are the second largest mountain ³_____ in Europe and home to brown bears, wolves and the lynx. You'll also find a number of thermal springs there.

The Turks and Caicos islands, just south-east of the Bahamas, have some incredibly ⁴_____ seas and a 14-mile barrier reef which makes it the perfect destination for scuba-diving and snorkelling.

The town of Nazare in Portugal has become a popular location for surfers since November 2017. This is when Rodrigo Koxa broke the world record after riding a huge ⁵_____ with a height of over 24 metres.

If you don't have much time, take a walk along the ⁶_____ River Thames. It's a great way to see many of London's popular tourist attractions such as Tower Bridge, the London Eye or the Houses of Parliament.

SHOW WHAT YOU KNOW

1 Complete the gaps with single words.

SURVIVING SCHOOL
Location, location, location

Do you go to school in an unusual place or make an unusual journey to get there? If so, tell us about it below:

Julia_D$ I go to an international school on the other side of Tokyo. Tokyo is a huge *city* and I have to catch a train, then the underground, then a bus to get to school. It takes nearly two hours and I hate it. ☹

Sonia_16 My family lives on a very small ¹_____, so I get a boat every day to get to school. I can't be late because there's only one boat in the morning.

Bret@home Australia is a huge ²_____ and my parents own a farm hundreds of kilometres from the nearest big town. There's no secondary school in our little community, so I have all my lessons online.

pinky I go to school near Cape Town in South Africa, and about 20 kilometres from my school is the point where two ³_____ meet. The Atlantic and the Indian. I think our school has the most beautiful location in the world.

8ball_16 I go to school in Istanbul, which is famous for being the only city in the world where two ⁴_____ meet. My school is in Asia, but when I look out of the window, I can see Europe.

hellokaty_14 Everyone has heard of the famous ⁵_____ in our city, but most people don't know that the city is also called Niagara Falls. In fact, my school is called Niagara Falls High School!

Kid_16 My family lives in Dubai very close to the ⁶_____. It hardly ever rains, but we regularly have storms – sand storms! When that happens, we have to stay indoors, so it's impossible to get to school.

Yoda_347 My parents own a restaurant high in the ⁷_____ and I have to get a cable car down to the town to get to school every day. Sometimes, if it's really windy, I just have to stay at home. ☺

4 Cross out the word which does **not** collocate.

1 **mountain** peak / ridge / middle
2 desert / remote / alone **island**
3 high / growing / rising **tide**
4 dangerous / ocean / high **current**
5 fast-flowing / slow-moving / easy-going **river**
6 furious / calm / rough **sea**
7 tidal / spacious / enormous **wave**

WORD STORE 5C | Word families

5 Choose the correct answers A–C.

1 Kilimanjaro is 5,895 metres ___ , which makes it the tallest mountain in Africa.
A high   B height   C heighten

2 What's the ___ of this river? Do you think we can swim across it?
A wide   B width   C widen

3 Travelling abroad definitely helps you to ___ your understanding of other countries and cultures.
A broad   B breadth   C broaden

4 If we don't ___ the support for our tent, I think it will fall down during the night.
A strong   B strength   C strengthen

5 Is it possible to ___ our stay in Scotland? We haven't seen the Highlands yet.
A long   B length   C lengthen

6 How ___ is the Grand Canyon? Does anyone here know?
A deep   B depth   C deepen

6 Complete each pair of sentences with the unused words from Exercise 5. Change the verb forms if necessary.

a My legs aren't <u>strong</u> enough to climb this big hill any more.
b I had no idea of the river's <u>strength</u>. I think we should turn back.

1 a What's the _____ of this hill? Can we climb to the top?
b If we can _____ the middle of the tent, I'll be able to stand up.

2 a The total _____ of this desert is impressive. It must take weeks to cross it.
b This lake is very _____ , so please don't take the boats too far out.

3 a How _____ do you think the gap is? Can I jump it safely?
b Oh, look. They've _____ the cycle paths in this park. Now we can ride side-by-side.

4 a Mum, how _____ will it take to get back to the car? I'm tired of walking now.
b Nobody knows the exact _____ of the Amazon River but some experts believe it's even 6,990 kilometres.

5 a I think they've _____ this swimming pool. My feet don't touch the bottom.
b Hranicka Propast in the Czech Republic is probably the deepest underwater cave in the world with a _____ of 473 metres.

SHOW WHAT YOU'VE LEARNT

7 Choose the correct answers A–C.

1 I love just lying on my back and floating on the ___ sea close to my beach home.
A calm   B heavy   C rough

2 Many species of animal will die ___ if we don't start protecting them soon.
A up   B down   C out

3 I won't go into that pool. The water's too ___ and you know I can't swim well.
A deep   B wide   C broad

4 The highest point of a mountain is known as the mountain ___ .
A range   B ridge   C peak

5 Let's see how far we can walk across the sand when the tide ___ out.
A comes   B goes   C stirs

6 It's dangerous to swim in ___ rivers because the water can carry you away.
A fast-flowing   B slow-moving   C winding

7 I have just ___ across an article about an amazing microscopic organism called a water bear.
A gone   B been   C come

8 Jamaica is one of the most famous ___ islands. It's very popular with tourists from Europe.
A remote   B desert   C tropical

9 Jenny goes to the gym every day to ___ her legs because next year she's going hiking in Spain.
A broaden   B widen   C strengthen

10 In the dry season, every car driving past our house ___ up clouds of dust.
A heats   B stirs   C makes

/10

GRAMMAR

5.2

Articles: no article,
a/an or *the*

SHOW WHAT YOU KNOW

1 Choose the correct answers (Ø = no article).

Greener than you think

People who have never been to ¹*the* / Ø London usually think that it's full of dirt, noise and endless concrete. And while this is partly true, it is also ²*a* / Ø city where you can feel the presence of ³*the* / Ø nature almost everywhere you go. The parks in ⁴*a* / *the* centre, including St. James' Park, Hyde Park and Kensington Gardens, create ⁵*a* /*an* huge green area that feels almost like ⁶*the* / Ø countryside. There are also ⁷*a* / Ø green squares that offer ⁸*a* / Ø break from ⁹*a* / *the* noise and pollution. To me, this modern metropolis still seems connected to ¹⁰*the* / Ø ancient land it was built on.

2 ★ Cross out *the* where it is not needed. One sentence is correct.

The government should spend more on ~~the~~ education.

1 Has Emily visited the Netherlands and the Germany?
2 In January 2013, only around 39% of people in the United States owned the passports.
3 The population of Iceland is less than half a million.
4 The citizens of Germany chose a female Prime Minister, and naturally she has promised to do more for the women of her country.
5 The biggest city in the China is the Shanghai. Around 16 million people live there.
6 The pollution is generally a problem in big cities, but the pollution in this city is worse than in most others.

3 ★★ Complete the protest signs with *a/an*, *the* or Ø.

Say **NO** to ¹___ plastic.

You never know when you might need ⟨a⟩ nurse. **More pay for nurses!**

²___ Amazon rainforest belongs to everyone.

There is an answer to war. ³___ answer is peace.

Save ⁴___ planet.

End ⁵___ racism **now!**

Graffiti is ⁷___ crime. Keep our city clean.

⁶___ TOKYO WANTS THE OLYMPIC GAMES!

---

4 ★★★ Complete the telephone conversation between Sally and Ken with *a/an*, *the* or Ø.

K: Hey, Sally. Have you heard of this new trend called plogging?
S: No, I haven't. What on earth does that mean?
K: Well, it comes from the Swedish word for 'pick up' and the English word 'jogging'.
S: But what is it? It sounds like some sort of name for ⟨a⟩ music group or something.
K: Not at all! Actually, it's ¹___ form of exercise that combines jogging with cleaning up ²___ rubbish that you see in the places where you go running. According to the media, it's ³___ most popular new trend of the year, and ⁴___ people are taking it up all over ⁵___ world.
S: So is it something you're interested in trying?
K: Well, I think it would be ⁶___ great idea for our running group. You know, people are always dropping litter in ⁷___ park where we run, and it would be great if we could get our exercise and improve ⁸___ environment at the same time. All you need to do is carry ⁹___ bag with you and wear ¹⁰___ gloves to protect your hands, and suddenly you're doing ¹¹___ good and keeping fit at the same time!
S: Well, we can certainly give it a try. It drives me crazy to see litter everywhere, so let's do something about it!

SHOW WHAT YOU'VE LEARNT

5 Find and correct the mistakes. In each sentence there is one mistake only.

We try to provide a food and water for the poorest families. *Ø food and water*

1 For me, Paris is a very special city. It's a city where I was born. _____
2 I'd like to become the journalist and report on our country's problems. _____
3 An economic development is a good thing, but not if it destroys the environment. _____
4 Pencils will not be allowed in the exam. Please bring the pen. _____
5 Hill that overlooks Barcelona is the best place to view the city. _____
6 Is this an only place to eat around here? _____

/6

GRAMMAR: Train and Try Again page 158

5.3

Collocations
• compound nouns

1 Read the dialogue between Michael and the presenter. Choose the correct options to complete the collocations in bold.

Extract from Student's Book recording 🔊 **2.25**

M: First of all, we have solar panels on the roof of the school. [...]

P: And will they ¹*use / provide / have* **power** for the whole school?

M: Yes, that's the idea. It will ²*pay / cost / save* **a lot of money on electricity.** [...]

***

M: Our Eco School garden will ³*eat / grow / cook* **vegetables** [...] and we'll also have chickens, rabbits and ducks.

P: And will they go into the school dinners too?

M: Ha ha, no. That would be terrible. They'll be pets and they'll be useful. They'll ⁴*throw away / use / eat* **the leftovers** from the kitchen and the chickens will ⁵*provide / eat / collect* **eggs.**

P: Very good. So what other plans do you have to make the school more environmentally friendly?

M: We'll ⁶*use / buy / make* **low-energy light bulbs** in all the classrooms. We'll also ⁷*clean / have / empty* **recycling bins** in every classroom and in the school grounds.

P: And what about your lessons – will they be different from non-eco schools?

M: Most of our lessons will be similar to lessons in any secondary school. But in our Science lessons we'll ⁸*focus / think / learn* more **on environmental issues** like climate change and global warming. Then, in our Technology lessons we'll ⁹*consider / learn / study* **about things like** renewable energy and even how to make solar panels.

P: I see. Well, we've almost run out of time. Thank you for talking to us about your project. It's very nice to meet a teenager who is so ¹⁰*confused / concerned / nervous* **about the environment.**

2 Complete the sentences with collocations from Exercise 1. Change the verb forms if necessary.

> If you turn down the heating at home, you'll use less energy and *save a lot of money on electricity*.

1 If Peter can't finish all the food on his plate, his dad always _____ .

2 The wind farm currently _____ for local houses and businesses.

3 The school now _____ outside the main building, so please separate your rubbish.

4 If you are really _____ , why don't you sell that big car and buy something greener?

5 To save energy, the council will make sure all the street lights in the city _____ .

6 Jeremy and Pat _____ , herbs, and fruit in their garden.

7 Vote for the Green Party. We promise to _____ , not on defence and industry.

8 At the moment in Physics, we _____ electricity and magnetism.

9 A local farm _____ all the eggs used in this restaurant.

WORD STORE 5D | Compound nouns

3 Choose the correct answers A–C.

1 There are recycling ___ in our apartment block, but some people still don't bother to separate plastic and paper.
   A bins   **B** panels   **C** issues

2 Despite all the evidence, there are still people who don't believe that climate ___ is real.
   A warming   **B** recycling   **C** change

3 This backpack has small solar ___ on it and you can actually use it to charge your phone.
   A panels   **B** climates   **C** light bulbs

4 Global ___ is causing the ice caps in both the Arctic and the Antarctic to melt.
   A environment   **B** warming   **C** change

5 Renewable ___ is the future. We can't continue burning fossil fuels forever.
   A energy   **B** recycling   **C** low-energy

6 The developing world is facing serious ___ issues such as air pollution and water contamination.
   A climate   **B** change   **C** environmental

7 Low-energy ___ last ten to fifteen times longer than ordinary ones.
   A bins   **B** light bulbs   **C** panels

1 Read the article quickly and choose the newspaper section that it should <u>not</u> appear in.
1 Environment news
2 Technology news
3 Tourism news
4 Winter sports news
5 Scandinavian news

A Very Bright Idea

The sun makes life on Earth possible. Almost all plants and animals rely on its warmth and heat to stay alive. For us humans, it also provides many simple pleasures such as long summer evenings, bright winter days and the feeling of warm sunlight on our faces. Imagine the frustration of living somewhere where, even when the sun is shining, people can't feel its heat or appreciate its light. The town of Rjukan, in Norway is just such a place.

For six months of the year, Rjukan, a town of 3,500 people located 100 miles west of Oslo, is cut off from direct sunlight by the steep forested hills that surround it. ¹_____ Of course, many Scandinavian towns and cities suffer from freezing cold temperatures in the winter months, but Rjukan's residents* have had to cope with a complete lack of sunlight as well. In an early attempt* to find a solution to this problem, a cable car was built in 1928, which allowed the town's citizens to ride to the top of the hill and top up* their vitamin D.

These days, however, the people of Rjukan can stand in their central square and enjoy the warmth and the light of the winter sun. How is this possible? What has changed? Well, the answer might seem like something from a science fiction story, but in fact it is reality. Authorities have placed three giant mirrors on top of the hills surrounding the town to reflect light down into the valley. ²_____ As a result of this investment the town now benefits from a 600-square-metre area of light which brightens the central square. 'We think it will mean more activities in town, especially in autumn and wintertime,' said Karin Roe, head of the town's tourist office. 'People will be out more.'

The mirrors are controlled by a computer to follow the sun and adjust to the best angle* to catch the rays* and reflect them onto the centre of the town. ³_____ However, it was only made possible with modern technology. Solar panels power equipment to automatically wash the mirrors and move them into position.

Steinar Bergsland, the town's mayor said, 'It is really special to stand in the light down on the square and feel the heat. This is for the pale little children of Rjukan.' A message on the Rjukan tourist website states, 'The square will become a sunny meeting place in a town which is otherwise in the shade.'*

⁴_____ A similar project was completed in Italy in 2006, when the residents of Viganella installed mirrors on the hills above their village to take advantage of the sunlight that shone there.

GLOSSARY

residents *(n)* – the people who live in a particular place or building

attempt *(n, v)* – try *(n, v)*

to top up *(v)* – to increase the level of something and make it full again, e.g. a drink or your mobile phone credit

angle *(n)* – the space between two straight lines that join each other; you measure it in degrees, e.g. 30, 45, 90

ray *(n)* – a straight, narrow line of light, e.g. from the sun, the moon or a laser

shade *(n)* – slight darkness or protection from the sun made by something blocking it, e.g. an umbrella

2 Read the text again. Complete gaps 1–4 with sentences A–E. There is one extra sentence.

A The huge mirrors were carried there by helicopters, as part of a project which cost 5 million kroner (£500,000). ☐

B This happens because between September and March the sun is so low in the sky that its light and warmth don't reach the small town at the bottom of the valley. ☐

C Environmentalists disapprove of the project, however. ☐

D However, Rjukan is not the only place to benefit from this kind of scheme. ☐

E The idea was first suggested 100 years ago by Sam Eyde, who was responsible for building the town of Rjukan. ☐

3 Read the texts again. Choose the correct answer A–D.

1 Which is <u>true</u> about the importance of the sun?
A It prevents humans from becoming frustrated.
B It is both practical and pleasant for people.
C Its warmth is appreciated everywhere on Earth.
D Every animal and plant needs it to live.

2 For half a year the town of Rjukan in Norway
A doesn't get direct sunlight because of its location.
B isn't the only Scandinavian town without sunlight.
C hasn't been able to find a solution to its problem.
D doesn't allow its citizens to stay in the valley.

3 Now the people of Rjukan
A can finally stand in its central square.
B are able to feel the sun in winter.
C have sunlight everywhere in the town.
D are organising more activities in cold months.

4 The newly installed giant mirrors
A make the town of Rjukan unique.
B can wash and move themselves.
C give the town a new meeting place.
D aren't a completely new idea.

4 Match the beginnings with the correct endings to make extracts from the text.

… many Scandinavian towns *suffer*   (f)
1 The mirrors (…) *adjust*   ☐
2 They installed mirrors (…) to *take advantage*   ☐
3 … the town now *benefits*   ☐
4 Sam Eyde (…) was *responsible*   ☐
5 … residents have had to *cope*   ☐

a *of* the sunlight that shone there.
b *from* a 600-square-metre area of light …
c *with* a complete lack of sunlight …
d *for* building the town of Rjukan.
e *to* the best angle to catch the rays …
f *from* freezing cold temperatures in the winter …

5 Complete the sentences with the combinations in italics in Exercise 4.

The air pollution in this city means that many residents <u>suffer from</u> serious allergies.

1 People in this region have learned to _____ the destructive effects of tropical storms.
2 Every person on the planet is _____ reducing global warming. We all need to change our behaviour.
3 It may take some time to _____ life in the countryside after living in the city for so many years.
4 We invite hotel guests to _____ our free airport bus service.
5 The only people who _____ illegal logging are the loggers themselves.

VOCABULARY PRACTICE | In the woods

6 Look at the vocabulary in lesson 5.4 in the Student's Book. Choose the correct words.

1 I was so thirsty that when I saw the fresh water flowing from the *spring / pond / clearing*, I ran and quickly began to drink.
2 The Grigson twins found a lovely little *clearing / trail / path* in the woods, so we decided to sit there and have a picnic.
3 It really is true that you can tell the age of a tree by counting the rings in its *branches / leaves / trunk*.
4 Often a tree's *leaves / roots / branches* do not actually reach deep underground. In fact, they grow horizontally and usually only sixty centimetres below the surface.
5 Don't get too close to that *hedgehog / skunk / squirrel* – it might get scared and spray you with its horrible smelling scent.
6 Most people know that *foxes / squirrels / hedgehogs* are related to dogs. But not many people know that over 10,000 live in London!
7 Cats might be cute but they are natural *predators / prey / roots* and hunt birds and mice for fun!

WORD STORE 5E | Verb phrases

7 Complete the text with the correct prepositions.

The last of our food had gone *off* and I was sure we would die ¹_____ hunger. Bradley and Cooper were speaking, trying to decide what we should do next. But I slept ²_____ most of their discussion, too exhausted to join in with them. One thing was sure, we couldn't continue to sit ³_____ doing nothing, just waiting to die. I was about to fall asleep again when a noise awoke me. Cooper was close by, searching ⁴_____ his bag. Then I heard another noise – off to my left. I turned and suddenly found myself face to face ⁵_____ what I believed to be a wild dog. Slowly, I reached ⁶_____ a food tin which was lying beside me, to throw it for the animal and gain time to defend myself if it decided to attack me. But at that moment the dog jumped at me and violently began to lick my face! Then I heard a deep voice calmly saying: 'Lilly, leave that man alone. I'm sure he doesn't want to be kissed by an old dog like you.' And then I burst into laughter. We were saved!

GRAMMAR

5.5 Non-defining relative clauses

SHOW WHAT YOU KNOW

1 Complete gaps *a* with a word from the box and gaps *b* with *which/that*, *where*, or *who/that*. There are two extra words in the box.

> bangle ~~coast~~ court embassy
> opponent ostrich pitch tour leader

The ªcoast is a place ᵇwhere the sea meets the land.

1 An ª_____ is a large flightless bird ᵇ_____ lives in Africa.

2 A ª_____ is a person ᵇ_____ travels with and looks after a group of tourists.

3 A ª_____ is a place ᵇ_____ cricket, football, rugby and hockey are played.

4 A ª_____ is a piece of jewellery ᵇ_____ is worn around the wrist.

5 An ª_____ is a place ᵇ_____ an ambassador and his/her staff work.

2 ★ Choose the correct relative pronoun.

⬤◯◯

SPARE BRAIN – your online encyclopedia

Tōhoku earthquake and tsunami

The 2011 tsunami in Japan, ¹*which / that* hit the Tōhoku region on the Pacific coast, was caused by a huge undersea earthquake. The earthquake, ²*what / which* was the most powerful ever to hit Japan, created waves of up to 40.5 metres high and killed over 15,000 people. In Sendai, ³*which / where* is the largest city in the Tōhoku region, the waves travelled up to ten kilometres inland. In Fukushima, ⁴*where / whose* Fukushima Daiichi Nuclear Power Plant is located, there was a major nuclear disaster. The World Bank, ⁵*who / whose* goal is to increase development and reduce global poverty, said that cleaning up and rebuilding after the tsunami would cost more than after any other natural disaster in world history.

---

3 ★ ★ Write sentences with non-defining relative clauses. Use the correct forms of the verb *be*.

Australia / sixth largest country in the world / home to a relatively small population

Australia, which is the sixth largest country in the world, is home to a relatively small population.

1 Sydney / the famous opera house can be found / not actually the capital of Australia.

_____

2 Australian actress Nicole Kidman / films include *Moulin Rouge* / actually born in Hawaii.

_____

3 Hugh Jackman / known for playing Wolverine in the *X-Men* films / from Sydney.

_____
_____

4 ★ ★ ★ Complete the text with the correct relative pronoun and add commas where necessary.

◯◯◯

SPARE BRAIN – your online encyclopedia

Charles Darwin

Charles Darwin.

Charles Darwin, *who* was born on 11 February 1809, was an English naturalist and geologist. He was the first person to suggest that all species evolved from a single original form of life. He also suggested the theory of natural selection ¹_____ attempts to explain why there are now so many different forms of life on Earth.

In the Galapagos Islands ²_____ Darwin studied local birds he found strong evidence to support his theories. Natural selection ³_____ is sometimes called 'survival of the fittest' is still the most popular scientific explanation for the variety of life found on our planet. Darwin ⁴_____ ideas were questioned at first is now famous as one of the most important thinkers in human history.

SHOW WHAT YOU'VE LEARNT

5 Complete the sentences using *who, whose, which* or *where* and the prompts in brackets. Do not change the order of the words. Change forms or add new words and commas if necessary.

Mount Vesuvius, *which is a famous attraction in Italy,* (be / fame / attract / Italy) last erupted in 1944.

1 The Louvre _____ (collect / include / paint) such as the Mona Lisa, is located in Paris.

2 My cousin, _____ (live / San Francisco / USA) has an apartment overlooking the city.

3 Our new car _____ (my dad / buy / recent) is environmentally friendly.

4 Spain, _____ (my two / sister / study) at the moment has a very diverse climate.

5 My neighbour _____ (son / meet / shop / centre) yesterday moved here only last year.

6 These new light bulbs _____ (use / little / electric / tradition / one) are actually quite expensive.

/6

GRAMMAR: Train and Try Again page 158

USE OF ENGLISH

5.6

Prepositions at the end of clauses

1 ★ **Choose the correct answers A–C.**

1 Elias: What do you think ___ when I say the word 'mountain'?

Roxanne: I don't know. Everest?

A of   B on   C to

2 Angelica: When you're in Spain, who are you going to stay ___ ?

Sophie: My cousin, Anna.

A on   B with   C by

3 Jules: Sleeping in a tent is something that I've never got used ___ .

Doug: Well, that's because you hardly ever go camping.

A by   B for   C to

4 Charlotte: Thank you for this Environmentalist Award. It's something I'm incredibly proud ___ .

Ingrid: You worked hard for it. Congratulations!

A to   B with   C of

5 William: I never leave rubbish on the grass! That's something I can't be criticised ___ .

Pearl: Sorry. I didn't mean to upset you.

A for   B by   C with

6 Mica: Hey, Travis. What are you listening ___ ?

Travis: It's actually the sounds of waves on the beach. It helps me relax.

A for   B on   C to

2 ★ ★ **Put the words in order to make sentences.**

is / Smoking / something / approve / not / I / of / .

Smoking is not something I approve of.

1 Green / passionate / something / is / Margaret / is / politics / about / .

_____

2 What / for / animals / wild / we / are / looking / ?

_____

3 Geography / in / an / is / area / that / I / want / succeed / to / .

_____

4 Destroying / to / forests / to / something / build / roads / is / I / object / .

_____

5 Which / for / head / of / the / two / hills / we / should / ?

_____

3 ★ ★ **Choose the correct words.**

1 She's the girl that I really want to speak *at / to / for*.

2 Is that the club you'd like to go *to / for / by*?

3 Who is that boy you were arguing *with /at / to*?

4 I find Joseph incredibly easy to work *out / with / in*.

5 Which teacher are you going to give that apple *up / for / to*?

6 How many voters did you manage to sign *out / up / off*?

4 ★ ★ **Choose the correct answers A–C.**

DAD GOES ZERO WASTE

The amount of waste my family produces is something I have always worried ¹___ . Putting several bags of rubbish into the bins every day is certainly not something to be proud ²___ ! The Zero Waste movement was an idea I became interested ³___ . The movement certainly has goals that I agree ⁴___ , but it all just seemed too difficult to try and produce no rubbish at all. Was it something my family could deal ⁵___ ? I didn't think so. Then I found a website which suggested smaller goals that we could focus ⁶___ . I mean things like reusing bags and containers or putting all of our vegetable waste into a bin for composting. But we still haven't found a solution for managing the packaging from new clothes and hair products, I'm afraid. When I say to my children, 'Isn't the environment something you care ⁷___ ?' they say it is, but they want to look good too! Well, none of us is perfect, but we do the best we can.

1 A for   B in   C about   D of

2 A at   B of   C in   D for

3 A about   B on   C to   D in

4 A with   B in   C from   D to

5 A about   B with   C from   D on

6 A in   B at   C about   D on

7 A for   B at   C about   D of

5 ★ ★ ★ **Complete the sentences using the prompts in brackets. Do not change the order of the words. Change forms or add new words if necessary.**

Bernice: Are there any *animals (that / which) you are interested in* (animal / you / interest)?

Anna: Well, I quite like bears.

1 Franklin: Putting glass recycling banks everywhere is a waste of money.

Dolores: So, which environment issues do you think _____ (govern / should / concentrate)?

2 Marvin: Bees are a good example of an animal _____ (person / rely).

Emil: Yes, we need them to keep the eco-system in balance.

3 Rory: Are you still here? _____ (who / you / wait)?

Melina: My Biology teacher.

4 Haley: Did you hear that Nancy was bitten by a snake?

Emma: I know. She's the last person that it _____ (can / happen).

5 Nicki: I don't give money to any charities.

Gregg: Why not? There must be _____ (thing / you / real / care).

5.7

A 'for and against' essay

1 Read the sentences of the essay below. Put them in the correct order. Use the linkers in bold to help you.

> [1] Countries often take pride in their cultural heritage and spend billions on protecting and promoting it.

> ☐ **Personally**, I hope that there will always be individuals who can give their time and energy to preserving culture until circumstances allow the government to take over.

> ☐ **On the one hand**, it seems obvious that all cultures are worth protecting, since every country has something unique to contribute to the world.

> ☐ **On the other hand**, the physical well-being of a country may have to be the main focus of its government. A country whose population lacks jobs, homes, medical care or education may not be able to afford to preserve or promote their cultural heritage because the population has more urgent needs.

> ☐ **For instance**, there are a number of unique languages in central Europe which are spoken by few people. These languages are important to their regions, and they should be protected and promoted, along with the art, music and traditions of these areas.

> ☐ **Furthermore**, countries which are engaged in conflicts may not be able to focus on cultural matters.

> ☐ **However**, is it really a good idea when they could use the money to improve the lives of their citizens?

> ☐ **In conclusion**, the current circumstances in a country may decide if they can protect their cultural heritage.

2 Look at the essay and the linkers in bold in Exercise 1. Which of the linkers in the text can be replaced with the linkers in the box?

> First of all   For example   In addition
> In my opinion   Secondly   To sum up

Personally, I think   = *In my opinion*
1 On the one hand   = _____
2 In conclusion   = _____
3 For instance   = _____
4 Furthermore   = _____

3 Read the first paragraph of the 'for and against' essay in Exercise 4 and decide which topic is being discussed.

1 'It would be better if everyone in the world spoke the same language.'   ☐
2 'Everyone in the world should learn to speak at least one foreign language.'   ☐
3 'All the world's school pupils should study the Mandarin language.'   ☐

4 Choose the correct linkers to complete the essay. Sometimes, more than one answer is correct.

Experts say there are about 6,500 different languages spoken in the world today. Huge amounts of money and time are spent on learning and translation, so it is not surprising that some people believe life would be simpler if we all spoke the same language. [1]*For example / However*, many other people feel that language is an essential part of identity and that having just one language would damage individual cultures.

[2]*On the one hand / On the other hand*, there are some good arguments for the idea of a single global language. [3]*Secondly / Firstly*, for politicians and business people, there would be no barriers to communication and doing business would be easier and cheaper. [4]*For instance / To sum up*, governments and international companies would not have to spend large sums of money on translation or multi-lingual staff. [5]*Secondly / Thirdly*, a single world language would probably be good for tourism. [6]*For example / For instance*, tourists would feel safer overseas and be more comfortable visiting certain countries if they knew they could communicate easily.

[7]*On the one hand / On the other hand*, there are several important arguments against a single global language. [8]*First of all / However*, a nation's language is a significant part of its culture and character. For example, when Poland was occupied by other countries in the past, the Polish language helped people preserve their identity and traditions. [9]*For instance / Furthermore*, many people get pleasure, satisfaction and even income from studying, using and teaching different languages. For them, a single global language would not be an advantage.

[10]*In conclusion / Finally*, although there are some reasonable arguments for the idea of a single world language, it is hard to imagine it could ever happen. [11]*Personally, I think / In my opinion*, if there ever was a single language, the world would be a far less interesting and varied place.

5 Complete the table with the words in the box.

> Finally   For instance   give a personal opinion
> give examples   introduce a conclusion
> list arguments   Personally, I think   show contrast

Linkers used to …

list arguments	First of all / Firstly / Secondly / 1 _____
2 _____	For example / 3 _____
4 _____	However / On the one hand / On the other hand
5 _____	In my opinion / 6 _____
7 _____	In conclusion / In summary

6 Read the task below. Then read the 'for and against' essay and complete the gaps with the correct form of the words in brackets.

> Write an essay on the topic 'Is Fair Trade really fair?' In the essay present arguments for and against this initiative, including examples and your own opinion.

Is Fair Trade really fair?

Consumers in many countries are becoming more and more aware of the harmful effects of human ¹_____ (CONSUME) and both the ²_____ (ENVIRONMENT) and ethical issues it creates. That is why the Fair Trade organisation was designed – to help and protect farmers in poor countries. It seems to be a good initiative, but is it really ᴬ*an / – / the* idea that we can fully approve ᴮ*of / on / with*?

On the one hand, Fair Trade tries to make sure that the producers in poorer countries earn more money. It helps farmers create a better infrastructure, ³_____ (STRONG) their position in the ⁴_____ (AGRICULTURE) sector, and invest their money wisely. Such a practice is definitely something everyone can agree ᶜ*at / for / with*.

Sadly, at the same time the Fair Trade model seems to challenge some ethical ⁵_____ (BELIEVE). For instance, some online sources suggest that in fact only a small number of farmers benefit from the system. In Africa, ᴰ*which / that / where* farmers need more support, just a few countries are helped. In addition, some studies claim that the poor communities receive only a small amount of the profit and that most of the money goes to the companies which transport, pack and sell the final product. Some experts say this is ⁶_____ (AVOID), but it is something that one may criticise the Fair Trade initiative ᴱ*for / by / with*.

In conclusion, it seems to me that Fair Trade is an initiative which only looks like a good idea. However, we need to remember it is also a business strategy that brings money to large and ⁷_____ (POWER) companies. In my opinion, we need to do more to make sure Fair Trade really helps the poor people and not only itself.

7 Read the essay again and choose the correct options A–E.

8 You are going to write a 'for and against' essay on the topic 'Money can buy happiness.' Mark these arguments as *F* (for) or *A* (against).

People get pleasure from nice possessions. ⬡F

1 Friendship and love don't cost anything. ⬡
2 In many places education and healthcare are not free. ⬡
3 If you have money, you can see the world. ⬡
4 Life is full of simple pleasures. ⬡
5 Happiness comes from achieving your goals. ⬡

> ### SHOW WHAT YOU'VE LEARNT

9 'Money can buy happiness.' Write an essay in which you present arguments for and against this statement and give your personal opinion. You can use the ideas in Exercise 8 to help you.

> ### SHOW THAT YOU'VE CHECKED

Finished? Always check your writing. Can you tick ✓ everything on this list?

In my 'for and against' essay:

• the first paragraph begins with general or factual comments about the topic.	⬡
• the first paragraph ends with a statement that mentions both sides of the issue.	⬡
• the second paragraph presents arguments for the topic and supports them with examples.	⬡
• the third paragraph presents arguments against the topic and supports them with examples.	⬡
• the final paragraph includes a summarising statement and my personal opinion.	⬡
• I have not used contractions (e.g. *I'm / aren't / that's*) or abbreviations (*info / CU / v. good*).	⬡
• I have checked my spelling.	⬡
• My text is neat and clear.	⬡

SPEAKING

5.8

Expressing and justifying
an opinion

1 Translate the phrases into your own language.

SPEAKING BANK

Describing, comparing and contrasting pictures

The three pictures show/
focus on/illustrate …

_____
_____

Picture X is/looks interesting/
attractive but …

_____
_____

Picture X is more … than the
other pictures.

_____
_____

Picture X isn't as … as the
other pictures.

_____
_____
_____

**Choosing one of the options
and justifying the choice**

I think the best option would
be X because …

_____
_____
_____

I prefer/I'd go for/I'd
(definitely) choose picture X
because …

_____
_____
_____
_____
_____

I like the (first/second) picture
best for two reasons. Firstly,
because … and secondly,
because …

_____
_____
_____
_____
_____

Out of these three pictures,
I'd choose picture X
because …

_____
_____
_____

**Explaining reasons for
rejecting other options**

The problem with picture X is
that …

_____
_____

Personally, I wouldn't go for
picture X because …

_____
_____
_____
_____

I wouldn't choose the picture
showing … because …

_____
_____

The reason I don't like X
is because …

_____
_____

**2 Read and complete the discussion between
a teacher and two students. The first letters are
given.**

T: OK, so tell me what you think about these three
posters. Which one should we display on the
school notice board?

S1: Well, t*he* t*hree* p*osters* i*llustrate* the
importance of recycling rubbish at school.
Poster 1 ¹i_____ fine b_____ it's very
simple and the picture is quite basic, so some
students might not notice it. It might be better
to have something more eye-catching. Pictures
2 and 3 ²a_____ m_____ attractive
t_____ the first one and they would both
be easier to notice from a distance or quickly as
you are walking past. I think the ³b_____
o_____ w_____ be poster 2 because
it's the brightest and most colourful.

S2: Personally, I ⁴w_____ g_____
f_____ poster 2 because I think it's a bit
too childish. It looks like it would be better for
a junior school or even a kindergarten. I like
the third picture ⁵b_____ f_____ two
r_____ . Firstly, because the design is
really attractive and appealing to teenagers
⁶a_____ s_____, b_____ it has
a very memorable message. I think everyone will
remember this rhyming phrase and the reference
to basketball makes recycling sound like a cool
thing to do. Lots of people are lazy when it
comes to recycling, but actually it's a really easy
way to live a greener life.

S1: Yes, I guess you're right. OK, so, ⁷o_____ of
t_____ t_____ posters, we would
choose poster 3.

T: Great, so let's go for number 3. I'll order some
more and we'll put them on the notice boards
and next to the recycling bins when they are
ready. Thanks for your help.

**3 Read the discussion in Exercise 2 again
and number the posters.**

Student A, look below. Student B, go to page 138.

1 **In pairs, ask and answer the questions.**

Talk about food.

1 When was the last time you ate an unhealthy snack? What was it?
2 Do you prefer wholemeal bread or white bread? Why?
3 What are the advantages of including fresh, raw food in your diet?
4 What's the best restaurant you've ever been to? Why?
5 You'd like to cook a balanced three-course meal for your friends. What are you going to cook and how?

2 **Look at the photo of a natural landscape. Take turns to talk about what you can see in your photos. Talk about the people, the place and the other things in the photo.**

3 **You and your friend are discussing ways you can help to stop climate change in your school. Here are some ideas. Talk together about the different ideas and say which would be most useful and why.**

4 **Talk about climate change.**

- Are you worried about climate change? Why?/Why not?
- What do you do at home to help stop climate change?
- Is it easy to recycle things where you live? Why?/Why not?
- What sources of renewable energy are used in your country?
- What are the dangers to animals from climate change?

VOCABULARY AND GRAMMAR

1 Match the correct halves of the sentences. Then complete the missing words. The first letters are given.

Some scientists say **renewable**　　　⨍

1 Since we started using **low-energy** ⬭
2 Here on the top there are **solar** ⬭
3 This is a **slow-moving** ⬭
4 The family spent four weeks on the **remote** ⬭
5 The boat was carried out to sea by the **strong** ⬭

a **p**_____ which provide power for the lights.
b **i**_____ away from the stress of modern life.
c **c**_____ created by the storm.
d **l**_____ **b**_____, we've saved a lot of money.
e **r**_____ which joins the Thames close to Oxford.
f **e**_nergy_ is the best alternative to nuclear power.

/5

2 Complete the sentences with the words in the box. Change the form if necessary. There are two extra words.

broad ~~come~~ deep die
go high long sleep

The tide _comes_ in very quickly at around midday, so we need to keep an eye on the time.

1 Travelling abroad can help to _____ your knowldege of other countries and cultures.
2 Has this cheese _____ off or is it supposed to have bits of blue in it?
3 We need to _____ the hole if we are going to plant this tree properly.
4 Polly _____ through the storm but woke up when I started preparing breakfast.
5 If they _____ that wall in front of our building, we will lose our view of the sea.

/5

3 Complete the sentences with the correct words. The first and last letters are given.

We'll continue along this narrow **p**_at_**h** until we get out of the woods.

1 The water in the **s**_____**g** is particularly clean and very good to drink.
2 As we walk through the forest, be careful not to walk into any low **b**_____**s** which can hit you in the face.
3 There's a large **p**_____**d** on the other side of the hill and we can go swimming in it when we get there.
4 Look at that little **s**_____**l** high up in the tree eating nuts. Isn't it cute?
5 Don't try to pick up that **h**_____**g** – those needles on its back are very sharp!

/5

4 Complete the sentences with the appropriate article (Ø = no article).

Ladies and gentlemen, we have landed in Ø Reykjavik. Welcome to Iceland.

1 Last night I had ___ strange dream. The dream was about my teacher.
2 When Clara leaves school, she wants to be ___ architect.
3 Did you know that ___ Moon is the fifth-largest natural satellite in the solar system?
4 ___ swimming pool at our school is very old and a bit scary.
5 ___ unemployment in the European Union has fallen recently.

/5

5 Add *who, which, where* or *whose* and commas to form sentences with non-defining relative clauses.

who
Katie⸲ lives next door⸲ looks after lost and injured animals.

1 _____
Stratford-upon-Avon I was brought up is famous as the birthplace of William Shakespeare.

2 _____
Singapore is an island country in south-eastern Asia is an extremely clean and tidy place.

3 _____
Prince George of Cambridge great grandmother was the Queen of England was born in 2013.

4 _____
Ganesha is a Hindu god has an elephant's head.

5 _____
Penang is an island off the coast of Malaysia is sometimes called the 'Pearl of the Orient'.

/5

6 Choose the correct answers A–C (Ø = no article).

BRAZIL'S DIVERSITY

Brazil, _A_ is the largest country by both land mass and population in ¹___ South America, has ²___ most diverse animal and plant life on our planet. It has many different types of mammals and fish, more than 40,000 plant species, and ³___ unknown number of insects. In fact, ⁴___ experts estimate that one acre of the Brazilian rainforest alone is home to as many as 70,000 kinds of insects. Some scientists actually found 700 different types of beetles living on a single tree. Sadly, large areas of the rainforest are being cut down every day. This means that many species might disappear before they are identified, ⁵___ will be a great loss.

	A	B	C
	(A) which	B where	C who
1	A a	B Ø	C the
2	A Ø	B the	C a
3	A a	B an	C the
4	A a	B the	C Ø
5	A which	B that	C whose

/5

Total /30

USE OF ENGLISH

7 Complete the second sentence so that it has a similar meaning to the first one. Use between two and five words, including the word in capitals.

Make these baked beans warm and then we can eat them. **HEAT**
If you _heat these baked beans up_, we can eat them.

1 I was swimming when I saw a shark right in front of me. **FACE**
I was swimming when I _____
_____ a shark.

2 There are 50 official States in America. **UP**
Officially, America _____
50 states.

3 Experts believe the dodo bird became extinct in around 1660. **OUT**
According to experts the _____
in around 1660.

4 It was extremely cold and that's why eventually the mountain climber didn't survive. **DIED**
The mountain climber _____
_____ the extreme cold.

5 I tried to get my bag but it was too far away. **REACHED**
I _____ but it was too far away.

/5

8 Complete the sentences using the prompts in brackets. Do not change the order of the words. Change the forms or add new words where necessary. Use up to six words in each gap.

This is _the tree I fell out of_ (tree / I / fall out) when I was seven.

1 Excuse me, _____ (be / park / near) here?

2 That's _____ (man / shoot / bird) in my garden last week.

3 Which _____ (be / much / pollute) city in China? Probably Beijing.

4 Apparently, there is _____ (tree / trunk) of over 2 metres in diameter near here. Can you see it?

5 Which is _____ (trail / we / follow) yesterday to get to the lake?

/5

9 Complete the text with the correct form of the words from the box. There are two extra words.

deep   die   differ   environment
globe   ~~recycle~~   renew   rise

Sometimes it is hard to know what we can do as individuals to help protect the environment. We carefully sort our trash for _recycling_, we consume as little water as we can and use low-energy light bulbs. We even campaign for the use of ¹_____ energy and try to make others aware of the problems we face. But then we read about the ²_____ tides in our oceans and many types of animals ³_____ out, and it all begins to look a bit hopeless. The truth is, however, that every small action we take makes a ⁴_____ and that if we make it clear to our governments and the businesses we buy things from that we are greatly concerned about ⁵_____ issues, the necessary changes might happen at an increasing rate.

/5

10 Choose the correct answers A–C.

Waylon: What should you do if you see ___ moving in bushes near you?
Mariah: I'm not sure. Stand still, maybe?
A a root   B a trunk   **C** a skunk

1 **Debra:** Did you know that although bears are ___ , they mostly eat grass and berries?
Zaynep: I didn't know that. So if one attacks me, I should give it some strawberries, right?
A prey   B predators   C animals

2 **Monty:** Some people actually believe ___ change isn't a global problem.
Craig: I know. Crazy, isn't it?
A climate   B weather   C atmosphere

3 **Leon:** Sometimes I just wish I lived on a ___ island. Don't you?
Roger: I'm not sure. Wouldn't you feel lonely?
A tropical   B desert   C remote

4 **Lily:** Do you feel that the days ___ ?
Josef: For sure. Look, it's half past seven and it's still light.
A get longer   B are going to lengthen
C are lengthening

5 **Kristen:** What's the ___ ?
Alicia: They eat small animals like birds, mice and rabbits, I believe.
A natural prey of a fox   B typical diet of a rat
C usual food of a dog

/5

Total   /20

73

6 Good health

VOCABULARY

6.1

Parts of the body • injuries
• body idioms

SHOW WHAT YOU KNOW

1 Label the body parts in the photos with the correct words.

big toe	11	knee	☐
bottom	☐	lips	☐
chest	☐	neck	☐
eyebrow	☐	shoulder	☐
fingernail	☐	tongue	☐
forehead	☐		

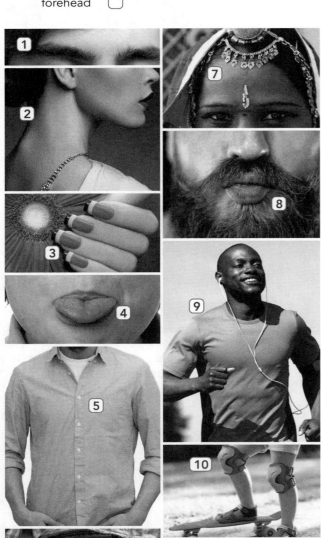

WORD STORE 6A | Parts of the body

2 Choose the correct words.

Aching muscles in your ¹*thumbs / thighs*? Relaxing leg massages only €10 for 30 minutes.

Add some more colour to your ²*cheeks / chin* with our new Fresh-Rose face powder. It's guaranteed to make you look younger and healthier.

Want a thinner ³*wrist / waist*?
Try our new diet today!

Weak ⁴*ankles / elbows* can make walking hard. Revolutionary Walk Tall Supports will help you take the next step to making walking fun again.

A soft mattress can be bad for your ⁵*rib / spine*.
Try HardMat for a good sleep and a good back.

3 Complete the sentences with the correct form of the unused words from Exercise 2.

Please, don't make me laugh. I hurt my <u>ribs</u> playing basketball and laughing is painful.

1 How can you write text messages so quickly? You must have super-powered _____ .
2 Don't put your _____ on the dinner table, Graham. It's bad manners.
3 This watch is too big for my skinny _____ . Maybe I can replace the strap with a shorter one?
4 I fell asleep on the tram and hit my _____ on the seat in front of me. Stupid me, eh?

WORD STORE 6B | Injuries

4 Complete the mini-dialogues with the correct forms of the verbs in the box. There are two extra verbs.

> bite   break (x2)   burn   dislocate
> get   ~~have~~   pull   sprain

A: Did you notice that Jack <u>has</u> a black eye? How did that happen?
B: He's taken up boxing.
1 A: Ouch! I've _____ my tongue.
B: Well, I warned you the soup was hot.
2 A: Troy's had a skiing accident. But it's quite funny actually.
B: Yes, so I've heard. He fell off the ski lift and _____ his shoulder.
3 A: Have you ever ᵃ_____ an arm or a leg?
B: I have actually. I ᵇ_____ my arm when I fell out of a tree. I was seven at the time.
4 A: Are you playing football with us tomorrow?
B: No, I can't. I've _____ my knee and can hardly walk.
5 A: What are those two small red dots on your ankle?
B: What? Where? Oh, no. I think I've been _____ by a snake.

5 Match the verbs and nouns from boxes A and B to complete the sentences. Use the verbs in the correct form. Some verbs are used more than once.

A (bite   break   burn   ~~dislocate~~   have   sprain)

B (ankle   bruise   dog   finger   hair
hip   insect   ~~thumb~~   toe   wrist)

Adam ªdislocated his ᵇthumb while he was playing basketball. Now he has to do everything with his left hand.

1 I can't stop scratching my leg. I think I've been
ª_____ by a(n) ᵇ_____ of some kind.
A mosquito, probably.

2 Granddad fell over and ª_____ his
ᵇ_____ . He said it wasn't that painful at the time but it really hurt when the doctors put it back into the right position.

3 A: Hey, Aidan. You ª_____ a huge
ᵇ_____ on your leg. How did you get that?
B: I was playing with my little brother and he kicked me. He's stronger than he looks!

4 Judy was ª_____ by a large ᵇ_____
when she was a kid, so she's scared of them now. In fact, she's even scared of my little poodle, Tammy.

5 I ª_____ my ᵇ_____ when I suddenly started running for the bus. I can hardly walk now.

6 A: How did you manage to ª_____ your
ᵇ_____ , Marta?
B: I was cooking on the barbecue and when I bent over the grill … Next time I will remember to put it in a ponytail or wear it in a bun.

7 I'm having trouble holding my pen because
I ª_____ a cut on my ᵇ_____ . I cut myself when I was chopping onions.

8 Ian ª_____ his ᵇ_____ when he kicked a basketball while wearing sandals. Apparently he had no idea those balls are so heavy!

9 When I fell off my bike, I put my hand down to protect myself. Unfortunately, my hand bent backwards and I ª_____ my ᵇ_____ .

WORD STORE 6C | Body idioms

6 Choose the best word to complete the idioms.

1 I've sprained my wrist and I can't lift anything heavy. Could you give me a *hand / heart / head* with my luggage?

2 When she showed us the bruise we couldn't believe our *hearts / legs / eyes*. It covered her whole thigh!

3 When Frieda's cat died, it broke her *leg / heart / head*. I told her it was just a cat and she slammed the door in my face. She was very upset.

4 What's it called again? You know … er … thingy. Oh … come on! It's on the tip of my *bottom / tongue / thumb*.

5 It's your birthday? Really? But I didn't get you anything ... or did I? Ha, ha, ha … I'm only pulling your *arm / tongue / leg*. Here's your gift. Happy birthday.

6 When I saw Jason dressed as Nurse Florence Nightingale, I laughed my *bottom / tongue / head* off.

SHOW WHAT YOU'VE LEARNT

7 Choose the correct answers A–C.

1 I hope I never __ my arm. It must be so painful.
   A rest   B pull   C break

2 Do people always kiss you on the __ in France when they say 'hello'?
   A wrists   B cheeks   C elbows

3 I stupidly hit myself in the face with my guitar and now I have a __ eye.
   A blue   B brown   C black

4 I've never seen anything so funny! I couldn't believe my __ .
   A eyes   B mouth   C ears

5 Lucy has a __ on her finger. She was picking up some broken glass in the park.
   A scratch   B cut   C chop

6 Jack __ his hand. He forgot to put the glove on when taking the pizza out of the oven.
   A burnt   B sprained   C dislocated

7 Why are you never bitten __ insects?
   A from   B by   C on

8 What is the actress in *The Hunger Games* called? It's on the tip of my __ . Jennifer something.
   A teeth   B tongue   C lips

9 I've hurt my __ and can't even lift this kettle. Could you please make me a cup of tea?
   A ankle   B waist   C wrist

10 Tracy always complains that her __ hurts when she stands up for more than an hour. I think she should go for some physiotherapy on her back.
   A hip   B spine   C toe

/10

Second Conditional
• wish / if only

SHOW WHAT YOU KNOW

1 Choose the correct meaning.

1 If I had a pair of winter boots, my feet wouldn't be cold.
   A The speaker's feet are cold.
   B The speaker's feet aren't cold.

2 My brother and I wouldn't fall out if he wasn't so immature.
   A The speaker's brother is immature.
   B The speaker's brother is not immature.

3 She'd need glasses if she was short-sighted.
   A She needs glasses.
   B She doesn't need glasses.

4 Peter, you'd find using these scissors more difficult if you were left-handed.
   A Peter is right-handed.
   B Peter is left-handed.

5 Polly wouldn't hang out with Ella if they didn't have so much in common.
   A Polly and Ella are very different.
   B Polly and Ella are very similar.

2 ★ Choose the correct words.

randomquestions.com

Today's online guest is British teenage rap-sensation

Mikey Silence

Latest questions (there are 171 people logged in)

20:08 **Clairewiththehair**

What would you do if you weren't a rapper?

Hi, Claire. If I ¹*wasn't / wouldn't be* a rapper, I ²*wouldn't be / 'd be* a doctor or a teacher because I'd like to do something to help other people.

20:07 **Sk8r_132**

If you ³*would have / had* a superpower, what would it be?

Interesting question Sk8r. I'd love to be able to fly. If I ⁴*would want / wanted* to get away from people for a while and be on my own or write some new lyrics, I ⁵*d fly / will fly* up to the clouds and just hang out there for a while. That would be pretty awesome.

20:05 **Lily422**

Which part of your body would you most like to change?

Woah! Lily that's a bit of a personal question, I'm pretty happy as I am to be honest. Nobody's perfect, but I don't really care what anybody else thinks. But I suppose I could change my height. If I ⁶*d be / were* taller I ⁷*d be / were* better at basketball. I love playing basketball, but I am kind of short 😞.

waiting for next question …

3 ★ ★ Write Second Conditional sentences using the information in bold and in brackets. Use commas where necessary.

I wish I didn't have this virus (I / go out and meet my friends)
I 'd go out and meet my friends if I didn't have this virus

1 **If only the exam was next week** (we / have a bit longer for revision)
If _____

2 **I wish my legs were stronger** (I / run much further)
I _____

3 **If only we lived on the coast** (I / walk on the beach every day)
If _____

4 **I wish you liked fish** (we / have a healthier diet)
We _____

4 ★ ★ ★ Write a second sentence to show that you would like the situation or behaviour to be different.

My brother borrows my clothes without asking.
I wish *my brother wouldn't borrow* my clothes without asking.

1 I have a dislocated finger.
If only _____
a dislocated finger.

2 My daughter never calls me.
I wish _____ call me sometimes.

3 Our school doesn't have recycling bins.
I wish _____ recycling bins.

4 My friend isn't talking to me.
If only _____ to me.

5 Fast-food is bad for you.
If only _____ bad for you.

SHOW WHAT YOU'VE LEARNT

5 Find and correct the mistakes.

If only driving lessons ~~would be~~ cheaper. *were*

1 If Lucas would have a suit, he'd wear it to the wedding. _____

2 We save a lot of money if we stayed over at Karen's house. _____

3 I wish I wouldn't be so pale-skinned. _____

4 I'd ate it if it wasn't so greasy. _____

5 If only broccoli tastes like chocolate. _____

6 I wish my shoes wouldn't smell so bad.

_____

/6

GRAMMAR: Train and Try Again page 159

1 Put the words in questions A–E in the correct order.

> *Extract from Student's Book recording* 🔊 **2.44**
>
> **A:** Hi Rob!
>
> **R:** Oh. Hi Anna. Listen, I need some advice.
>
> **A:** Sure. *you / know / what / need / to / do* <u>What do you need to know</u> ?
>
> **R:** Well, I'm taking part in [this] cycle ride and I want to raise some money ¹___ charity. **A** *do / that / know / do / I / can / you / how* _____ ?
>
> **A:** Sure – I did the London Marathon last year. [...] You have to ask your friends to sponsor you. In other words, they support you ²___ giving you money. You have to set up a webpage first.
>
> **R:** Okay, **B** *do / I / sort / of / webpage / information / put / what / the / on* _____ ?
>
> **A:** You explain what event you're doing – so you're going to do the London to Brighton Cycle. Then you put some information ³___ the charity you want to support. **C** *are / you / in / charity / which / interested* _____ ?
>
> **R:** I want to do it ⁴___ the British Heart Foundation.
>
> **A:** OK, great. **D** *have / any / do / you / reason / particular* _____ ?
>
> **R:** Yes, it was my grandmother's idea – my grandfather died ⁵___ a heart disease.
>
> **A:** Okay, so you can say on the webpage that you're doing it ⁶___ memory of your grandfather. Then you share the page ⁷___ all your friends and family. It's a good idea to send it ⁸___ all the adults you know because people our age don't have any money!
>
> **R:** Okay, that's good advice. **E** *by / pay / credit / they / card / do* _____ ?
>
> **A:** Yes. Most people give ⁹___ £5 and £20.

2 Complete gaps 1–9 with the correct answers A–C.

	A	B	C
1	to	from	for
2	with	on	by
3	under	about	next to
4	for	at	behind
5	with	of	over
6	to	on	in
7	with	of	to
8	for	to	by
9	about	over	between

REMEMBER THIS

It is not easy to know which prepositions come after which verbs. Remember that different combinations are possible, depending on context. For example, many verbs can be followed by either *for* + noun or a *to*- infinitive.

*I want to **raise** money **for charity**.*
*I want to **raise** money **to help** heart attack victims.*

3 Read REMEMBER THIS. Choose the correct words.

1. a I'm afraid you'll have to pay *to / for* see a private doctor.
   b Please pay *to / for* your popcorn before you start eating it!
2. a Visitors: queue here *to / for* the aquarium.
   b Do we queue here *to / for* buy a ticket for the match?
3. a Messi has scored seventeen goals so far this season *to / for* his team.
   b England need to score one more goal *to / for* become world champions.
4. a Matthew is very serious about basketball. He always plays *to / for* win.
   b In my opinion it's not right that foreign players play *to / for* the national team.
5. a Darling, I promise I'll always be there *to / for* you.
   b Don't worry about your sprained ankle. We'll be there *to / for* help you get up the stairs.

WORD STORE 6D | Charity fund-raising

4 Complete the adverts with the correct form of the words from the box.

> donate   set up   share   sponsor
> raise   take part   train

> **Have you** ever wanted to <u>raise</u> **money** for a specific **charity** but never knew **how to do it?**
> # Well, now you can!
> Our company can help you to ¹_____ a simple webpage for the charity of your choice and make it easy for anybody to ²_____ money to help the organisation you really care for.
> **All financial and legal matters are covered by us too!**
> Check us out at: www.startacharity.com.pr

> This year's
> # Mortgate Charity Marathon
> will take place soon. If you would like to ³_____ in the run, you should **start** ⁴_____ **for it** now!
> You'll need to be fit to run the whole 23 miles. If you want to ⁵_____ someone who is running in the race, you can do that here. To help us collect as much money as we can this year, please ⁶_____ this webpage with friends and family.

5 Find and correct the mistakes.

1. Many of my family members have offered to sponsor for me when I run in the charity race. _____
2. My classmates and I have decided to donate money at people who have lost their homes in the fire. _____
3. We are going to set out a webpage to advertise our 'Save the Old School' campaign. _____
4. I trained on the race for weeks, but I still didn't manage to run the whole way. _____
5. A great way to raise money to a good cause is to sell T-shirts with a positive message on them. _____

1 Read about Jack Andraka's invention. Why is the article called *A Lot of Light Bulbs*?

1 Because Jack Andraka invented several new types of light bulb. ☐

2 Because light is an important element in Jack Andraka's invention. ☐

3 Because Jack is like Thomas Edison, the inventor of the light bulb. ☐

A Lot of Light Bulbs

A On first impressions, Jack Thomas Andraka is a pretty normal young American. A former student of North County High School, near Baltimore, he was born in 1997, and <u>raised</u> in Maryland on the east coast of the US. His father is a civil engineer and his mother an anaesthetist,* and originally his family comes from Poland. Jack is a keen scout who likes white water rafting. He enjoys Maths, reading on his Kindle and watching the TV series *Glee* and *Bones* in his free time.

Sounds pretty average, right? Well, in fact Jack is anything but average. He is the winner of several major science awards, the subject of a number of documentary films and a regular speaker at scientific and educational conferences around the world. Why? Because, despite his young age, he is also a world-famous inventor, pioneering cancer researcher, and proof that you don't necessarily need to have a lifetime of experience or to work among other professionals to be able to invent something truly life-changing.

B After the sad death of a family friend from pancreatic* cancer, the same very serious illness that killed Apple-founder Steve Jobs in 2011, teenage Jack began doing research into the life-threatening condition. He discovered that one of the reasons so many people died from this particular type of cancer was because there was no cheap and reliable test that allowed doctors to diagnose the illness early enough to save the patient. Amazingly, Jack <u>thought of</u> a way to develop a simple test using things he had learned in his Biology class at school and through scientific journals and articles, some of which he <u>found by chance</u> online. But Jack needed money, the assistance of experienced scientists and a laboratory to <u>continue</u> the development of his idea, so he <u>contacted</u> around 200 research professionals to ask for help. Unfortunately, 199 of the replies were negative, but the 200th from Dr Anirban Maitra, a Professor at Johns Hopkins School of Medicine, was the one that Jack was waiting for. So, with the help of Professor Maitra and the use of his lab, Jack successfully developed a test for pancreatic cancer that is 168 times faster, 400 times more sensitive and 26,000 times less expensive than the current diagnostic tests. The test is even effective for two other types of cancer as well.

C In 2012, Jack received the grand prize of the Intel International Science and Engineering Fair for his invention. He returned to school to finish his education and in 2015 became a student at Stanford University, but since his success his life has changed. He has met Bill Clinton and Barack Obama, and been interviewed by the BBC, CNN and many other radio stations, television channels and newspapers around the world. Jack hasn't <u>stopped</u> inventing, and is currently working with a group of other prize-winning students on a device* the size of a mobile phone that can diagnose a wide range of illnesses instantly and without a blood sample. Sounds like something from *Star Trek*? Well, yes. That's where the inspiration came from.

Professor Maitra is enthusiastic about Jack's ideas and his future. He spoke to a newspaper reporter and compared Jack to Thomas Edison, the inventor of the light bulb. The professor called him the Edison of our times and promised there were going to be a lot of light bulbs coming from Jack in the future.

YOUTH AWARD

GLOSSARY

anaesthetist (n) – a medical professional who specialises in stopping patients from feeling pain during surgery

pancreatic (adj) – from *pancreas* (n); the pancreas is located near the stomach and produces insulin

device (n) – a machine or tool that does a special job. A synonym for *gadget*

2 Read the text again. In which part of the text A–C do we learn that

1 Jack believed he had found the cause of so many deaths from a particular disease? ☐

2 some of Jack's ideas come from the field of popular culture? ☐

3 few people were initially interested in Jack's ideas? ☐

4 Jack's story shows that being a successful inventor does not depend on your experience or profession? ☐

3 Read the text again. For questions 1–5, choose the correct answer A–D.

1 In the first paragraph, the writer
   A explains how Jack is.
   B describes Jack's interest in science.
   C describes Jack's personality and looks.
   D explains how normal Jack is.

2 Jack began the research into his invention because of
   A the death of someone famous.
   B an interesting Biology class at school.
   C the loss of a friend.
   D something he read in a scientific journal.

3 Which organisation helped Jack develop his invention?
   A North County High School
   B Johns Hopkins School of Medicine
   C Apple
   D Intel

4 The text says that Jack's test for pancreatic cancer
   A doesn't require a blood sample.
   B was inspired by *Star Trek*.
   C is not as fast as current tests.
   D can also help patients with other kinds of cancer.

5 What is the main message of this article?
   A Young people can achieve amazing things.
   B You can invent something extraordinary by accident.
   C Even the most serious types of cancer are treatable.
   D Very few organisations are willing to help young inventors.

4 Match the phrasal verbs below with the underlined synonyms in the text.

carry on   *continue*
1 brought up   _____
2 came across   _____
3 got in touch with _____
4 came up with   _____
5 given up   _____

5 Complete the sentences with phrasal verbs from Exercise 4. Change the form if necessary.

They *carried on* walking until they reached the fence that surrounded the mysterious building.

1 One day, if I become a parent, I hope to _____ my kids in a world where men and women are truly equal.

2 I wasn't planning to buy you a gift but then I _____ this in the market and I just had to get it.

3 Uncle Steve has _____ smoking four times this year. It's obviously not working.

4 Lindsay _____ the idea for a surprise party for Damien. He absolutely loved it.

5 David, your teacher _____ me today to say that you haven't been to school all week.

VOCABULARY PRACTICE | Health issues 1

6 Look at the vocabulary in lesson 6.4 in the Student's Book. Complete each pair of sentences with the correct form of the words from the box.

> allergy condition cut epidemic
> ~~pain~~ surgery team ward

I've got stomach *pain*. I think I ate too many sweets.
Shelley usually has muscle *pains* after playing tennis.

1 Ellen's got a nut _____ , so she can't eat a lot of products I enjoy.
Between 1–2 percent of adults and 5–8 percent of children in the UK suffer from food _____ .

2 The local _____ is closing down, so we'll need to find another doctor.
There are plenty of doctor's _____ in my area but I hardly ever get ill.

3 Is that a shaving _____ on your face? Why not use an electric razor instead?
There are quite deep _____ and you may need stitches to stop the bleeding.

4 Flu _____ have caused millions of deaths over the years. Luckily, we have fewer nowadays.
In case of a cholera _____ , drink only bottled water and keep your hands clean.

5 Your wife is in the maternity _____ , Mr Jones. And congratulations on a beautiful baby girl!
There are two children's _____ in this hospital. Your son is in the one in Building D.

6 Simon is in a stable _____ , so all we can do now is wait.
After the bus accident, the hockey team were in a serious _____ . Fortunately, they all made a good recovery.

7 St Michael's Hospital is looking for experienced paramedics to join their three new emergency _____ .
The rescue _____ took a helicopter to the top of the mountain.

WORD STORE 6E | Health issues 2

7 Match the beginnings with the correct endings to make sentences.

Doctors shouldn't only treat   ⓗ
1 I would have   ☐
2 It's nothing serious, Ms Smith. I'll just write ☐
3 What do you call a woman that delivers ☐
4 Luckily, I've never caught   ☐
5 Somebody who works to save   ☐
6 Last week I had to give   ☐
7 If you continue to eat so much, you'll gain ☐

a first aid to an old man who fell down in the street.
b weight and then have to go on a diet.
c a disease that was very serious.
d a prescription for some tablets …
e lives deserves a lot more respect in society.
f babies? Oh, yes. A midwife.
g a panic attack if I had to speak in front of a crowd.
h patients' physical problems. They should care about their mental well-being too.

SHOW WHAT YOU KNOW

1 Complete the beginnings of the sentences with the Past Perfect form of the verbs in brackets. Then match them to the endings.

Jack and I _hadn't met_ (not/meet),   (e)

1 Chiara _____ (break) her arm once, ◯
2 Alice _____ (forget) to get changed, ◯
3 Ken _____ (lose/touch) with Amy, ◯
4 Emma _____ (not/study) meteorology, ◯

a so she arrived at school in her slippers.
b so she didn't know a lot about the weather.
c so he was surprised when she called.
d so she knew how much it hurt.
e so I didn't recognise him.

2 ★ **Choose the correct answers.**

1 If Jack and I had met, I would've recognised him.
real past event: We _met / didn't meet_.
real past result: I _recognised / didn't recognise_ him.

2 Chiara wouldn't have known how much it hurts when you break your arm if she hadn't done it once.
real past event: Chiara _broke / didn't break_ her arm once.
real past result: She _knew / didn't know_ how much it hurt.

3 If Alice hadn't forgotten to get changed, she wouldn't have arrived at school in her slippers.
real past event: Alice _forgot / didn't forget_ to get changed.
real past result: She _arrived / didn't arrive_ at school in her slippers.

4 Ken wouldn't have been surprised when Amy called if he hadn't lost touch with her.
real past event: Ken _lost touch / didn't lose touch_ with Amy.
real past result: He _was / wasn't surprised_ when she called.

5 Emma would have known a lot about the weather if she had studied meteorology.
real past event: Emma _studied / didn't study_ meteorology.
real past result: She _knew / didn't know_ a lot about the weather.

6 If I had felt an earthquake before, I wouldn't have been so terrified when it struck.
real past event: I _had felt / hadn't felt_ an earthquake before.
real past result: I _was / wasn't_ terrified when it struck.

3 ★ ★ **Complete the dialogue with the correct form of the verbs in brackets. Use short forms.**

At the summer house …
A: What a long journey. Open the door, Dan.
D: You've got the keys.
A: What? I texted you to say bring the spare ones.
D: What? If you _'d texted_ (text) me, my phone
   ¹ _____ (go beep).
A: Well, I definitely texted you. You ² _____ (see) the message if you ³ _____ (look) at your phone. I've lost my keys.
D: But … why didn't you say something before we left? Anne, we are 200 kilometres from home!
A: We'll have to break a window.
Later in the hospital …
D: Ouch!!!
N: Sorry, Mr Finch but I have to clean the cut.
A: I'm sorry, Dan.
D: It's not your fault, Anne.
A: But if I ⁴ _____ (not/lose) the keys, you ⁵ _____ (not/cut) your hand and we wouldn't be here in the hospital.

4 ★ ★ ★ **Complete the dialogues using the Third Conditional. Use short forms.**

A: I was in a bad mood last night. I shouted at Sally and we had an argument.
B: (stay calm / not fall out)
   Oh dear. If _you'd stayed calm, you wouldn't have fallen out._

1 A: Phew, I really thought I'd left my passport at home.
   B: (miss the flight / you forget it)
     We _____

2 A: Chris fell off his bike yesterday. The bruise on his forehead was huge.
   B: (not hurt himself / have his helmet on)
     It's his own fault, Louis. He _____
     _____

3 A: That food was so spicy.
   B: (not be so spicy / not use so much chilli sauce)
     It _____

SHOW WHAT YOU'VE LEARNT

5 Complete the sentences using the prompts in brackets. Do not change the order of the words. Change the forms and add new words if necessary.

Our opponents wouldn't have won _if you had scored a/ that goal_ (you / score / goal).

1 _____ (you / leg / not / be / cold) if you had worn long trousers last night.

2 If the clothes in the sales had been cheaper, _____ _____ (I / spend / much / money).

3 Ben wouldn't have spoken to me again _____ _____ (I / remember / his birthday).

4 Last year our _____ (electric / bill / be / small) if we'd bought low-energy light bulbs.

5 Daisy wouldn't have burnt herself yesterday _____ _____ (she / use / glove / kitchen).

6 _____ (you / buy a ticket / early), we wouldn't have missed the train.

/6

GRAMMAR: Train and Try Again page 159

6.6

Clauses of purpose

1 ★ **Choose the correct answers A–C.**

1 Tina: Why are you getting married again, Grandad?
Grandad: I'm getting married __ .
- **A** so as not to be alone
- **B** in order to be not alone
- **C** not to be alone

2 Ed: I go to the gym to build up muscle.
Bob: I go __ lose weight.
- **A** to not
- **B** so as to
- **C** so not

3 Meg: Why did you leave the room when Jenny fell over?
Jess: I left the room __ laugh my head off in front of her.
- **A** so as to
- **B** so that
- **C** so as not to

4 Ted: You're wearing eye make-up?
Andy: Yes, __ try to cover up my black eye.
- **A** to not
- **B** to
- **C** in order not to

5 Ollie: What are those tablets for?
Ella: I take them __ get car sick.
- **A** so as to not
- **B** in order not to
- **C** in order to

6 Mum: Put the oven gloves on __ you don't burn your hands.
Amin: OK, Mum.
- **A** so that
- **B** in order to
- **C** so as not to

2 ★ ★ **Match the sentence halves.**

This clinic carries out studies on volunteers in order
1 We ask you to be very quiet so as
2 Follow these simple tips
3 You can use this electronic device
4 Use these headphones so that
5 Warm up before any physical activity in order

- **a** to track how many steps you take each day.
- **b** you aren't disturbed by noise while you are studying.
- **c** to limit the amount of sugar in your diet.
- **d** not to disturb the students in the lab.
- **e** not to injure yourself.
- **f** to understand what keeps people awake at night.

3 ★ ★ **Connect the sentences using the word in brackets. Add any words you need. Use between two and four words.**

I took the medicine _so as to_ (as) get better.
1 I went to the doctor _____ (that) I could get a blood test.
2 I use an electric razor _____ (not) cut myself.
3 I eat healthily _____ (order) put on weight.
4 I never rush anywhere _____ (in) reduce the chances of having an accident.
5 I avoided the dog _____ (so) be attacked.

4 ★ ★ **Complete the second sentence so that it means the same as the first.**

I don't work at weekends because I want to relax.
I don't work at weekends so _as to relax_.
1 I take allergy tablets because I want to control the symptoms of hay fever.
I take allergy tablets so _____ .
2 I'm joining the emergency team because I want to save lives.
I'm joining the emergency team in _____ .
3 Janet is taking time off work because she needs to recover from her illness.
Janet is taking time off work to _____ .
4 I always sleep eight hours a night because I don't want to be tired during the day.
I always sleep eight hours every night so that _____ .
5 I don't eat breakfast because I want to lose weight.
I don't eat breakfast so as _____ .

5 ★ ★ ★ **Complete the text with one word in each gap.**

How to avoid common sports injuries

To many people, doing sports means occasionally getting injured. But, you can do several things _to_ help you avoid getting a common sports injury.

Firstly, it's important to warm up so ¹ _____ to slowly raise the heartbeat and warm the muscles. This should be for a minimum of ten minutes and at lower intensity than your main sporting activity. Next, focus on your technique. Many sports injuries are the result of doing something wrong. Understand fully what you are doing ² _____ avoid making mistakes. An experienced trainer is required early on so ³ _____ you don't learn bad habits.

After your training, you need to warm down. This stage of your routine is important so as ⁴ _____ to suffer from sore muscles the next day. Like the warm-up, take 10 minutes in ⁵ _____ to allow your heartbeat and body temperature to return to normal. And finally, relax. A tired body is more likely to pick up an injury, so be sure your body is well-rested before the next exercise session.

1 Read the factual article below and choose the best title for it.

- a Health is important
- b How to live a long life
- c Live Strong, Live Long

Experts agree that if we were more carefree, we would live longer, happier lives. **Additionally** Ⓐ, we should eat a healthy, natural diet and stay active. Sounds easy, doesn't it? Unfortunately, it's not so simple. Even the place where you live can make a difference.

According to scientists, there are a number of places around the world where citizens live longer. In Sardinia, men live for a surprisingly long time. Many of them are shepherds and they eat mainly goats' cheese and milk. **¹As well as that** ◯, they spend a lot of time outside **²in order to** ◯, look after their sheep. They are **³also** ◯, very relaxed. **⁴In contrast** ◯, the women are not as active and live to a more normal age.

If you lived in Okinawa, a Japanese island, you could also reach a very old age. Understandably, this is for slightly different reasons. Most people have a garden to grow their own food. **⁵As a result** ◯ people are active and get a lot of natural sunlight. They eat food from their gardens **⁶so as not to** ◯, waste money, and they make sure not to overeat, **⁷so** ◯ they stop eating when they are 80% full. **⁸Therefore** ◯, they stay fit and strong.

Unfortunately, walking around with sheep and growing vegetables is not an option for those of us who live in cities and have school or jobs to attend. **⁹However** ◯, we can try to have the same positive attitude that is common to the people of Sardinia and Okinawa **¹⁰so that** ◯ we can grow very old too.

2 Read the article in Exercise 1 again. Label the linkers in bold: *C* (show contrast), *A* (add information), *R* (show result) or *P* (show purpose).

3 Match beginnings 1–5 with endings a–e. Then complete the sentences with the linkers from the box.

> additionally   although   as a result
> as well as   ~~in order to~~   so as not to

It's important to eat a balanced diet *in order to*   ⒡

1 People are eating more and more fast food. _____ ◯
2 I spend two hours in the gym every week. _____ ◯
3 You should warm up before you exercise _____ ◯
4 _____ going to bed early, ◯
5 Scientists advise sleeping with the windows open, _____ ◯

- a I cycle to work every day.
- b you should avoid coffee in the evening.
- c hurt yourself.
- d it's too cold where I live.
- e they are overweight.
- f stay healthy.

4 Read the factual article *So you think social media is bad for you?* Choose the correct words a–f.

5 Look at the words in bold in the article in Exercise 4. Find pairs of synonyms.

Teenagers = *youngsters*

1 _____ = _____
2 _____ = _____
3 _____ = _____
4 _____ = _____
5 _____ = _____

So you think SOCIAL MEDIA is bad for you?

Teenagers face lots of criticism for spending too much time online, and **social media** is often the reason. ᵃ*Hopefully, / Clearly,* if **youngsters** spent all their time on these platforms, they wouldn't complete homework assignments on time. On top of that, they might come across online bullies and, ᵇ*obviously / surprisingly,* they may be out of shape as a result of being inactive. Therefore, should we be **disconnected** all the time?

ᶜ*Interestingly, / Probably* research shows a number of **benefits** for people who regularly use **online networks**. First of all, social media users have better relationships with friends and family, both online and offline. They are more sensitive and have a better ability to understand people's **feelings**. As a result they find it easier to share their own **emotions**.

Additionally, online friends can be anywhere in the world. This is ᵈ*naturally / unfortunately* a great opportunity to learn about other cultures and communities.

Finally, people who use social media often use these platforms to play games. ᵉ*Fortunately / Unfortunately,* experts say this is good for us. Gamers are often better at visual tasks and get higher scores on tests connected to space and coordination.

ᶠ*Certainly / Sadly,* there are many **advantages** to being part of an online community. With that in mind, next time your parents tell you to get **offline** and 'live in the real world', just share some of this **information** with them.

If you can't remember the **advice**, just check online!

6 Read the task below. Then read the factual article and complete gaps a–f with the words from the box.

> You have been asked to write an article for your school magazine about ways to help the environment. Include and develop these points:
> - Give your factual article a catchy title.
> - Include experts' opinions and official data.
> - Use direct questions and different words and phrases to make the article interesting for the reader.
> - Finish your factual article with a summary.

> additionally   as a result   hopefully
> research shows   sadly   unfortunately

A **Healthy Planet** for a Healthy **Body and Mind**

'If only people ¹_____ (take) more care of the environment!' That's what my six-year old nephew said to me and he is right. To feel happy and healthy people need fresh food, water and air.

ᵃ_____ I started looking for ways to help the planet. There are many alarming statistics about the effects humans have on the planet, and ᵇ_____ , many scientists think we've reached the point of no return. But how much can we really do to make a difference?

ᶜ_____ that we need to change our habits and recommend renewable energy and recycling. Obviously, these things are great but many people can't include them in their daily lives. ᵈ_____ where I live there are no recycling bins and my family can't afford solar panels.

However, there are things everyone can do to help with environmental issues. Clearly, anyone can raise money and donate it to a green charity. ᵉ_____ we can write letters to local supermarkets asking them to use less plastic. Obviously, if big supermarkets ²_____ (not/start) using so much plastic, we ³_____ (not/produce) so much pollution in the first place.

Naturally, if everybody ⁴_____ (make) one or two small changes, the world ⁵_____ (become) a greener, cleaner place and everyone ⁶_____ (be) much healthier ᶠ_____ things will gradually start to change.

Read the article again. Complete gaps 1–6 with the correct form of the words in brackets to make Second and Third Conditional sentences.

8 You have decided to write a factual article to raise awareness about living a healthy lifestyle in your home town. Include and develop these points:
- Give your factual article a catchy title.
- Include experts' opinions and/or official data.
- Use direct questions and different words and phrases to make the article interesting for the reader.
- Finish your factual article with a summary.

Finished? Always check your writing. Can you tick √ everything on this list?

In my factual article:

• I have included a catchy title.	☐
• I have given experts' opinions and/or official data, e.g. *According to research … Statistics show …*	☐
• I have asked direct questions to engage the reader, e.g. *But what do we really know about it?*	☐
• I have used a range of linkers to make my text clear and logical, e.g. *Additionally, As a result, In contrast*	☐
• I have used a range of vocabulary and synonyms to avoid repeating words, e.g. *teenagers / young people.*	☐
• I have ended the text with a summary.	☐
• I have divided my work into paragraphs.	☐
• I have checked my spelling and punctuation.	☐
• My text is neat and clear.	☐

SPEAKING

6.8 At the doctor's surgery

1 Translate the phrases into your own language.

SPEAKING BANK

Treatment

You need to take antibiotics. _____

You need to put a fresh bandage / a plaster on it. _____

You need a few stitches. _____

I need to check your blood pressure / pulse, etc. _____

I don't think you need an X-ray / operation, etc. _____

I'm not going to give you an injection. _____

We need to bring the swelling down. _____

You need to take painkillers to ease the pain. _____

You need to put ice / ointment, etc. on your ankle. _____

REMEMBER THIS

Ouch is a word for the sound that you make when you feel sudden pain. Such sounds are called interjections. Other examples include: *achoo* – the sound of a sneeze, *oops*, a sound you make when you make a mistake, or break or drop something, *phew*, a sound to express relief, and wow, a sound to express amazement. Look in a dictionary or online for more interjections like these.

2 Read REMEMBER THIS. Complete the dialogues with the correct words from the box.

(achoo phew oops ouch ~~wow~~)

A: Look! I fell over and didn't scratch or cut myself.
B: *Wow*! That was lucky.

1 A: _____ !
B: Bless you. Here's a tissue.

2 A: Did you just put my ointment on your arms instead of sun cream?
B: _____ !

3 A: _____ ! I nearly dropped this bottle of medicine.
B: You should be more careful.

4 A: This won't hurt.
B: _____ ! What did you just say?

3 Choose the correct words.

1 You're bleeding again. We need to *take / put / bring* a fresh bandage on your arm.

2 I'm afraid this cut is going to *need / put / take* a few stitches.

3 The doctor *checked / brought / put* my blood pressure and listened to my lungs.

4 Did you *take / put / bring* that ointment on your elbow?

5 Fortunately, I don't think you *bring / take / need* an operation. You're a very lucky boy!

6 I need to *take / put / give* you a little injection. It won't hurt, I promise.

7 The ice will *put / check / bring* the swelling down on your wrist.

8 You need to *take / bring / put* painkillers for the pain.

9 The doctor told me to stay home and *give / put / take* antibiotics for a week.

4 Complete the gaps in the conversations with the correct words.

Doc: We need to put some *ice* on this bruise.
Timmy: Ouch, it's really cold!

1 Amy: How long do I have to take the _____ ?
Doc: For ten days – it's a very serious infection.

2 Greg: Is the cut on my arm very deep, doctor?
Doc: I'm afraid so. You'll need a few _____ , to stop it bleeding. Now, where's my needle?

3 Doc: Please sit down and I'll check your _____ . Put this on your arm, please.
Jon: OK, doctor but I should tell you that I ran all the way here.

4 Doc: You might have a broken rib. We'll need _____ to see the bone and be 100 percent sure.
Oliver: That's the last time I ever play basketball with my sister, doctor!

5 Fiona: Is it dangerous to travel to a tropical country?
Doc: Yes, and that's why I'm going to give you some _____ so you don't catch any diseases.

6 Doc: This cream should help bring the _____ down.
Emily: Thank you, doctor. I can't even put my foot in my shoe at the moment.

7 Doc: If you've got a bad headache, just take these _____ with some warm water.
Olaf: Thank you, doctor. How many tablets can I take per day?

8 Rob: Doctor, I've cut my finger on a piece of paper.
Doc: Oh, that's nothing serious! Let's wash it and then put a(n) _____ on it.

Student A, look below. Student B, go to page 139.

1 In pairs, ask and answer the questions.

Talk about the environment.

1 Tell me about three things you have done at school to help the environment.

2 Is it the responsibility of each individual person or the government to take action on environmental issues? Why?

3 What do you think is the best form of renewable energy? Why?

4 Would you prefer to come face to face with a skunk or a bear? Why?

5 In what ways can oceans be dangerous?

2 Discuss this question together. Take different sides of the argument during your discussion. 'Is it acceptable to test new medicines on animals?' Decide who is going to take each side. Then share your ideas.

3 Look at the two photos showing people raising money for charity. What can you see in the photos? Have you ever done something to raise money for charity?

4 Read the instructions on your card and role-play the conversation.

Student A:

The situation:

You are a doctor and Student B is a patient. Ask about what the problem is, how it happened and his/her symptoms. Then decide what advice to give. Will you send the patient to hospital? Will he/she need an operation? Will he/she need any medicine?

Your goal:

To treat your patient successfully.

VOCABULARY AND GRAMMAR

1 Choose the correct answers A–C.

Remember to fasten your helmet strap under your _chin_.
A elbow   B waist   (C)chin

1 Shelly danced for 24 hours non-stop and __ £200 for charity.
A rose   B raised   C recovered

2 Jamie almost __ a panic attack when he saw how high the balcony is.
A had   B did   C made

3 When I told Sarah what had happened, she __ her head off. I didn't expect her to find it so funny.
A pulled   B broke   C laughed

4 Karen __ money every month to a different charity. Maybe we could do that too?
A donates   B raises   C sponsors

5 What's her name again? Oh, it's on the __ of my tongue.
A tap   B tip   C top

/5

2 Complete the sentences with the correct form of the words from the box. There are two extra words.

chin   hand   heart   jaw   leg   ribs   thighs   ~~tongue~~

Be careful not to burn your _tongue_ when you drink this tea. It's really hot.

1 I wasn't serious, Kathy! You don't owe me any money. I was only pulling your _____ .

2 When my grandmother had to sell her old house, it broke her _____ .

3 Leah needs some help with her Maths homework. Can you give her a _____ ?

4 I don't like these jeans. They're the wrong shape for my legs. They make my _____ look really fat.

5 One of Sam's _____ was broken in the car accident. He says it really hurts when he laughs.

/5

3 Match a word from box A with a word from box B to complete the sentences. There is an extra word in box A.

A   broken   flu   nut   ~~serious~~
    shaving   sore   stomach

B   allergy   ~~condition~~   cut
    epidemic   finger   pain

The woman is in a _serious condition_, so she needs to stay in hospital.

1 I've got a _____ because I was sending text messages all night.

2 Why have you got toilet paper stuck to your face? Do you have another _____ ?

3 I'm not surprised Archie has _____ after eating all that chocolate.

4 There's a _____ in town, so I'm going to get an injection against it.

5 Donna has a _____ , so she tends not to eat chocolates or biscuits just in case.

/5

4 Complete the sentences with the correct forms of the words in brackets.

I wish I _wasn't_ (not/be) so tired because I'd really love to go out tonight.

1 If Claire _____ (not/feel) ill, she would definitely go to the gym.

2 Damien wishes he _____ (have) more money so he could take Nicole to an expensive restaurant.

3 If motorists _____ (not/drive) so close to each other on the motorway, there would be far fewer accidents.

4 If the government made healthcare free for everyone in the country, we _____ (pay) much higher taxes.

5 If only ice cream _____ (be) good for me. I'd be the healthiest person alive.

/5

5 Decide which prompt goes in each gap and then complete the Third Conditional sentences. Use short forms.

Jack ᵃ_wouldn't have been late_ if he ᵇ_hadn't stopped_ to watch the football match. **not stop / not be late**

1 Erin ᵃ_____ the other skier if she ᵇ_____ so quickly. **hit / not turn**

2 I ᵃ_____ to pay for everyone if I ᵇ_____ how expensive it was here. **know / not offer**

3 If Jill ᵃ_____ her shoulder, she ᵇ_____ in the match yesterday. **not play / hurt**

4 If Connor ᵃ_____ three bars of chocolate, he ᵇ_____ . **not eat / feel sick**

5 The doctor ᵃ_____ on time if she ᵇ_____ her car keys. **not lose / be**

/5

6 Choose the correct answers A–C.

Hi Clara,

I'm writing to you from hospital. I hurt my back really badly and needed an operation on my _C_ . I'm doing OK and, according to the doctors, in a ¹__ condition, which is good news. I asked if I could go home this morning. The doctor said that if I went home, I ²__ the strong painkillers they give me here. He says I need to stay for another two days. I wish I ³__ because I miss normal food. If Mum ⁴__ me food from home, I wouldn't have eaten anything this week. But I shouldn't complain too much. It must be hard to ⁵__ all the patients here.

Are you coming to visit me tomorrow? If you do, can you bring me some magazines? I'm BORED BORED BORED!

See you x

A chin   B wrist   (C)spine
1 A safe   B stable   C serious
2 A wouldn't get   B won't get   C didn't get
3 A can leave   B could leave   C leave
4 A didn't bring   B wouldn't bring C hadn't brought
5 A deal   B care   C treat

/5

Total   /30

7 Choose the correct answers A–C.

In the end, the doctor refused to give me ___ .
A said he wouldn't give
(B) a prescription.
C a receipt.

1 I landed on my side ___ my knee.
A in order to sprain
B so that I hadn't sprained
C so as not to sprain

2 If I had played with my little brother more carefully, I ___ .
A didn't break a toe
B couldn't have broken a toe
C wouldn't have a broken toe

3 I think ___ . Look at these marks on his ankle.
A he bit a rat
B a rat was bitten by him
C he was bitten by a rat

4 Jake ___ a webpage about volunteering to help sick children in hospital with me.
A set up
B shared
C took part in

5 Oliver ___ me in the mini-marathon, so he was very upset when I dropped out.
A had sponsored
B has sponsored
C will sponsor

/5

8 Complete the sentences using the prompts in brackets. Do not change the order of the words. Change the forms or add new words where necessary. Use up to six words in each gap.

Tony _wouldn't have caught a disease_ (not / catch / a disease) if he hadn't forgotten to take his tablets.

1 I would have called the rescue team _____ (if / know) it was an emergency.

2 We left home early _____ (order / not / be) late for the meeting with the nurse.

3 You can put on _____ (my jacket / so / keep) warm if you like.

4 Julie _____ (wish / not / be / allergy) to chocolate because she loves the taste so much.

5 If only Mary _____ (not / have / bruise) on her arm – she could wear the short-sleeved dress she loves.

/5

9 Complete the second sentence so that it has the same meaning as the first. Use between two and five words, including the word in capitals. Do not change the word in capitals.

Tony forgot to use kitchen gloves and burnt his fingers on the hot pan. **REMEMBERED**
Tony wouldn't have burnt his fingers on the hot pan _if he had remembered_ to use kitchen gloves.

1 James has decided he isn't going to play the match on Sunday. **TAKE**
James has decided _____ in the match on Sunday.

2 I need to get in shape because of the marathon next month. **TRAIN**
I need to _____ marathon next month.

3 Paddy regrets not knowing how to give first aid. **WISHES**
Paddy _____ how to give first aid.

4 I think it would be a good idea to speak to your doctor first. **IF**
I would speak to your doctor first _____ you.

5 You were exhausted because you had worked too much. **NOT**
If you hadn't worked too much, _____ exhausted.

/5

10 Complete the text with the correct form of the words in the box. There are two extra words.

day   dislocate   ~~interesting~~   obvious
operate   sprain   stitch   surgeon

Medical help to get you back on track

Professional athletes depend on their bodies working well in order to succeed. _Interestingly_, recent studies have shown that many of them have a reaction to pain that is different to what most of us experience. This is because physical pain is so much a part of their ¹_____ lives. For example, a ballet dancer who experiences muscle pain might simply assume that they've had a hard workout and just stretch or take a hot bath to feel better. A runner who has ²_____ an ankle might just wrap it in an elastic bandage and keep on running, hoping it will get better on its own. This is ³_____ the wrong approach, as any doctor will tell you, and can lead to long-lasting injuries. Fortunately, more and more professional athletes have easy access to doctors and physical therapists, which means that they can more easily prevent and deal with injuries. They don't even need to go to a doctor's ⁴_____ , because most services are available where they train. Of course, nothing makes an athlete happier than to hear the words, 'I don't think you need a(n) ⁵_____ .' Because they are getting help earlier, they are more likely to avoid serious problems and to have longer careers as well.

/5

Total /20

87

7 The art of entertainment

VOCABULARY

7.1

Entertainment • people in
entertainment • phrasal verbs

SHOW WHAT YOU KNOW

1 Choose the odd one out.

1	ballet dancer	actor	singer	sculpture
2	documentary	fantasy	horror	science fiction
3	news bulletin	thriller	crime drama	period drama
4	game show	talent show	soap opera	reality TV
5	orchestra	composer	conductor	painter
6	plot	portrait	setting	soundtrack

2 Complete the sentences with words from Exercise 1.

I never watch _period dramas_ because I prefer shows
set in modern times.

1 Did you watch the latest _____ ? There
was a big accident near our flat half an hour ago.

2 I liked the music from the film so much that I bought
the _____ on CD.

3 _Dynasty_ was an American _____ made
in the 80s and shown on TV all over the world.

4 It might only be an animation film but the
_____ is too complicated for me. I've
no idea what's happening.

5 Who's your favourite _____ ? I love
Monet and Munch. And Salvador Dali's not bad.

WORD STORE 7A | Entertainment

3 Choose the correct verbs.

1 In 2017, Ed Sheeran ᵃ_played / appeared_ in an
episode of _Game of Thrones_. He ᵇ_acted / played_
the part of a Lannister soldier in the episode
Dragonstone.

2 Jay-Z and Bruce Springsteen are the two artists that
have _signed / made_ the biggest recording contracts
– both $150 million. Robbie Williams is third with
a contract valued at $125 million!

3 You don't need to ᵃ_write / have_ great reviews to
ᵇ_have / make_ a hit single but it certainly helps.

4 The garage rock band Severe Tire Damage were
the first band to perform live on the Internet. Their
concert _got / was_ streamed in June 1993.

5 Pink Floyd ᵃ_released / sold_ the album _Dark Side of
the Moon_ in 1973 and it ᵇ_has got / has been_ in the
charts for a total of 861 weeks – that's over 16 years!

6 In 2014, Prince ᵃ_did / made_ a live secret gig in
London in front of 75 people. In fact, legends such
as Neil Young, Jack White and Tom Waits have all
chosen to ᵇ_play / perform_ small venues in the UK in
recent years.

**4 Complete the radio announcement with the missing
words in the correct form. The first letters are given.**

'It can take time for a **b**_and_ to go from playing
small ¹v_____ which hold only a few
dozen people to big stadiums that hold
tens of thousands, but for one band success
has come quickly. It started when The Opal
Orange's first song had great ²r_____ in the media.
This resulted in the band having a hit ³s_____ with
their first CD back in January. Since then, the band have
stayed in the ⁴c_____ with all of their other songs
getting into the top 10. They've just signed a ⁵r_____
contract with a big record company and will ⁶r_____
their first album in August. They're doing a number of
live ⁷g_____ around Europe, and fans that can't
get tickets will be pleased to hear that the concerts will
be ⁸s_____ live in cinemas. Singer Tom Bradley has
also ⁹a_____ in the fantasy TV series _Games of Kings_
where he plays the ¹⁰p_____ of Prince Ludo.'

REMEMBER THIS

viewer (n) – someone who watches a TV programme
audience (n) – a group of people who come to watch
and listen to someone giving a speech or another live
performance
spectator (n) – someone who watches a sporting event
or other competition
listener (n) – someone who listens to the radio

**5 Read REMEMBER THIS. Complete the sentences with
the correct word.**

The number of live _spectators_ is now so low that
organisers of horse racing events are offering other
forms of entertainment on the day. These include
such family favourites as dog shows, live music and
open air discos.

1 Regular _____ to BBC Talk Radio will
already know that there has been a change to
schedules …

2 After the mayor's emotional speech, the
_____ rose to their feet and started
clapping and cheering.

3 The TV broadcast of Prince Harry and Meghan
Markle's wedding attracted around 750 million
_____ worldwide.

WORD STORE 7B | People in entertainment

6 Complete the sentences with the correct form of the words from the box.

> audience   cast   drummer   ~~guitarist~~
> musician   songwriter   viewers   vocalist

The lead *guitarist* played one of the best solos I've ever heard.

1 Each episode of *Game of Thrones* is watched by around 12 million ª_____ and every member of the ᵇ_____ who stars in the show is now incredibly famous.

2 When the ª_____ of the band started to sing the band's greatest hit, the ᵇ_____ went wild.

3 The _____ dropped his sticks and the band had to stop playing. It was really quite embarrassing.

4 Paul McCartney is a talented _____ as well as singer. He can play the guitar, bass, piano and drums among other instruments.

5 Bob Dylan is the singer-_____ that won the Nobel prize for Literature in 2016 for creating 'new poetic expressions within the great American song tradition.'

WORD STORE 7C | Phrasal verbs

7 Match the beginnings with the correct endings to make sentences.

A

We're going to miss the start of the film if Marley doesn't turn ⬡ e

1 I want to get creative again, so I'm thinking of signing ⬡

2 Even the most famous and successful celebrities have to start ⬡

3 Don't ask Clarke to play live on stage yet because she'll mess ⬡

4 The new album by J. Cole is going to come ⬡

a up for a photography class.
b out at the bottom.
c out soon.
d up the guitar solo.
e up soon.

B

1 The school's theatre club has this crazy idea of putting ⬡

2 Fernando isn't enjoying the book club, so I don't think he's going to carry ⬡

3 Life's much too short to beat yourself ⬡

4 It's normal to be nervous the first time you go on stage but it quickly wears ⬡

5 I don't want to be mean but at 17 you're far too old to take ⬡

a off.
b on coming.
c up about things.
d up ballet.
e on a musical.

8 Complete the dialogues with the verbs from Exercise 7 in the correct form.

1 **Rudi:**   The new superhero film *comes* out on Thursday. Do you want to go to the Arizona Cinema with me and George to watch it? We've got an extra ticket.

  Claud: Sure. What time should I _____ up at the cinema?

  Rudi: Be there at 6:30 and we can grab a coffee first, OK?

2 **Beckie:**   Next week is the last lesson of our singing course. Are you going to ª_____ up for the next level?

  Vilma: I don't think I'll ᵇ_____ on with my career as a vocalist, to be honest. I'm not good enough.

  Beckie: Oh, come on! If Leonard Cohen could sing, you certainly can!

3 **Daniel:**   I can't believe I came last in the TV talent show. How embarrassing. Was I really that bad? Will the feeling of being a complete loser ever ª_____ off?

  Rebecca: Of course it will. Don't ᵇ_____ yourself up about it. You were much better than some of the other people.

4 **Moira:**   Hi, Joe. Listen, I'm ª_____ on a show at school and I'm looking for some people to act on stage. It's nothing too complicated and you won't need to say anything.

  Joe: Oh, I don't know. That kind of thing isn't for me. I'd probably ᵇ_____ something up and fall over or something.

  Moira: Hmm. OK. Well, I thought I'd ask.

SHOW WHAT YOU'VE LEARNT

9 Choose the correct answers A–C.

1 How long has this song been __ the charts? I'm bored of hearing it now.
  A in   B on   C at

2 I can't sing at all, so we need to find a __ for our band.
  A musician   B gig   C vocalist

3 We turned __ late. The play had already started.
  A up   B out   C in

4 If you could __ in any TV series, which one would you choose and why?
  A stream   B appear   C show

5 Our band doesn't play pop music, so we'll never have a __ single.
  A great   B big   C hit

6 Who's the __ guitarist in Guns N' Roses again?
  A main   B head   C lead

7 Gabriel really wants to put __ an end-of-year show for the teachers, so I think we should help him.
  A on   B up   C off

8 The *Mamma Mia Here We Go Again!* musical has great __ in this online film magazine.
  A previews   B revisions   C reviews

9 Wow, I never knew you'd taken __ the violin.
  A on   B up   C to

10 We've been practising our songs for months and we think we're ready to do our first live __ .
  A gig   B venue   C play

/10

SHOW WHAT YOU KNOW

1 Put the words in order to complete the conversation between Mum, Dad and Kirsty.

D: Kirsty, please tell me we are not watching *The X Factor*.

K: You *watch / said / could / I* _said I could watch_ it tonight.

D: No, I ¹*could / you / watch / said* _____
_____ it upstairs.

K: Dad!

D: What? The other day I ²*I / television / said / was / taking back / my* _____
on Saturday nights. I want to watch the Grand Prix.

K: *(shouting)* Mum! *The X Factor* has started!

D: Kirsty! Last Saturday night, I ³*told / you / bought / I / had* _____
a second television for exactly this kind of situation.

M: *(enters room)* Oh. Did you ⁴*The X Factor / that / say / started / had* _____ ?

D: But … the Grand Prix.

M: There's another television upstairs, Walter.

2 ★ Write reported speech as direct speech. Pay attention to the underlined words.

Margaret Mead said that thanks to television, for the first time the young <u>were seeing</u> history before it <u>was censored</u> by their elders.
Margaret Mead: *'Thanks to television, for the first time the young are seeing history before it is censored by their elders.'*

1 Peter J. Laurence said that television <u>had changed</u> the American child from an irresistible force into an immovable object.
Peter J. Laurence: '_____
_____.'

2 Christine Amanpour said <u>she</u> <u>believed</u> that good journalism, good television <u>could</u> make our world a better place.
Christine Amanpour: '_____
_____.'

3 ★ ★ Match the reporting verbs with the definitions.

Minister for Culture Embarrassed in Television Interview

Last night on Channel 10 News, the Minister for Culture <u>claimed</u> that young people were happier these days than when he had been young. The journalist Mandy Striker <u>pointed out</u> that there was no real proof of that, and politely <u>suggested</u> that happiness was very difficult to measure. The minister <u>explained</u> that his statement was based on meetings he had had with young people and parents in local schools in his area. He <u>added</u> that his own teenage children were also living full and happy lives. The minister then asked Ms Striker if this was reasonable evidence. Ms Striker <u>replied</u> that not all young people were as lucky as those who lived in the area where the minister lived. This morning the red-faced minister promised there would be a nation-wide survey into young people's levels of happiness.

gave a reason for something   _explained_
1 said that something was true   _____
2 answered   _____
3 said more about something   _____
4 told someone something that they
  didn't know or hadn't thought of   _____
5 said something in an indirect way   _____

4 ★ ★ ★ Read the direct speech. Choose the correct reporting verb. Then complete the gaps with the correct forms of the verbs in brackets. Change any other words if necessary.

'Honestly, please believe me, I really didn't know she was a drug dealer.'
The TV presenter ᵃ*suggested /*(claimed) he ᵇ<u>hadn't known</u> (not/know) that the woman had been a drug dealer. He begged the court to believe ᶜ<u>him</u>.

1 'We don't think the programme is suitable for children.'
When a journalist asked why the programme had been banned, the members of the panel ᵃ*added / replied* that, in ᵇ_____ opinion, they ᶜ_____ (not/think) the programme was suitable for children.

2 'Don't tell everyone, but maybe you should wait until next week. There's probably going to be a sale here.'
I was in the electrical store a few weeks ago and the assistant winked at me and ᵃ*replied / suggested* that the ᵇ_____ week there ᶜ_____ (probably/be) a sale ᵈ_____ .

3 'Leo can take my car. I won't need it because I'm working from home today.'
Leo wanted to borrow his dad's car, but his mum ᵃ*added / suggested* that he ᵇ_____ (take) hers. She ᶜ_____ (not/need) it because she was working from home ᵈ_____ day.

SHOW WHAT YOU'VE LEARNT

5 Rewrite the direct speech as reported speech.

'I will miss the last part of this TV series tomorrow.'
It was a long time ago, but I remember she said <u>she would miss the last part of that TV series the following day</u>.

1 'We're going to be on television next week.'
Two months ago, they said _____
_____.

2 'I'm meeting your sister here later today.'
We were in the café and Dad told me _____
_____.

3 'We saw you both last month.'
It was back in January when they told us _____
_____.

4 'I can't give you her phone number now.'
Jason said _____
_____.

5 'Your concert is cancelled.'
We were very disappointed when the organiser told us that _____
_____.

6 'I'll see you tomorrow.'
Six days ago she told him _____
_____ , but then she never came back.

/6

1 Complete the expressions in bold in the extracts with the words from the box.

> common   expression   feel   ~~formula~~
> himself   laugh   spans   stupid

Extract from Student's Book recording 🔊 **3.13**

1 A viral video is a video that becomes popular very quickly through the Internet. People share the video through social media and email. [...] There isn't a *formula* **for** a viral video hit. But the most popular ones **have three things in** ¹_____ . Firstly, [they're really] short. People **have short attention** ² _____ , especially when they're looking at websites, so the most successful viral videos are around three minutes long. Secondly, they stir up your emotions – they may be funny, sad, shocking, entertaining or even extremely annoying, but they **make viewers** ³_____ **something**. The third ingredient is story. Many of the most popular viral videos tell a [simple] story and the ones with an inspirational ending are the most memorable.

2 My favourite videos are the ones that **make you** ⁴_____ . It's usually because somebody **does something** ⁵_____ – for instance, there's a video of a man who dives into a frozen swimming pool. Well, I say he dives, but of course he hits the ice and slides across the swimming pool. How can you be so stupid? [...]. I couldn't believe it! [...] I love the one where a baby bites his brother's finger. The little brother puts his finger in his baby brother's mouth, and **surprise, surprise***, the baby bites it. I love **the** ⁶_____ **on the baby's face** – he's very pleased **with** ⁷_____ .

2 Complete the sentences with words and expressions from Exercise 1. Change the verb forms if necessary.

> People ask me what the formula *for* success is. I tell them it's hard work and good timing.

1 Viv loves spending time with Dave. He _____ her feel happy and relaxed.

2 I love visual comedy. It _____ me laugh more than any joke could.

3 Emma and Karen both got top marks in the test, so they were very _____ with themselves.

4 Did you see the expression _____ Kieran's face when he heard he had won? He looked really surprised.

5 Danielle, I've _____ something really stupid. I forgot to pay the deposit and we've lost the booking.

6 Lindsay and I aren't friends anymore. We just don't have anything _____ common.

7 This game is only suitable for children over the age of six. Younger children's attention spans are too _____ to enjoy it properly.

3 Match the adjectives below with underlined synonyms in the text.

	happy	=	*pleased*
1	brief	=	_____
2	amusing	=	_____
3	straight-forward	=	_____
4	foolish	=	_____
5	irritating	=	_____
6	disturbing	=	_____

REMEMBER THIS

1 The expression *surprise, surprise,* can be used when something unexpected and pleasant happens. *I asked her out on a date and surprise, surprise, she actually said yes!*

2 In contrast, it is often used ironically, when someone has done something, or something has happened that was actually very predictable and therefore is not a surprise. *He was late on Monday and Tuesday, and surprise, surprise, he was late again on Wednesday.*

4 Read REMEMBER THIS. Is meaning 1 or 2 expressed in Extract 2 in Exercise 1?

WORD STORE 7D | Collocations

5 Complete the reviews with the correct form of the words from the box.

> emotion   span   surprise (x2)   ~~upload~~   view   viral

Website of the year

My choice is SnappyVid. OK, websites for *uploading* your home-made videos are nothing new. But this site is perfect for people that have a short attention ¹_____ because videos must be shorter than 45 seconds. And best of all, to ²_____ a video all you need to do is to choose a topic and say it into your microphone.

Advert of the year

Adverts in this category need to go ³_____ – if they don't, very few people will see them! Fortunately, everybody saw the Mango Munchies advert that contains an element of ⁴_____ which made it unique among this year's ads. Oh, and Mango Munchies taste great too!

Film of the year

Documentaries are not usually fun but *Down by the Sea* really took me by ⁵_____ . Firstly, it really made me laugh (which is not easy to do!) and secondly, it stirs up ⁶_____ in very unusual ways. I won't say anything more, other than watch this film today!

1 Read the text and match headings A–F with parts 1–4. There are two extra headings.

A Getting a Clearer Picture
B Television Goes Mobile
C Hi-tech Becomes Old-tech
D What Day? What Time? What Channel?
E The Internet Replaces Television
F Stay in your Seat, Stay in Control

1 _____

If your grandma or grandpa were <u>lucky</u> enough to have a television in their bedroom when they were your age, they probably felt pretty cool, even if it was black and white, weighed about 20 kg and had an antenna that looked like a metal coat hanger. **A___** The technology of televisions has changed so quickly that it's not surprising some of the most <u>sophisticated</u> features of the TV sets of the past seem rather silly these days. In this week's article, check out these old TV technologies, but while you are laughing, remember that many <u>modern</u> gadgets will seem just as ridiculous to the youngsters of tomorrow.

2 _____

'Stay tuned!' is something you still occasionally hear people on television say when they are really asking you not to switch off or change the channel. The phrase has lost its original meaning, which referred to 'tuning' early analogue televisions (adjusting* them to get the best quality picture) by turning a big dial,* or wheel, on the front. Later televisions had <u>individual</u> channel buttons, but for each button there was still a tuning dial located behind a little plastic door on the front of the set. These dials were often tiny and <u>tricky</u> to turn, so some manufacturers used to sell their sets with a little plastic stick that you would put into a hole and turn until the picture was clear enough to watch. **B__** Nowadays, thank goodness, televisions 'tune' themselves automatically.

3 _____

When your grandparents were young, 'channel surfing' actually required physical effort because to change the channel you had to stand up, walk across the room and press a button on the television. **C___** Eventually, remote controls were invented, but the first ones actually had a wire that stretched across the room from the remote to the television. Later more boxes appeared – video recorders, satellite tuners and so on – and with those came <u>additional</u> remote controls. Eventually, when it became impossible to open the living room door because of all the different remotes, universal controllers became popular and one small device could finally control all the different boxes in your living room! Now, with the help of the right app, it is becoming more and more common to use a mobile phone or tablet to control all the various media devices in your house, though some homes still have more remote controls than hands to operate them.

4 _____

Not so many years ago, viewers had no choice but to wait a week for the next episode of their favourite TV programmes to be shown. **D___** It was not unusual for people to plan their week around the TV schedule and, if they were busy at the time of their favourite show, they either missed it or found space on a video tape, set the video recorder for the right time and hoped the tape didn't run out before the programme had finished. These days, TV schedules are still printed in magazines and some newspapers. However, they are much less <u>significant</u> because of 'catch-up' TV channels, <u>on-demand</u> Internet TV services such as Netflix or I-player, and of course legal and illegal downloading.

Television and the technology associated with it is changing constantly and if you have children, by the time they are your age, flat-screen, HD and 3D will probably seem as silly and old-fashioned as black and white, two channels only, and a coat hanger for an aerial.

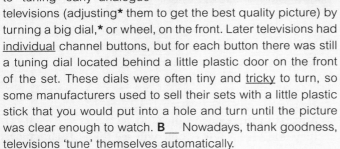

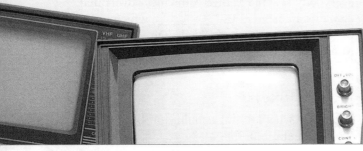

GLOSSARY

adjust *(v)* – to change or move something slightly to improve it or make it work better

dial *(n)* – the wheel-like part of a radio or old-fashioned television that you turn to find a different station or channel

2 Read the text again and complete gaps A–D with the missing sentences below. There is one extra sentence.

1 If you lost this little tool, the entire set became useless. ◯

2 These first colour television sets were extremely expensive. ◯

3 People would check the weekly TV schedule in a magazine or newspaper and highlight the shows they really wanted to watch. ◯

4 Now, just a few decades later most of us carry small, powerful, high-definition, full-colour, multi-media devices in our bags and pockets. ◯

5 Actually, this wasn't such a big problem, because for a long time there were only two or three channels to choose from. ◯

3 Match the underlined adjectives in the text with synonyms below. Use a dictionary if necessary.

fortunate = *lucky*   4 single   = _____

1 important = _____   5 instant   = _____

2 advanced = _____   6 contemporary = _____

3 more   = _____   7 difficult   = _____

REMEMBER BETTER

When you learn a new word (verb, noun or adjective) or if you want to learn more about a word you already know, look in a collocation dictionary or online and make a note of some common collocations in which it is used.

And the *lucky winner* of tonight's lottery is ticket number 459!

That was a *lucky escape*. If we hadn't been late, we would've been on the train that crashed.

Did you really know the answer or was it a *lucky guess*?

VOCABULARY PRACTICE | Phrases related to reading

4 Look at the vocabulary in lesson 7.4 in the Student's Book. Complete the quotes about reading with the correct form of the words in brackets.

'While a lot of people nowadays reach for their e-books or tablets when they want to read, most people agree that reading the *old-fashioned* (FASHION) way – i.e. a paper book – actually
1 _____ (ENHANCE) the reading process.'

'For readers who can feel 2 _____ (DISTRACT) by over-complicated plots and a large cast of characters, some of George R.R. Martin's books can be challenging. This is not the case with his short story *The Monkey Treatment*. I guarantee you will find this tale both easy to 3 _____ (FOLLOW) and gripping to read.'

'Anybody who is 4 _____ (CRITICISE) of e-books should pause for a second and realise that we should be encouraging young people to read however they choose to. Reading anything at a young age helps to improve
5 _____ (LITERATURE) rates and this can't be a bad thing.'

---

5 Complete the sentences with the verb or noun forms of the word in capitals.

CREATE
a I've got a great idea! Let's *create* a band website where people can stream our music.
b Improvisation is the *creation* of spontaneous music.

1 **ACCOMPANY**
a I often study or clean the house to the _____ of music.
b Jones, please _____ me to the head teacher's office now.

2 **DISTRACT**
a Sorry, what did you say? I was _____ by that loud banging. What is that noise?
b There are too many _____ at home, so I often do my homework in the library.

3 **ENCOURAGE**
a I never thought I could act but my parents _____ me and I've been quite successful.
b James isn't very self-confident but with a little _____ he performs quite well.

4 **ENGAGE**
a Ms Hay is known for her _____ in politics and environmental issues.
b Fiona never has any free time. She's always _____ in one activity or another.

5 **ENHANCE**
a What can I do to really _____ my singing skills?
b We have made a lot of _____ to the equipment in our music venue.

6 **ENTERTAIN**
a The _____ industry is worth over $2 trillion a year, apparently. Wow!
b Grandad's in the garden _____ the kids with his magic tricks.

7 **IMPROVE**
a We have seen great _____ in communication technology over the years.
b If you want to _____ at anything, you must practise, practise, practise.

8 **MEMORISE**
a _____ techniques such as the Memory Palace are designed to help you remember things in great detail.
b How have you _____ so much information? I forget most things moments after I hear them!

'Unlike a film, reading a book leaves something to the 6 _____ (IMAGINE), and this is very often more engaging than simply being shown everything on the big screen.'

'I always prefer to review a book 7 _____ (POSITIVE) but I'm finding that very hard with Edward Lowell's *The Paper Plant*. This novel is 8 _____ (BASE) on the real life of a nineteenth century factory owner and seems an inappropriate subject for a book of any kind. What was Lowell thinking?'

GRAMMAR

Reported speech
– questions and
imperatives

SHOW WHAT YOU KNOW

1 Complete the dialogue with Grandma's questions.

Grandma: *What are you going to wear to the party?*
Lori: I'm going to wear a black dress and high heels.
Grandma: ¹_____
_____
Lori: I'm going with my friends and my fiancé.
Grandma: ²_____
_____
Lori: Yes, I have got a fiancé, Grandma.
Grandma: ³_____
_____
Lori: Yes, he's nice.
Grandma: ⁴_____
_____
Lori: You are going to meet him next month at my birthday party.

2 ★ Katy is talking to her friend about a journalist from a teen magazine she met in a café yesterday. Choose the correct option to complete the sentences. Then match them with the reported answers a–f.

Yesterday, the journalist said …
1 Do you come here often?
2 Can I buy you a coffee?
3 What is your hobby?
4 Have you got a best friend?
5 Where did you meet her?
6 What is she like?

Today, Katy is telling her friend …
1 He asked me *did I go there / if I went there* often.
2 He asked whether he *can / could* buy me a coffee.
3 He asked me what *my hobby was / was my hobby*.
4 He asked me *did I have a best friend / if I had a best friend*.
5 He asked me where *I had met / did I meet* her.
6 He asked me *what was my best friend like / what my best friend was like*.

a I said I had met my best friend at a party.
b I told him it was sport.
c I said he could buy me a coffee.
d I told him my best friend was fantastic.
e I said 'yes' I had a best friend.
f I said I went there most lunchtimes.

(a) ( )
(b) ( )
(c) ( )
(d) ( )
(e) ( )
(f) (1)

3 ★★ Look at Rosie's list and complete her conversation with her friend Poppy.

Record of horrible things my big sister has said to me

Monday	Tuesday	Wednesday
1 be quiet	3 grow up	5 go away
2 don't annoy me	4 don't be stupid	6 stop writing lists

P: How are things with your sister, Rosie? Are you still writing your list?
R: Yes, I am. I'll tell you. On Monday she *told me to* be quiet and ¹_____ annoy her. On Tuesday she ²_____ grow up and ³_____ stupid, and on Wednesday she ⁴_____ go away and asked me ⁵_____ lists.
P: Oh, Rosie. Poor you.
R: Yeah, she's pretty mean, but then she's got her exams coming up soon, so I have decided to forgive her.

4 ★★★ Complete the reported questions and answers from Exercise 1. Use short forms.

Grandma asked Lori *what she was going to wear* to the party.
Lori said she *was going to wear* a black dress and high heels.
1 She also asked her ᵃ_____ to the party with.
Lori said she ᵇ_____ with her friends and fiancé.
2 Then she asked her ᵃ_____ a fiancé.
Lori said she ᵇ_____ a fiancé.
3 After that, she wanted to know ᵃ_____ nice.
Lori said her fiancé ᵇ_____ nice.
4 Finally, she asked ᵃ_____ meet him.
Lori told her grandma ᵇ_____ meet him the following month at her birthday party.

SHOW WHAT YOU'VE LEARNT

5 Report the questions and instructions. Use short forms.

M: Have you arrived safely?
Mum called as soon as the plane landed and *asked me if I had arrived safely*.
1 **M:** What was the flight like?
She _____ .
2 **M:** Have you been through passport control yet?
Then she _____ .
3 **M:** Did you remember to collect your luggage?
She even _____ .
4 **M:** Don't forget to change some money.
Next, she _____ .
5 **M:** How are you getting to your aunt and uncle's house?
Still more questions! She _____
_____ .
6 **M:** Say 'hello' to everyone from me.
Finally, she_____
I'm looking forward to a little time away from home.

/6

GRAMMAR: Train and Try Again page 160

1 ★ **Choose the correct answers.**

1 Did Chiara give you *a / –* good advice on what to do?
2 How *much / many* information can you give me on your singing classes?
3 I'm making *a / –* very slow progress in my sculpture lessons.
4 Please pass me a pair of *scissor / scissors*.
5 I really like *this / these* trousers. Can I try them on?
6 Whose black jeans *is this / are those*?

2 ★★ **Find and correct the mistakes.**

The ~~headquarter of Disney is~~ in Burbank, California.
the headquarters of Disney are

1 Wow! You've bought lots of new furnitures since I last came here. _____
2 Oh, no. The airline has lost my luggages. What am I going to wear on the beach? _____
3 I'm afraid the news aren't very good. You haven't won the art award. _____
4 Can I name a famous actor without any hairs? Hmm. Patrick Stewart from *Star Trek* and *X-Men*? _____
5 I've got lots of favourite TV serieses – too many to name, in fact! _____

3 ★★ **Complete the sentences with the words in brackets in the correct form. Do not change the order of the words. You may need to add words. Use between three and six words.**

Don't worry, *the police are coming* (police / be / come) and will be here very soon to control the crowd.

1 I know I'm supposed to be a vampire but these _____ (tooth / be / sharp) and I keep biting my own tongue.
2 Isn't it funny that there _____ (be / many / sheep) than people in New Zealand?
3 Neil Armstrong and Buzz Aldrin _____ (be / first / man) to stand on the moon.
4 Norah can't dance at all. She _____ (got / two / left foot), as we often say.
5 Eeeek! There _____ (be / three / mouse) in the cupboard above the sink. How did they even get there? Somebody please get them out now.

4 ★★★ **Complete each gap with one word.**

(Not) Acting as a Child?

Shirley Temple

How to become a child actor? I've done *some* research on it recently and it's easier than you think.

Firstly, the good news [1]_____ that there is real demand for child actors. Did you know that Disney themselves employ over 1,000 [2]_____ every year? So, wherever you live, look for places where you can begin your acting career. There will be people in your area who work for theatres, schools and churches that may need your skills.

Secondly, practise at home. Learn lines from your favourite films or TV [3]_____ and read them aloud dramatically. Use simple props to help you get into character: a pair of dark [4]_____ to become a police officer, for example.

And finally, if one day you find yourself in front of a camera or on a stage, don't forget your [5]_____ and always be polite. Nobody wants to work with a troublesome star – no matter how young or old!

5 ★★★ **Complete each gap with one word.**

A: Hey, I have some new *information* for you! I'm sure it's something you don't know.
B: Well, go on then. Tell me, tell me!

1 A: Don't you think _____ is boring?
B: Not me. I'm really fascinated by politicians and what is happening on our political scene.

2 A: My company's headquarters _____ moving to Spain.
B: I know. What are you going to do?

3 A: Could you give me some _____ on how to become famous?
B: Certainly. Always work hard and look good.

4 A: Philip's _____ into Chinese poetry is absolutely fascinating.
B: He knows a lot about Chinese history and philosophy too.

5 A: Do you know that some species of _____, like salmon, are able to live in both seawater and freshwater?
B: Yes, I've read about it. It's amazing.

95

1 Complete the dialogues with extreme adjectives. The first letters are given.

1 M: Well, that was a really **t**errible (very bad) meal! And extremely expensive. I'm ¹**d**_____ (very disappointed) after spending so much money on that!

R: Actually my food was ²**d**_____ (very tasty) and I think the chef is absolutely ³**b**_____ (very talented). Besides, I think it's ⁴**h**_____ (very funny) that you say that now after eating everything. And rather quickly I might add.

M: That's not fair. I was so ⁵**s**_____ (very hungry) that it was ⁶**i**_____ (not possible) not to eat whatever they put in front of me.

2 J: That was an absolutely ⁷**a**_____ (very good) concert, Oli. Thanks again for inviting me. The band were ⁸**f**_____ (very good)!

O: Oh, man. I'm ⁹**e**_____ (very happy)! I've wanted to see them play live for years. I knew they were good but that was ¹⁰**e**_____ (very good)! And the way they played the songs differently to how they sound on the albums was also ¹¹**f**_____ (very interesting)!

J: I agree. They're very talented.

2 Choose the correct modifier.

Telly-Addicts: last night on the box

Last night's television highlight was definitely the ¹*absolutely / rather* fascinating BBC2 documentary *Icemen* about the lives of fishermen in Iceland. Some of the fishermen's stories were ²*rather / absolutely* sad, but ³*very / absolutely* interesting, and the shots of the Icelandic coastline were ⁴*very / absolutely* gorgeous.

Also worth watching was Channel 4's new quiz *What's Up?* which was presented by the ⁵*extremely / absolutely* talented Rosie Perks and her ⁶*very / absolutely* funny partner Richard Bond. Though many of the questions on the show are ⁷*quite / absolutely* impossible to answer, we still found it ⁸*really / absolutely* entertaining from start to finish.

3 Complete the puzzle using the clues below and find the word connected with the topic of this lesson which is hidden in the grey boxes.

- two adjectives which mean very bad
- one adjective to describe nice tasting food
- one modifier for base adjectives
- one modifier for extreme adjectives
- five adjectives which mean very good

The hidden word: _____

4 Read the article and number the paragraphs in the correct order. Then choose the most interesting title.

1 The Village Anniversary ◯
2 Last Weekend was Nice ◯
3 A Bright, Beautiful and Busy 400th Birthday ◯

Abbeydale Village News

A ◯ Saturday began with an early morning fun run. It was <u>nice</u> / *lovely* weather and when the sun rose, the sky turned a(n) ¹<u>very</u> / _____ pretty orangey-blue colour. When the runners reached the finish next to the abbey, the sun was already high in the sky, the music had started and the smell of ²<u>nice tasting</u> / _____ food was everywhere.

B ◯ Unfortunately, the traffic in the village was ³<u>bad</u> / _____ . Trying to drive through the village was almost impossible and the sound and smell of the cars was ⁴<u>bad</u> / _____ . Maybe next year one of the farmers' fields outside the village can be used as a car park.

C ◯ It is not often you get to say 'happy 400th birthday!' but that's exactly what we did in our village last weekend. 400 years ago, a group of monks decided to build an abbey, or church next to the river, and our village grew up around it. The ruins of the abbey are still standing today and that's where the anniversary celebrations were held.

D ◯ Except for the traffic, it was a ⁵<u>nice</u> / _____ day. I think every town and village should have a day when they celebrate their community and its history.

E ◯ By midday, everyone from the area was there enjoying the ⁶<u>nice</u> / _____ sunshine. All around the ruins, there were colourful market stalls and people selling ⁷<u>nice</u> / _____ local food. There were some great live bands and a(n) ⁸<u>really</u> / _____ fabulous play which told the story of the village.

5 Replace the underlined words in the text with more descriptive alternatives from Exercise 3. Use each word only once. Sometimes more than one answer is possible.

¹b			l		l					t	
²t				i		b		e			
³a	b										y
⁴a			z				g				
⁵f			t	a	s						
⁶l		v			y						
⁷e	x		r					l	y		
⁸d		l		c							
⁹a		f									

6 Read the task below. Then read the article and complete it with the correct form of the words in brackets.

> You recently watched a celebrity wedding on TV. Write an article reviewing the programme. Include and develop these points:
> - Say briefly what happened on the day and give your opinion on the importance of filming such events.
> - Share your impressions of the programme you watched and suggest how similar TV programmes could be improved in the future.

◉◯◯

A Day to Remember!

I recently watched the live TV <u>broadcast</u> of a celebrity wedding. Although I told my friend that I ¹_____ (be) ᴬ*rather / absolutely* sceptical about it, afterwards I admitted that I ²_____ (enjoy) watching the programme. I now consider such events as ᴮ*absolutely / very* engaging and valuable.

It began with shots of the ᶜ*absolutely / very* magnificent ³_____ (locate), a beach in Hawaii. The cloudless sky, clear water and golden sand make it certainly an ideal place to get married! The show's hosts then mixed with the crowd of ᴰ*rather / really* familiar faces, other A-list ⁴_____ (celebrity), asked them how they ⁵_____ (feel), if they were nervous, and spoke with them in a relaxed manner.

Next was the ⁶_____ (marry) ceremony itself. The bride and groom looked ᴱ*really / very* fantastic in their wedding ⁷_____ (cloth). They told us how much they ⁸_____ (love) each other and the camera showed guests with tears in their eyes.

One thing I thought was missing from the show was an interview with the celebrity couple before the ceremony. If it had been included, it would have been ᶠ*extremely / quite* nice to hear them share their ⁹_____ (feel) and say why they ¹⁰_____ (choose) to get married in this way. However, this is a small criticism of what was a(n) ᴳ*very / absolutely* wonderful television event.

Read the article again. For questions A–G, choose the correct words. Sometimes both answers are correct.

SHOW WHAT YOU'VE LEARNT

8 A television production company recently spent a day filming part of a reality TV show called 'Our School's Got Talent' at your school. Students showed artwork, put on plays and sang, danced and performed in front of the cameras. The production company organised food and a party at the end of the day to say thank you. They also said they would come back next year to film again. Write an article and review the event.
- Describe and give your opinion on the various events of the day.
- Make some suggestions for next year's event.

SHOW THAT YOU'VE CHECKED

Finished? Always check your writing.
Can you tick √ everything on this list?

In my article reviewing an event:

• I have begun with an interesting, funny or unusual title to attract the reader's attention.	☐
• I have held the reader's attention with an introduction which asks a question or gives interesting facts.	☐
• I have described the event using a variety of adjectives and modifiers.	☐
• I have made my descriptions interesting by describing what I saw, heard, smelled and tasted.	☐
• I have included personal opinions and suggestions.	☐
• I have finished with a recommendation for the reader.	☐
• I have checked my spelling and punctuation.	☐
• My text is neat and clear.	☐

SPEAKING

Asking for permission
• polite requests

1 Translate the phrases into your own language.

SPEAKING BANK

Asking for permission

Can/Could I/we …?
_____
_____
_____

Is it OK if I/we …?
_____

We were wondering if I/we could …?
_____
_____
_____
_____

Do you mind if I/we …?
_____
_____

Giving permission

Well OK, I suppose so.
_____

Yes, that's fine. No problem.
_____
_____

Sure, I don't see why not.
_____
_____

No, not at all, go ahead.
_____

Refusing permission

I'm sorry but …
_____

I'd like to help but I'm afraid …
_____
_____

I'm afraid …
_____

Yes, I do actually.
_____
_____

2 Put the words in order to make polite requests.

mind / photograph / take / do / if / you / we / your
Do you mind if we take your photograph ?

1 here / mind / you / if / do / I / sit
_____ ?

2 you / if / were / could / we / wondering / we / ask / a question
_____ ?

3 the channel / it / is / I / if / OK / change
_____ ?

4 me / you / lend / could / your / bike
_____ ?

5 toothbrush / I / can / your / borrow
_____ ?

3 Choose the correct options to complete the responses to the requests in Exercise 2 then mark each response as G for giving permission or R for refusing permission.

Yes, (I do actually)/ go ahead. I'm afraid I don't like being in photographs. [R]

1 Yes / No, not at all. No one is sitting there. ◯

2 Yes that's fine / I'd like to help but I'm rather busy at the moment. ◯

3 No problem / I'm sorry but I'm watching this programme. ◯

4 Sure / Not at all, I don't see why not. Do you want to borrow my helmet too? ◯

5 Well OK, I suppose so / not although it's a bit disgusting. ◯

REMEMBER THIS

Remember that after requests with
Do you mind if I/we …
you say _no_, meaning
'No, I don't mind' (i.e. it's OK) to give permission;
you say _yes_, meaning
'Yes, I do mind' (i.e. it's not OK) to refuse permission.

4 Complete the dialogues with phrases. Some letters are given.

Conversation 1: Floyd and Marjorie

In the shopping centre car park …

F: Hi, sorry to disturb you, but [a]I w_as_ w_ondering_ i_f_ I c_ould_ ask you to watch my shopping while I go and get some change for the parking machine? There are too many bags to carry down those stairs again and if I leave them here, I know someone will steal them.

M: No, [b]n_____ a_____ a_____ young man, you [c]g_____ a_____ .

F: Really? How kind! Back in two minutes!

Conversation 2: Duncan and Mum

D: Mum?

M: Yes, Duncan?

D: [a]D_____ you m_____ i_____ I borrow your car tonight?

M: [b]S_____ , I don't s_____ w_____ n_____ .

D: Really? Fantastic!

M: There's hardly any petrol in it though, so you'll have to fill it up.

D: No problem … oh … er … Mum?

M: Yes, Duncan?

D: [c]C_____ I borrow some money?

M: Well Duncan, [d]I'_____ l_____ to h_____ but I think I gave you £20 yesterday, didn't I?

D: Oh … er … oh … yes! Yes, of course you did, sorry. I'll use some of that.

Student A, look below. Student B, go to page 140.

1 In pairs, ask and answer the questions.

Talk about health.

1 Have you or has someone you know ever broken a bone? What happened?

2 What should you do when you have a black eye? Why?

3 Why do you think people have panic attacks?

4 Have you ever helped someone in need in your country or abroad? How?

5 When was the last time you pulled somebody's leg? What happened?

2 Look at the photo of the music event. Take turns to talk about what you can see in your photos. Talk about the people, the places and the other things in the photo.

3 You and your friend want to start doing a hobby related to music. Here are some of the things you could choose. Talk together about the different ideas and say which you would enjoy most.

4 Talk about making music.

- Would you rather play music or make music? Why?
- If you were a musician, would you prefer to make music by yourself or with friends? Why?
- Who is your favourite musician or songwriter of all time? Why?
- If you could play any venue, where would you play? Why?
- If you released an album, what would it be like? Why?

VOCABULARY AND GRAMMAR

1 Choose the correct words.

I love the ending to this film. Because we don't really know what happened, it *leaves* / *lets* / *plays* something to the imagination.

1 You're in a band, aren't you Jake? Have you ever *appeared* / *done* / *played* a venue that holds more than fifty people?

2 In my opinion, the best way to *gain* / *take up* / *improve* literacy rates is to promote reading and reduce children's time in front of the television.

3 I always listen to classical music when I read. I feel it somehow *increases* / *enhances* / *exaggerates* the reading experience.

4 Quite a few actors have *released* / *realised* / *reviewed* albums, you know. David Duchovny, Keifer Sutherland, Hugh Laurie, Scarlett Johansson ... Some of them are even pretty good!

5 In order to *view* / *review* / *make* a video on this website, please click the green 'play' button at the bottom of the screen.

/5

2 Complete the sentences with the correct form of the words from the box. There are two extra words.

> beat   carry   feel   mess
> release   sign   stir   upload

I've been kicked out of the band because I keep *messing* my solo up.

1 It's important not to _____ yourself up but rather look on a failure as something to learn from.

2 Lorna has _____ up for the local theatre group. She's always loved acting and can't wait to perform in a play.

3 Jack _____ a video of me dancing at his party. Luckily, he deleted it when I asked him to.

4 When I was a student I had trouble concentrating and often _____ distracted when I needed to work or study. It's better now, fortunately.

5 Hugo doesn't usually like folk music but these songs really _____ up emotions in him. I thought he was going to cry at one point.

/5

3 Complete the sentences with the correct words. The first and last letters are given.

The **c**as**t** of the new *Fantastic Beasts* film is awesome! Eddie Redmayne, Johnny Depp, Zoe Kravitz, ... and Jude Law is Dumbledore!

1 Most people agree that Agatha Christie's greatest **c**_____**n** was Hercule Poirot, the fictional Belgian detective. His death was even announced on the front page of The New York Times!

2 I read some of my poetry in a café last week. There were only about fifteen people in the **a**_____**e** but they seemed to like it.

3 Live music is my favourite form of **e**_____**t**. I try to go to a concert at least once a month.

4 Adele is the **s**_____**r-s**_____**r** who wrote and sang the James Bond title tune *Skyfall*.

5 Ringo Starr from the Beatles is the only famous **d**_____**r** I can name. They're not usually as well-known as guitarists or singers.

/5

4 Find and correct the mistakes.

TV presenter: 'Your new show is the best you have ever done.'
The TV presenter ~~said~~ the star that his new show was the best he'd ever done. *told*

1 Natalie: 'I am watching a film, Caroline.'
Natalie told Caroline I was watching a film. _____

2 Sophia: 'I haven't been to the cinema yet'.
Sophia added she didn't go the to cinema yet. _____

3 Tim: 'I missed the last episode yesterday.'
Tim said he had missed the last episode yesterday.
_____

4 Mollie: 'We'll meet here at six o'clock.'
Mollie said we'll meet there at six o'clock. _____

5 Ben: 'It can't be the same actor.'
Ben pointed out that it can't be the same actor.
_____

/5

5 Read the conversation between Phil, the head of a drama school, and Ruby. Use reported speech.

P: Do you really want to be an actress?
He asked me if *I really wanted to be an actress*.

R: Yes, I do.

P: Are you sure? Most actresses don't become rich or successful.
He asked me whether ¹_____ and said that most actresses didn't become rich or successful.

R: I'm sure.

P: Have you ever studied drama?
He asked me if ²_____ .

R: No, I haven't.
I said no, I ³_____ .

P: Can you act?
He asked me whether ⁴_____ .

R: Yes, I can.

P: Show me.
He asked me ⁵_____ .   /5

6 Choose the correct answers A–C.

> I took Grandma to buy a new TV last weekend. The shop assistant asked us what kind of TV we A interested in and Grandma ¹__ a black and white TV that was square and had at least four channels. The assistant told Grandma ²__ colour TVs these days and that they all ³__ more than four channels.
>
> In the end, the assistant and I persuaded her to buy a little colour TV. Altogether it cost £99.99 which I thought was ⁴__ , Grandma thought it was extremely expensive. Of course, her disappointment quickly ⁵__ off and now she loves her little TV and says it was worth every penny ☺.

(A) were	B are	C have been
1 A said she has wanted		B said she wanted
C said she wants		
2 A they only sold	B he's only sold	C we only sell
3 A have had	B had had	C had
4 A a good value	B good value	C good values
5 A went	B turned	C wore

/5

Total   /30

7 Complete the text with the correct form of the words in brackets.

A VERY GOOD NOISE

To many people there is nothing more annoying than the sound of a child banging on drums or making loud screeching noises when they practise on a violin. But in fact, a child who shows an interest in music should receive _encouragement_ (ENCOURAGE).

It turns out that playing a musical instrument has many benefits. Firstly, experts agree that because of the level of focus required, learning an instrument can help in the ¹_____ (MEMORISE) of facts such as historical dates and mathematical formulae. What's more, few people would argue that it's a better form of ²_____ (ENGAGE) than, for example, playing computer games or spending time on social media.

A musician in the home can also provide ³_____ (ENTERTAIN) at family meetings and, with the ⁴_____ (ACCOMPANY) of other family members either singing or playing along, can be both a fun and ⁵_____ (DEEP) engaging way to spend time together with loved ones at a special time of year.

/5

8 Choose the correct answers A–C.

What it takes to have a hit

Have you ever wondered why some series become hugely successful while others don't? What is their secret? Here are a few ideas:

1 The series has to come _A_ at the right time, for example when the book it is based on is still very popular.

2 It should be ¹__ on a widely-available platform so that many people have access to it.

3 It should contain a(n) ²__ of surprise. When shows are too predictable, their popularity soon wears ³__ . And, of course, every episode needs to end with a cliffhanger.

4 Having big names in the ⁴__ is not that important – it is enough if the actors are able to create characters that feel real.

5 Great ⁵__ don't really matter that much either – usually people start watching a series when a friend recommends it.

	Ⓐ out	B in	C off
1	A released	B streamed	C played
2	A element	B span	C part
3	A out	B off	C away
4	A cast	B audience	C venue
5	A charts	B contracts	C reviews

/5

9 Complete the second sentence so that it has a similar meaning to the first one. Use between two and five words, including the word in capitals.

'The guests became emotional during the presentation.' **STIRRED**
Luke said that the presentation _stirred up the guests'_ emotions.

1 Was understanding the plot of this book easy?
FOLLOW
Did you _____ the plot of this book?

2 Alicia Vikander stars as Lara Croft in the new *Tomb Raider* films. **PART**
Alicia Vikander _____
Lara Croft in the new *Tomb Raider* films.

3 The popularity of the sculpture completely surprised me. **BY**
I was completely _____
the popularity of the new sculpture.

4 The film *Bohemian Rhapsody* is about the life of Freddie Mercury and his band Queen. **ON**
The film *Bohemian Rhapsody*
_____ the life of
Freddie Mercury and his band Queen.

5 I was so happy when my book received positive reviews. **REVIEWED**
I was so happy when my book was
_____ .

/5

10 Choose the correct answers A–C.

Jonathan told us that he ___ a recording contract with Mercury Records.
A just signed   Ⓑ had just signed
C has just signed

1 Seeing and hearing Josie sing karaoke that evening ___ . It was so funny.
A I should only smile   B I would only laugh
C really made me laugh

2 Jason informed us that our advert with the bird playing drums ___ .
A has gone viral   B had gone viral
C had been a virus

3 You should never ___ when they are trying their hardest.
A be too critical of somebody
B be a critic of somebody
C be criticised by somebody

4 I only ever buy paper books because I prefer ___ .
A reading old-fashioned books
B old-fashioned reading
C to read the old-fashioned way

5 Adam said that the loud music ___ concentrate on his work.
A distracts him and he can't
B was distracting him and he couldn't
C was a distraction which he couldn't

/5

Total   /20

8 Modern society

VOCABULARY

8.1

Crime and criminals
• people involved in a crime case
• the justice system

SHOW WHAT YOU KNOW

1 Complete the information with the words from the box. There are two extra words.

> city   elections   people   politics   population
> prime   state   system   ~~United~~

FACTSFOCUS.COM   [US politics   🔍]

You searched for ... US politics here are the best results:

There are 50 states in the _United_ States of America. The total **1**_____ of the US is over 300 million. Washington D.C. is the capital **2**_____ . The political **3**_____ is called a Federal Constitutional Republic. There isn't a **4**_____ minister in the US. The President is the head of the government and also the head of **5**_____ . The American people choose the president in presidential **6**_____ every four years.

WORD STORE 8A | Crime and criminals

2 Look at the crime report and complete the sentences. The first letters are given.

Last year's city crime figures:
5 people killed . . . . (up 20%)
68 houses robbed . . . .(down 17%)
43 people attacked and robbed . . . . (up 4%)
114 car thefts . . . . (up 12%)
122 buildings attacked (windows broken, graffiti, etc.) . .(down 1%)

Last year …
5 people were **m**_urdered_
1   68 houses were **b**_____
2   43 people were **m**_____
3   114 cars were **s**_____
4   122 buildings were **v**_____

3 Choose the correct verb to complete the sentences. You may need to change the form of the verb.

DEAL / STEAL
1   a   The teenager that _dealt_ drugs outside the cinema was arrested and charged.
   b   Somebody _____ my wallet from my bag yesterday.

MUG / MURDER
2   a   I read that another person was _____ in the High Street last night. Fortunately, they only took his money and his phone and didn't hurt him.
   b   See, the man wasn't _____ after all – it was an accident.

PIRATE / SHOPLIFT
3   a   Plenty of shops use basic methods of security to stop people from _____ things.
   b   Many countries are becoming stricter on cyber-criminals who _____ software and stream films or music illegally.

ROB / BURGLE
4   a   Hank was _____ last week on the way home. They took his wallet and smartphone.
   b   Most of the people that try to _____ a house aren't professional criminals.

SET / VANDALISE
5   a   The statue of the famous politician was _____ by protesters.
   b   The protesters _____ fire to a car and then ran through the park to escape the police.

4 Choose the correct words.

1   Police statements claim that last week's fire at the NuVu Cinema was *arson / arsonist*

2   'My life as a *drug dealer / drug dealing*.' Read our shocking interview with an ex-criminal

3   DVD *piracy / pirate* falls as more people download films legally online

4   Film star tells her terrible secret: 'I was a celebrity *shoplifter / shoplifting*'

5   Police question students after *thieves / thefts* steal exam papers from city school

6   Street cameras fail to decrease the number of *vandalism / vandal* cases in local area

7   High Street *robbery / robber* caught by 78-year-old Maggie Pearson

8   Government announces *muggings / muggers* to get stricter sentences

9   *Burglary / Burglar* gets away with cat worth £5,000

10   Investigation continues into *murder / murderer* of Count Wardling

WORD STORE 8B | People involved in a crime case

5 Choose the correct answers A–C.

Conversation 1

Al: Do you know any ¹__ ?

Bea: Yes, I do. My next door neighbour was arrested for drug dealing.

Al: Really? What happened?

Bea: Very early one morning, five ²__ came round and took her away. The case went to court and the ³__ sentenced her to five years in prison.

1 A criminals   B arsonists   C judges
2 A muggers   B police officers C burglars
3 A victim   B suspect   C judge

Conversation 2

Agnes: Have you ever been a ⁴__ of a crime?

Ben: Luckily not, but I have been a ⁵__ . I saw a woman get mugged and have her handbag stolen.

Agnes: Wow. Did you have to give evidence to the police?

Ben: Sure. I described the man who did it and they arrested a ⁶__ . Then I had to point him out from a line of men that looked alike.

4 A suspect   B victim   C criminal
5 A murderer   B pirate   C witness
6 A victim   B suspect   C judge

WORD STORE 8C | The justice system

6 Complete the court notes with the words from the box. There are three extra words.

> arrested   charged   collected   ~~committed~~
> ended   guilty   interviewed   not guilty
> released   sentenced   went

Case number 004256

Notes:

25/01 a crime (burglary) was _committed_.

26/01 a suspect was ¹_____ and ²_____ with a crime.

26/01 the victim and suspect were ³_____.

27/01 evidence was ⁴_____.

14/03 the case ⁵_____ to court.

14/03 the judge decided the man was ⁶_____.

16/03 the man was ⁷_____ to 16 months in prison.

---

7 Complete each pair of sentences with the same answer A–C.

1 Lena's grandmother was __ on the London underground train going from Northwood Hills to Watford.
   Four men __ a bank and then drove away in a blue van.
   A stolen   B robbed   C mugged

2 The detective __ evidence from the scene of the crime and put it secretly in his pocket.
   Everybody I knew __ stamps as a hobby when I was a kid.
   A collected   B made   C watched

3 The accused was __ and sent to prison for three years.
   Have you __ your phone?
   A charged   B sentenced   C committed

4 Three teenagers were arrested for dealing __ in the nightclub.
   The doctor gave my aunt some strong __ to cure her illness.
   A medicine   B items   C drugs

5 How many points did the __ give the last singer?
   You must be very responsible to be a __ in a court of law.
   A judge   B suspect   C witness

6 The __ was once a successful local businessman.
   Ella __ me of using her laptop without asking her first.
   A murdered   B robbed   C accused

7 The police __ everybody in the room to find a suspect.
   Hey look! It's the woman that __ me for that accountancy job last week.
   A chatted   B spoke   C interviewed

8 Did you know that Beyoncé has __ a new album? It came out on Monday.
   The police __ me because I'm not guilty, that's why!
   A sentenced   B released   C committed

9 After four years the trial finally __ and everybody could return to their normal lives.
   I won't tell you how the book __ but be prepared for a surprise.
   A ended   B stopped   C closed

10 Apparently, somebody __ fire to the school on Sunday but very little damage was done.
   I'd like to __ up my own business as a jeweller one day in the future.
   A did   B set   C put

/10

GRAMMAR

8.2

The Passive

1 Complete the sentences with the correct passive form of the verbs in brackets. Use short forms.

YouTube *was started* (start) by an American, a Taiwanese and a Bangladeshi.

1 YouTube _____ (create) on Valentine's Day 2005.

2 The first video, called 'Me at the Zoo' _____ (not/post) until April 2005.

3 Currently, around a hundred hours of video _____ (upload) to YouTube every minute.

4 'Gangnam Style' by Psy _____ (watch) more than 2 billion times since it was posted.

5 YouTube _____ (buy) by Google in 2006 for US$1.65 billion.

6 A lot of money _____ (make) by people who have started successful YouTube channels.

2 ★ Choose the correct forms.

1 The crown jewels of England *have kept / have been kept* at the Tower of London for over 600 years.

2 *Will the student meeting be held / Will we hold the student meeting* in the cafeteria?

3 Until recently, prisoners in this jail *weren't being given / weren't giving* basic medical care.

4 Jennifer's dress *didn't design / wasn't designed* by Marc Jacobs. It's an Armani.

5 The plants are dying because they *aren't watering / aren't being watered* regularly.

6 *Are the school gates unlocked / Do they lock the school gates* at 8 a.m. every morning?

3 ★★ Read Kitty's message then complete the sentences with the correct passive forms.

Hi Henry,

Robin and I have finally organised everything for Nina's leaving party. We're not holding it at Big Mike's Burger Restaurant anymore, because they are renovating the place that weekend ☹. Anyway, we have decided that we will hold it at Pizza Land instead (Nina's dad hasn't paid the deposit yet, but he promised to do it soon). The Eatout website recommends Pizza Land, so it should be OK. I invited Jim, but unfortunately he can't make it. Everyone else has said yes, so there will be 9 of us. A mini-bus will pick everyone up from Robin's house at 6 p.m.

C U then ☺

Kitty xx

Everything *has been organised* by Robin and Kitty.

1 The party _____ at Big Mike's Burger Restaurant.

2 Big Mike's Burger Restaurant _____ that weekend.

3 Instead, the party _____ at Pizza Land.

4 The deposit _____ by Nina's dad yet.

5 Pizza Land _____ by Eatout.

6 Jim _____ by Kitty but he can't make it.

7 Everyone _____ from Robin's house at 6 p.m.

4 ★★★ Make the active sentences passive and add *by + person/thing* to the sentences using the words in the box.

the amateur theatre group   the director and the editor
~~the factory workers~~   the Kenyan runner   the nurse
the Physics teacher

They produce 100 mobile phones per hour here.
100 mobile phones per hour are produced here *by the factory workers*.

1 We are performing *Les Miserables* this year.

_____
this year _____ .

2 She injected me with a steroid.

_____
with a steroid _____ .

3 They were editing the film at the studio.

_____
at the studio _____ .

4 He has broken the marathon world record again.

_____
again _____ .

5 She will give out the exam papers in five minutes.

_____
in five minutes _____ .

5 Complete the notices with the correct forms of the verbs in brackets.

This bridge *was rebuilt* (rebuild) in 2010 using EU funds.

1 Tomorrow at 2 p.m. the water _____ (turn off) for half an hour.

2 The swimming pool _____ (clean) at the moment and will reopen in 20 minutes.

3 My bike _____ (steal) from here last night. Please call 409 709 if you saw or heard anything.

4 Rubbish _____ (collect) once a week on a Thursday morning.

5 This week's prize _____ (not/collect). Please check your ticket and contact us if you are the winner.

6 The council removed the recycling bins from this location as they _____ (not/use). Your nearest bins are now at the end of Pope Street.

/6

GRAMMAR: Train and Try Again page 161

LISTENING LANGUAGE PRACTICE

Collocations • prison

1 Read the interview between the presenter and Daniel. Choose the correct verb patterns to follow the verbs in bold a–h.

Extract from Student's Book recording 🔊 **3.30**

P: How many of the other young offenders were as motivated as you [...]?

D: Not many. A lot of them are happy the way they are and don't **want** ᵃ*to change / changing.*

P: Is it true that some young offenders **like** ᵇ*be / being* in prison because they have a better life inside than outside?

D: Yeah. That's definitely true. One of my mates was homeless ¹___ he came ²___ prison. He was worried ³___ being released – ⁴___ prison he got food and clean clothes and a warm cell. Outside, he was living in a box ⁵___ the street. The day he was released, he walked ⁶___ the prison car park and smashed the windows on five cars in the car park. He was back here ⁷___ a few days.

P: Hm, well that brings me to another point. The government **want** ᶜ*to improve / improving* conditions in young offenders' prisons. But some people say that this is wrong. They say that these are young people who have committed crimes and they **should** ᵈ*to be punished / be punished.* One prison guard said, 'They have education, they have a gym and television – it's like a holiday camp!' What do you say to that?

D: But it's not a holiday camp – we can't see our friends or our family. Doors are locked. I don't want to go back there. If you want young people to change, you **can't** ᵉ*lock / to lock* them in a cell and **expect them** ᶠ*changing / to change.* You **have to** ᵍ*educate / educating* them and **make them** ʰ*believe / to believe* that there is a better life in front of them. Simple as that.

2 Choose the correct prepositions A–C to complete gaps 1–7.

1 **A** after	**B** before	**C** during
2 **A** onto	**B** by	**C** into
3 **A** about	**B** for	**C** of
4 **A** on	**B** to	**C** in
5 **A** by	**B** on	**C** along
6 **A** into	**B** in	**C** on
7 **A** with	**B** before	**C** in

3 Use the prompts in bold to complete the prisoners' words with the correct verb patterns and tenses.

should / be
You *should be* very careful who you talk to. There are some very dangerous men in here.

1 **not want / leave**
I _____ prison because outside, I'll be homeless, jobless and poor.

2 **not expect / anyone / visit**
Well, I really _____ me now while I'm in here. I never had any friends and my family don't speak to me after what I did.

3 **have to / spend**
Most days, we _____ 22 hours in our cells. We only come out for meals and exercise.

4 **make / us / clean**
The prison guards _____ our cells every morning last week.

5 **like / share**
Nobody in here _____ a cell. One of the worst things about prison-life is the lack of privacy.

6 **can't / remember**
I've been locked up for so long that I _____ what it feels like to be free.

WORD STORE 8D | Prison

4 Choose the correct verbs from the box to complete the pairs of sentences. Change the form if necessary. There are two extra words.

> ~~break~~   have   lock   make
> punish   release   serve   take

a You *broke* the rules of the game, so you have to go back to the beginning.

b My mum says she has never *broken* the law in her life, but I don't believe her.

1 **a** On holiday in Greece last year, Dad was _____ up in a cell for two days because the police thought he was someone else. It sounds funny now but it was terrifying at the time.

b Joanne said she is just _____ the office and will be here in five minutes.

2 **a** In the UK, you can be _____ with a £1,000 fine for dangerous cycling.

b Although the football player received a red card, the referee did not _____ the team further by awarding a penalty kick.

3 **a** It is unlikely that this man will ever be _____ from prison. He is simply too dangerous.

b Are they _____ your grandad from hospital?

4 **a** In our hotel breakfast is _____ from 6.00 to 11.30 a.m.

b My next door neighbour is _____ a sentence for cruelty to animals. They should have locked him up and thrown away the keys!

5 **a** Can you be an English teacher if you _____ a criminal record?

b Aunt Josephine _____ been a police officer for over twenty years and she still says it's the best job in the world!

The Shawshank Redemption
• definitions • verb phrases
• synonyms

1 Read the text quickly and decide why it was written.

1 To describe a film and give an update on its star's current work ☐

2 To describe a film which shows what life is like in modern prisons ☐

3 To describe a film in which prisoners were used as actors ☐

 Film Focus

A Portrait of Life <u>Inside</u>

A According to many viewers and critics, *The Shawshank Redemption** is one of the greatest films ever made. It is a prison-drama adapted from a short story by Stephen King, and in the year of its release, it was nominated for 7 Oscars including best actor, best picture, best screenplay based on another source and best cinematography. Although it is set <u>behind bars</u>, it tells a heart-warming story of friendship and hope. It did not make a lot of money when it was first shown in cinemas and it won none of the awards for which it was nominated, but today it is loved by fans of cinema everywhere around the world. In fact, since 2008, it has been the number one film on the well-known film review website IMDB (Internet Movie Database). This puts it one place above Francis Ford Coppola's classic mafia movie *The Godfather* from 1972, starring acting legends Marlon Brando and Al Pacino.

B Set shortly after the end of the Second World War in the mid-1940s, *The Shawshank Redemption* tells the fictional story of Andy Dufresne, a young and successful banker who is <u>convicted</u> of the murder of his wife and her lover. Based in the state of Portland, Maine, one of nineteen American states without the death penalty, Andy is instead <u>sentenced to life imprisonment</u> in Shawshank Prison. Over the next twenty years, Andy, played by actor Tim Robbins, learns to adapt to life in prison with the help of his friend Ellis 'Red' Redding, an older <u>convict</u> played by Hollywood favourite Morgan Freeman. It would ruin the film to give away too many further details of the story here. However, it won't spoil it to say that the plot shows the power of hope, courage and determination, even in situations that at times seem incredibly cruel and hopeless.

C *The Shawshank Redemption* was filmed in the early nineties, and to prepare for his starring role, Tim Robbins spent time locked up alone in a real prison <u>cell</u>. Now, more than 20 years later, Robbins is back in prison. Thankfully, he is not there as an <u>inmate</u> this time, but as a teacher who gives acting lessons to prisoners in a medium-security <u>jail</u> in California. The project has been running for several years with the help of a theatre company* called 'The Actor's Gang,' which was started by Robbins in the 1980s. In an interview with CBS News, Robbins explained that the opportunity to act provides prisoners with a break from prison routine and a chance to explore new emotions and realities. When he was asked whether prisons should be offering such enjoyable activities to inmates who have been found guilty of serious crimes, Robbins replied that the acting classes were not about having a good time but were actually hard work which was physically tough and required* a high level of discipline, commitment* and courage. He also said that none of the prisoners who completed the programme had <u>reoffended</u> and returned to prison after they were <u>released</u>.

GLOSSARY

redemption *(n formal)* – saving someone or being saved from evil
theatre company *(n)* – a group of actors, dancers or singers who work together

require *(v)* – need
commitment *(n, u)* – the hard work and loyalty someone gives to an organisation, activity, etc.

2 Read the text again. Match sentences 1–4 to paragraphs A–C. Two sentences match one paragraph.

1 The film does not present a pessimistic view of relationships between people. ☐

2 Tim Robbins experienced life as a prisoner to add authenticity to his performance. ☐

3 *The Shawshank Redemption* is not based on real-life characters or events. ☐

4 The film became more appreciated by audiences years after it was made. ☐

3 Read the text again. Choose the correct answer A–D.

1 Which of the following is true about *The Shawshank Redemption*?
A It got many movie awards.
B It was based on a book.
C It was a financial success.
D It has always been popular.

2 What do we learn about the plot of the film?
A It is based on events that really happened.
B Its hero faces capital punishment.
C It shows the cruelty of inmates.
D It is about not giving up in life.

3 Why did Tim Robbins go back to prison?
A He wanted to share his acting skills with people who had committed crimes.
B He became an inmate to be able to take up acting lessons.
C He tried to recreate his starring role in the same conditions.
D He wanted to see what it was like to be locked up again.

4 In his interview with CBS news Tim Robbins talked about
A why he took a break from his routine.
B the true nature of being an actor.
C the purpose of prison activities.
D why his students turned to crime.

4 Match the definitions with underlined words and phrases in the text.

two informal phrases meaning 'in prison'

inside & *behind bars*

1 two phrases meaning 'prisoner'
_____ & _____
2 another word for 'prison' _____
3 found guilty of a crime _____
4 sent to prison for life by a judge _____
5 a small room in which prisoners are locked _____
6 let out of prison _____
7 committed another crime after leaving prison
_____

REMEMBER BETTER

In addition to translations of useful words and phrases in your vocabulary notes, try to write definitions in English if you can. This will help you increase your range of vocabulary and encourage you to think in English, not in your own language.

VOCABULARY PRACTICE | Verb phrases

5 Look at the vocabulary in lesson 8.4 in the Student's Book. Complete the sentences with the words from the box.

> advantage day deed difference
> hand ~~return~~ reward suspicion time

A true favour is when you ask for nothing in *return*.

1 I like doing volunteer work because I feel like I'm making a real _____ .

2 The woman in the shop gave me back too much money. When I tried to explain the mistake, I was met with _____ . Unbelievable!

3 It costs nothing to do a good _____ such as help somebody with their bags or hold a door open for them.

4 Don't rush, Will. Take _____ to do it properly or don't do it at all!

5 When somebody doesn't thank me for helping them, I always feel they've taken _____ of me.

6 Look at that poster. The owners are offering a _____ of £200 to the person who finds their lost cat.

7 When Alice agreed to go out with me on Saturday, it really made my _____ .

8 Mina is so kind. She's always offering me a helping _____ because she knows I have trouble working and studying at the same time.

WORD STORE 8E | Synonyms

6 Complete the radio interview with the correct words. The first few letters are given.

C: On the line right now we have a caller who would like to remain **anon***ymous* . Let's call him Jim. Hello, Jim.

J: Hi, Carol. First I'd like to say that I know I have a **¹sus**_____ mind sometimes. After all, I am a detective. However, I really feel that the **²cyn**_____ remarks made by your colleague Brian Fray about rising crime are no **³triv**_____ matter. It's a big deal! And as a police officer I took the comments very personally.

C: OK, Jim. Please continue …

J: Well, to begin with I know that both myself and my colleagues are **⁴ful**_____ in our work. We get a great sense of satisfaction catching criminals and protecting innocent people. So, when somebody says the police do not care about crime … for me that's a **⁵maj**_____ issue. Furthermore, I think it's highly irresponsible of your journalist colleague to say this and I want him to resign.

C: You want Brian Fray to resign? Because of what he said?

J: That would be **⁶wel**_____ news, yes. Today, ideally.

C: Well, we'll need to … oh, hang on! Brian has just walked into the studio. Brian? Brian, are you OK?

B: I've just been mugged. Right outside the studio. What do you think about that, Jim? Jim? Are you there, Jim?

1 Complete the sentences with verbs from the box. Change the forms if necessary. There are two extra verbs.

> build ~~cut~~ fix massage
> pierce redecorate whiten

Dean *cut* his own hair. It looked terrible.

1 Meggy _____ her own teeth. After two weeks she couldn't see any difference.
2 Mike attempted to _____ his own back. He couldn't reach.
3 Martha wanted to _____ her own ears. She wasn't brave enough.
4 George tried to _____ his own computer. He made it worse.

2 ★ Choose the correct option to complete the sentences and questions about the people in Exercise 1. Then fill the gaps with the correct profession from the box. There are two extra words in the box.

> body piercer dentist doctor ~~hairdresser~~
> physiotherapist mechanic technician

Now, Dean ᵃ*cuts his hair* / *has his hair cut* by a ᵇ*hairdresser*.

1 Next time, Meggy ᵃ*is whitening her teeth* / *is going to have her teeth whitened* by a ᵇ_____ .
2 Mike ᵃ*didn't massage his back* / *didn't have his back massaged* by a ᵇ_____ .
3 Why didn't Martha ᵃ*pierce her ears* / *have her ears pierced* by a ᵇ_____ ?
4 After he failed to do it himself, George ᵃ*fixed his computer* / *had his computer fixed* by a ᵇ_____ .

3 ★★ Look at Paris's list. Complete the sentences and questions with the correct form of *have/get something done*.

Paris's beauty list

Every week:
  Hair washed and styled (get)
  1 Nails painted (get)

Last month:
  2 Eyebrows shaped (have)
  3 A facial done (get/?)

Next Month:
  4 Back massaged (have)

Already done this year:
  5 Tattoo removed (have)

Still to do:
  6 Teeth whitened (have)

Paris *gets her hair washed and styled* every week.

1 Paris _____ every week.
2 Last month, she _____ .
3 Did she _____ last month?
4 Next month, she _____ .
5 She _____ already _____ this year.
6 She _____ yet this year.

4 ★★★ Complete the dialogue between a TV presenter and Clara with the correct form of *have something done*. Use short forms.

P: Today in the studio we have teenage author Clara Dickens, whose book *Bringing up my Parents* became an international bestseller. Clara, has success changed you?

C: Well, I guess I'm the same person. I have the same friends and go to the same school and still work hard. I mean I *don't have my homework done* (not/do/homework) for me or anything, but yes, in some ways life is different now.

P: How is it different?

C: Well, I'm not like a big Hollywood celebrity or whatever, but I'm into fashion and stuff, so since my success, I ¹_____ (make/some nice clothes) for me. Oh, and I also have very big feet, so I used to find it difficult to find shoes that fit, but now I ²_____ (design and fit/shoes) especially for me.

P: What about your parents, the subject of your book?

C: Well, I couldn't have done it without them, so I wanted to thank them, of course. At the moment, we ³_____ (redecorate/house), and Mum is going to the dentist regularly because she ⁴_____ (completely redo/her teeth). Dad likes old motorbikes, so he ⁵_____ (build/new garage) for his bikes.

P: Great. So let's talk about your new book …

5 Rewrite the sentences and questions using the correct form of *have something done*.

We changed the locks after the burglary.
We *had the locks changed* after the burglary.

1 Fiona colours her hair green every year for St Patrick's Day.
  Fiona _____ every year for St Patrick's Day.
2 A doctor is checking Isobel's eyes on Friday.
  Isobel _____ on Friday.
3 Unfortunately, they didn't deliver Scott's package yesterday.
  Unfortunately, Scott _____ yesterday.
4 Is somebody redecorating your aunt's kitchen at the moment?
  Is your aunt _____ at the moment?
5 Have they repaired your bike yet, Paul?
  Have you _____ yet, Paul?
6 Linda and Beth don't whiten their teeth.
  Linda and Beth _____ .

/6

GRAMMAR: Train and Try Again page 161

1 ★ **Choose the correct answers A–C.**

1 **Flora:** How long have you and Sally known ___ ?
 Janine: Since we were five, I think.
 A yourselves
 B yourself
 C each other

2 **Toby:** Can you show me how to shut down these computers?
 Lou: Don't worry, they turn ___ off after 5 minutes.
 A itself
 B themselves
 C one another

3 **Haley:** Why is Mary taking up karate?
 Tammy: She wants to learn how to protect ___ .
 A herself
 B by herself
 C her

4 **Earnest:** I need your help to write this newsletter.
 Hugh: Why can't you do it ___ ?
 A by myself
 B yourself
 C itself

5 **Ashley:** Shall we ask Whitney to help us with the project?
 Mark: No, I think we should do it ___ .
 A each other
 B one another
 C ourselves

2 ★ ★ **Complete the sentences with the correct form of the words from the box and reflexive pronouns. There is one extra word.**

> blame cut ~~enjoy~~ introduce love
> prepare repair teach wash

The party was great. We really *enjoyed ourselves* .

1 It wasn't your fault, Larry. Don't _____ .
2 Jenny didn't have a Spanish teacher. She _____ .
3 It's better to have two cats rather than just one! They both stay cleaner because they _____ .
4 Be careful with that knife. You might _____ .
5 Adam and I are getting married. We really _____ .
6 The two new students walked into the room and _____ .
7 I passed my driving test first time because I really _____ .

3 ★ ★ **Complete the text with the missing words.**

A helping hand

Have you ever asked *yourself* what you can do to make the world a better place? One thing you can do is volunteer and help others who may be unable to help ¹_____ . This is exactly what Nigel Courtney did. Nigel, 16, first volunteered last year by helping an elderly neighbour, Arthur, in his garden. The garden is large and because Arthur is old, he is unable to care for the garden ²_____ . 'I can't manage by ³_____ ,' said Arthur, 'but with Nigel's help the garden now looks great once again.'

Soon, Nigel found ways to help others too: 'I noticed that many homeless people have dogs for company because they get lonely living by ⁴_____ . The owners love their dogs but they have problems getting food for them.' Nigel arranged for donations of dog food to be collected outside a supermarket and then distributed among the homeless. Does Nigel really expect nothing in return for his efforts? 'Helping other people is a reward in itself,' he said. 'I'm happy to help other people and truly believe that we should all help ⁵_____ . Maybe one day when I need help, somebody will be there for me.'

4 ★ ★ ★ **Complete the second sentence so that it has a similar meaning to the first. Use no more than six words, including the word in capitals.**

Stacy and Lou painted their own house.
BY
Stacy and Lou *painted their house by themselves*.

1 Paul and Andy refused to shake hands.
 ANOTHER
 Paul and Andy didn't want _____
 _____ .

2 Jo isn't very good at saying what she means.
 EXPRESS
 Jo finds it _____
 _____ .

3 The three boys decided to tidy the park without the help of others.
 BY
 The three boys decided to _____
 _____ .

4 Adam and Mateo – please stop misbehaving!
 BEHAVE
 Adam and Mateo – please _____
 _____ !

5 When did Hugh and Justin start to work together?
 EACH
 How long have Hugh and Justin _____
 _____ ?

WRITING

8.7
An opinion essay

1 Complete the linkers in the sentences. The first and last letters are given.

1 To b**egin** with, I think it's wrong to suggest …

2 I w_____d like to p_____t o_____t that not everyone feels the same about …

3 For i_____e, there are currently several female prime ministers who …

4 It s_____s to me t_____t we need to change our attitude towards …

5 L_____y, we must not forget that …

6 In c_____n, if we are really serious about saving the planet, then …

7 P_____t another w_____y, it is not acceptable for children to …

8 M_____r, such changes would also benefit …

2 Match linkers from Exercise 1 to each description.

A introduce body paragraphs   ①&⃝

B give personal opinion   ⃝&⃝

C give examples ⃝

D add further support ⃝

E emphasise a point by repeating it ⃝

F introduce the conclusion ⃝

3 Read the sentences A–I from an opinion essay and then put the essay in the correct order.

A ① I grew up with two loving parents, both of whom spent as much time with me as possible and gave me the attention and care that I needed.

B ⃝ This is because they carry the baby for nine months when they are pregnant and then, in most cases, feed them directly when they are first born.

C ⃝ However, I do believe that women make better parents than men.

D ⃝ To begin with, mothers have a greater physical connection to their child than a father.

E ⃝ Finally, in many households it is still traditionally women who stay at home to look after a child while fathers go to work.

F ⃝ For example, many young girls prefer to play with dolls and look after them like real children rather than play (or fight) in the park like young boys tend to do.

G ⃝ Secondly, women tend to be less aggressive and more sensitive than men. They also have a natural tendency to show affection and care for others.

H ⃝ In conclusion, there are a number of physical and social factors which make women better parents. Although more and more fathers are looking after their children at home nowadays, the physical bond between a father and child can never be as close as that between mothers and their children.

I ⃝ In my view, young children are therefore very familiar and comfortable with being cared for by the mother and many young girls see this as a role that they themselves will have one day.

4 Read another essay below and decide which question the student has answered.

1 Do children really need both a mother and a father to bring them up? ⃝

2 Why are mothers generally thought to be better parents than fathers? ⃝

3 Which of your parents had the biggest influence on you as a child? ⃝

5 Replace the words in bold with linkers from Exercise 1. Sometimes more than one answer is possible.

I was raised by my mother and father and benefited from the influence of them both during my childhood. **As far as I am concerned** 2 or 4, men and women may provide different things for their children and influence them in different ways, but it is incorrect to suggest that women are better parents than men.

First of all / ᵃ_____ , it seems to me that in the early years the physical connection between mother and child is often stronger than with the father. This is almost certainly because the woman carried the child inside her for nine months and because she is able to feed the child with her own milk. However, **in my view** / ᵇ_____ this does not mean she is a better parent. For instance, fathers who hold, bathe, dress and change their babies can also develop strong physical bonds with their children. **In addition** / ᶜ_____ , many babies are fed from a bottle meaning that a father can feed his child just as well as a mother.

Next, I would like to point out that both parents are equally able to entertain, educate and care for their child as it grows. Often women spend more time with young children because many couples decide that the man will go to work and the woman will stay with the children. However, this does not make the man any worse as a parent. **For example** / ᵈ_____ , if the woman went to work and the man stayed at home, there is no reason why he could not look after the child just as well as his partner.

Finally / ᵉ_____ , men and women are equally able to provide good role models for their children. Of course, it seems logical that girls will learn more about being female from their mother, but the opposite is also probably true. **In other words** / ᶠ_____ , boys will probably learn more about what it means to be male from their father. In addition, it is almost certainly more important that parents teach their children to be good people, regardless of their gender, and men and women are equally able to do this.

In summary / ᵍ_____ , I think men and women are equally good at being parents, and I also think that the ideal approach for parents and children is for partners to share the responsibility for raising a family.

6 **Read the task below. Then read the essay and complete gaps 1–9 with the correct words A–D.**

> Is prison the best way to teach young criminals to be better citizens? Write an opinion essay in which you express your opinion. Include and develop these points:
> - State whether you agree or disagree with the question.
> - Provide arguments to support your personal opinion.

Most people agree that somebody who commits a crime should ¹_____ . **A**_In addition / As far as I am concerned_, however, and especially in the case of young offenders, we can do more than lock them ²_____ in a cell.

B_To begin with / Moreover_, the fact that these criminals are young means new skills and patterns of behaviour can still ³_____ . Instead of making them serve a ⁴_____ in prison where they may become more aggressive, anti-social, and possibly continue committing crimes in the future, there are programmes to help them become better citizens.

C_Put another way / For instance_, in Australia there are organisations in which young criminals help train dogs that care for disabled people. **D**_I would like to point out / In addition,_ that in this kind of work both patience and a sense of responsibility ⁵_____ . **E**_In my view / Moreover_, a large part of training these animals stresses rewarding good behaviour, which can be a valuable lesson to the youngsters who have ⁶_____ the law.

F_Finally / For example_, while working with the dogs, the young offenders learn compassion towards others. They gain confidence in their own abilities and develop skills which help them find employment in the future. **G**_In addition / In other words_, tests show they become less likely to harm ⁷_____ or others.

H_Secondly / In summary_, a young criminal ⁸_____ the chance to be a better person. Instead of punishing them ⁹_____ , we can help them to become valuable members of a community. **I**_In my view / For instance_, taking this opportunity away from them is harmful both to the individual and to society as a whole.

1	**A** punish		**B** punished	
	C be punished		**D** punishment	
2	**A** out		**B** up	
	C off		**D** down	
3	**A** learn		**B** be learnt	
	C to be learnt		**D** learning	
4	**A** crime		**B** judge	
	C prison		**D** sentence	
5	**A** are needed		**B** is needed	
	C will be needed		**D** were needed	
6	**A** broke		**B** been broken	
	C broken		**D** breaking	
7	**A** each other		**B** themselves	
	C yourself		**D** ourselves	
8	**A** can give		**B** should be given	
	C is given		**D** gives	
9	**A** badly		**B** awfully	
	C hardly		**D** severely	

Read the essay again and choose the correct answers A–I.

8 **If young people behave badly, should their parents accept responsibility and also be punished? Write an opinion essay. Include and develop these points.**
- State whether you agree or disagree with the question.
- Provide arguments to support your personal opinion.

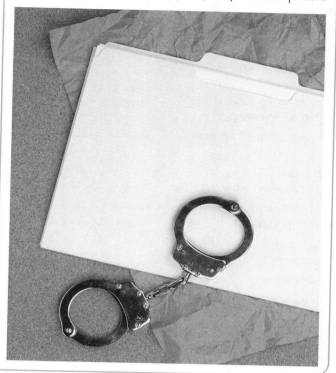

SHOW THAT YOU'VE CHECKED

Finished? Always check your writing. Can you tick ✓ everything on this list?

In my opinion essay:

• in the introductory paragraph I have introduced the topic and clearly stated my point of view.	☐
• in the body of the essay I have included two or three paragraphs with more detailed personal opinions and supported these with reasons and examples.	☐
• in the conclusion I have included a summary of my main point of view and used different words to the statement in the introduction.	☐
• in the conclusion I have included a final comment which leaves the reader with something to think about.	☐
• I have used a variety of linkers to help the reader to follow my essay.	☐
• I have used formal language.	☐
• I have not used emoticons ☺ or abbreviations (info / CU / gr8).	☐
• I have checked my spelling and punctuation.	☐
• My text is neat and clear.	☐

SPEAKING

Opinions: talking about advantages and disadvantages

1 Translate the phrases into your own language.

SPEAKING BANK

Talking about your skills and interests

(Cooking) isn't my thing at all. _____

You're really good at (Maths/swimming). _____

I'm not (patient) enough. _____

I'd rather (visit an elderly person). _____

I'm really into (vintage clothes). _____

Giving and explaining an opinion

In my opinion … _____

To be honest, I think/don't think … _____

What I mean is … _____

In fact … _____

Talking about advantages and disadvantages

There are a lot of advantages/disadvantages … _____

One/Another benefit is that … _____

The main advantage of voluntary work is that … _____

There are drawbacks too. _____

One of the main disadvantages of voluntary work is that … _____

Another disadvantage of voluntary work is that … _____

2 Complete the dialogue between Rachel and Leah. The first letters are given.

R: I've decided I want to **d**o **s**omething **t**o **h**elp **o**ther **p**eople, Leah. The thing is I don't know what I could do. Have you got any ideas?

L: Well, you're ¹**r**_____ **g**_____ **a**_____ making conversation. Why don't you volunteer to call on an elderly person and chat to them? You've always got something to say.

R: Are you saying I talk too much?

L: Ha ha! You? Talk too much? Of course not. Seriously though, I think you'd be really good at it. I'm ²**n**_____ patient **e**_____ myself. It wouldn't be my thing. ³**I**_____ **r**_____ organise a sale to raise money for charity, or something.

R: ⁴**T**_____ **b**_____ **h**_____ , I think I'd prefer to do that too. We could do it together. We could cook something and sell it during lunch break at school.

L: Cool. Actually, I talked to Katy and Sally about this yesterday and they ⁵**w**_____ **r**_____ **i**_____ the idea too. The four of us could bake some cakes and organise a sale together.

3 Complete the sentences with the singular or plural form of *advantage*, *disadvantage*, *benefit* or *drawback*. Use each word no more than twice.

1 One _benefit_ of being an only child is that you get all your parents' time and attention.
One of the main ᵃ_____ is that you don't have another young person to play with or talk to at home.
Another ᵇ_____ is that your parents might be overprotective because they only have one child.
Another ᶜ_____ though is that you don't have to share a room with your brother or sister.

2 There are ᵃ_____ to single-sex schools. For example teenagers are less distracted by the opposite sex while they are at school and tend to study more effectively as a result.
One of the main ᵇ_____ of single-sex schools is that boys and girls don't learn about their differences and similarities.
Another ᶜ_____ is that exam results are usually better in single-sex schools.
One ᵈ_____ is that one of the joys and challenges of being young is interacting with the opposite sex.

4 Choose the correct words to complete the dialogue.

Lena: In my ¹*opinion / meaning* there are a lot of ²*drawbacks / benefits* to being a man. For example, one of the main ³*disadvantages / advantages* is that it is easier for men to get highly-paid and powerful jobs.

Joey: I guess so, though in ⁴*fact / honest* I think that is slowly changing, isn't it? ⁵*How / What* I mean is there are more well-paid and high-powered women than there used to be.

Lena: Well, yes, but to be ⁶*true / honest*, I think there is still a long way to go.

Joey: I'm sure you're right, but it's not all great being a man, you know. There are ⁷*drawback / drawbacks* too.

Lena: For example?

Joey: Er … well, er … we have to shave every morning.

Lena: Oh, poor you! It must be awful. And you coul[d] cut yourself. How do you cope?

Joey: Are you being sarcastic, Lena?

Lena: Me? Never …

Student A, look below. Student B, go to page 141.

1 In pairs, ask and answer the questions.

Talk about entertainment.

1 Tell me about the last live concert you attended.
2 If you were a musician, would you rather sign a recording contract with a big music company or make music in small clubs? Why?
3 Would you prefer to be a great drummer, lead guitarist or singer-songwriter? Why?

4 Have you ever been to a music festival? What was it like?
5 Would you ever sign up for a reality TV programme? Why?/Why not?

2 Discuss this question together. 'Is the main purpose of a prison to punish a criminal or to help him/her not to break the law again when he/she is released?' What do you think?

3 Look at the two photos showing criminal activity. What can you see in the photos? Which do you think is more serious? Why?

A

B

4 Read the instructions on your card and role-play the conversation.

Student A:

The situation:
You and Student B are discussing placements for voluntary work. There are two places available: one is at a youth centre helping young people with their Maths and one is at an old people's home, keeping elderly people company. Discuss the advantages and disadvantages of both placements, talk about your skills and interests and decide which you will do.

Your goal:
You want to work at the old people's home.

VOCABULARY AND GRAMMAR

1 Complete each pair of sentences with the same answer A–C.

I don't believe that you have never __ the law.
Ouch! Ouch! Ahhhh! Oh my finger hurts so much!
I think it must be __ .
(A) broken B committed C released

1 The missing boy's father __ a reward for any information about his son.
I __ to pick Sally up after school, but she said 'no.'
A gave B asked C offered

2 I was surprised that after helping me Mike asked for absolutely __ in return.
Elizabeth said __ about the accident, not a word.
A nothing B anything C something

3 My request to leave school early was __ with suspicion by my teachers.
Have you ever __ somebody rich and famous?
A seen B met C watched

4 The fact that Charlotte remembered my birthday and gave me a call really __ my day.
Sean really didn't want to go to the party, so he __ an excuse and stayed at home.
A made B gave C did

5 The concert has become this summer's __ event.
My uncle was a sergeant __ in the army.
A serious B common C major

/5

2 Complete the sentences with the missing adjectives. The first letters are given.

I don't have a **s**uspicious mind. I just want to know where you were and who you were with.

1 I'm not **f**_____ in my job. I think I'll look for something more rewarding.

2 Many people that report a crime wish to remain **a**_____ and not give their name to the police.

3 I've never been arrested so no, I don't have a **c**_____ record.

4 Please stop being so **c**_____ . Can't you say something positive for a change?

5 The fact that you lied to me is not a **t**_____ matter. For me it's a big issue.

/5

3 Complete the sentences with the correct forms of the words in brackets.

I think Claudio _really took_ (real / take) advantage of me and won't repay my kindness and generosity.

1 The man _____ (severe / punish) for the crime.

2 The woman said she _____ (not / be / shoplift) but had simply forgotten to pay for the make-up.

3 After three weeks the police still had no idea who the _____ (arson / be).

4 There has been an increase in the number of _____ (violence / mug) in the area.

5 Phillip _____ (commit / pirate) when he copied the computer game for himself.

/5

4 Complete the sentences with the correct passive forms of the verbs from the box. There are two extra verbs.

burgle ~~find~~ finish hunt
miss put renovate wash

Painite is one of the rarest minerals on Earth. It _is found_ in Myanmar in south-eastern Asia.

1 The dodo, a large flightless bird, _____ until it disappeared completely in the 17th century.

2 Fiona's house _____ twice this year. How unlucky!

3 The old school sports hall _____ at the moment, so all our PE lessons are held on the field.

4 Our car _____ when the accident happened. The handbrake failed and the car rolled into the wall.

5 We're here to say goodbye to Mr Thomson. Mr Thomson, you _____ by all your students.

/5

5 Write sentences or questions from the prompts. Use the structure *have something done* and the correct tense.

suit / dry-clean
Charlie _had his suit dry-cleaned_ just before the wedding.

phone / fix
1 Emma _____ twice this month and today she's having problems with it again.

health / check
2 Our dog _____ by the vet later this afternoon. He hates the vet.

replace / headphones
3 I _____ free of charge when they stopped working after a week.

you / phone / take away
4 _____ ever _____ by the teacher?

make-up / do
5 _____ by a professional make-up artist? She looks amazing!

/5

6 Choose the correct answers A–C.

This year's School Charity Day is coming up next month. Any ideas for ways to raise money are always _B_ and, of course, anyone that wishes to offer a ¹__ hand on the day should let us know asap. Who can forget last year's big event when the head teacher ²__ by the school nurse? Or when the whole of year 7 ³__ and cleaned cars for money in the local village? In total, over £400 ⁴__ for the animal rescue centre and we hope to beat that sum next month.

So, if you fancy doing a ⁵__ deed, join us on the 25 May to help the local orphanage.

A welcoming (B) welcome C welcomed
1 A helpful B helping C helpless
2 A shaved his hair off B had his hair shaved off C was having his hair shaved off
3 A got together B were got together C had got together
4 A raised B was raised C were raised
5 A high B great C good

/5

Total /30

7 Complete the text with the correct form of the words in brackets.

THE TRUE detective

Being a real-life private *detective* (DETECT) is not as exciting as fans of Sherlock Holmes or Hercule Poirot may imagine. To begin with, most of the time they don't deal with actual ¹_____ (CRIME) like robbers or thieves at all. Their customers usually want somebody to be found or they have a friend or partner that is a ²_____ (SUSPICION) in a case where no crime has been committed – such as cheating or lying in some way. Heroic and dramatic acts like catching a mastermind bank ³_____ (ROB) or rescuing people on the streets from a heartless ⁴_____ (MUG) is not how detectives earn a living. Indeed, even solving local ⁵_____ (BURGLE) is not something that your average private detective would be interested in because it doesn't help pay the bills.

/5

8 Complete the sentences with the correct form of the words in brackets. Do not change the order of the words. You may need to add words. Use up to five words in each gap.

The accused *was found not guilty* (find / not guilty) and left the court with a big smile on his face.

1 The judge _____
(prepare / her / trial) by re-reading the case notes.

2 Last week, two _____
(thief / be / charge / steal) my car. They were twelve years old!

3 At the beginning of our relationship Laura and I
_____ (promise / another / we) would be honest about our feelings.

4 The two vandals accused me of breaking the window but in fact they _____
(break / it / they).

5 How many _____ (robbery / commit) every day around the world? Millions?

/5

9 Complete each pair of sentences with the same answer A–C.

Do you think giving £10 a month to charity can make a __ ?
What's the __ between your phone and mine? They look the same to me.
A change   B point   Ⓒ difference

1 Did you remember to __ the back door?
They're going to __ him up in a cell for twenty years.
A shut   B close   C lock

2 Theresa is __ a sentence for selling pirate software.
Mum is __ dinner in a few minutes, so help me set the table.
A doing   B serving   C making

3 What's the __ in reading this newspaper? There's nothing in it except celebrity gossip!
Catching criminals gives me a real sense of __ . But being a police officer is a tough job.
A point   B purpose   C reason

4 Please take __ to do the report carefully.
What __ are we going to meet Clarke and Justin?
A time   B effort   C hour

5 I've booked the __ for Sunday and we can play for two hours.
The case goes to __ next month.
A field   B pitch   C court

/5

10 Complete the second sentence so that it has a similar meaning to the first. Use between two and five words.

Steve definitely didn't copy my homework.
My *homework definitely wasn't copied* by Steve.

1 The police officer warned the man to put down the gun.
The man _____
the gun down by the police officer.

2 Did we send the latest report to the judge?
Was _____ the judge?

3 We haven't arranged a date for the trial yet.
A date for the trial _____ yet.

4 The charity organisation opposite the library often helps homeless women.
Homeless women _____
the charity organisation opposite the library.

5 The two men noticed that a police officer was following them.
The two men noticed that _____
_____ a police officer.

/5

Total   /20

115

Translate the phrases into your own language.

People

Age

in his early twenties _____

in his late twenties _____

in his mid-twenties _____

in his teens _____
middle-aged _____

Personality

carefree _____
caring _____
come across as _____
courageous _____
cynical _____
decisive _____
determined _____
disobedient _____
distrustful _____
down-to-earth _____

easy-going _____
friendly _____
generous _____
hard-working _____
honest _____
hopeful _____
hopeless _____
human trait _____
inspiring _____
kind _____
kindness _____
modest _____
mysterious _____
nervous _____
open to _____
patient _____
polite _____
popular _____
positive _____

rebellious _____
reliable _____
resilient _____
rude _____
sceptical _____
selfish _____
sense of humour _____
shallow _____
successful _____

superstitious _____
suspicious _____
take after _____

vain _____
well-mannered _____

Feelings and emotions

admire _____
appreciated _____
be the centre of attention _____

blame yourself _____
care a lot about _____
devastated _____
enjoy yourself _____
feel comfortable in your own skin _____

fulfilled _____
impressed by _____
lonely _____
pleasures of life _____

stir up _____
welcome _____

Appearance

bald _____
blond/blonde _____
comb hair _____
dark hair _____
fall over something _____

hair straightener _____

long hair _____
look _____
look like _____
medium height _____
nail clippers _____
scruffy _____
short _____
short hair _____
skinny _____
slim _____
stare _____
straight hair _____
wear make-up _____
well-built _____

Body parts

ankle _____
arm _____
bottom _____
cheek _____
chest _____
chin _____
elbow _____
eyebrow _____
finger _____
fingernail _____
foot/feet _____
forehead _____
heel _____
knee _____
lips _____
neck _____
rib _____

shoulder _____
spine _____
stomach _____
thigh _____
thumb _____
toe _____
tooth/teeth _____
waist _____
wrist _____

Clothes and accessories

ankle boots _____
bandanna _____
bangles _____
baseball cap _____
beanie _____
blouse _____
brightly-coloured _____
casual _____
cool _____
cotton _____
dark suit _____
denim jacket _____
distressed jeans _____
ethical brand _____
fabric _____
faded jeans _____
fashionable _____
fast fashion _____
fast-drying _____
fleece _____
fur-lined _____
garments _____
hard-wearing _____
high heels _____
in fashion _____
jumper _____
leather belt _____
leggings _____
necklace _____
out of fashion _____
patterned _____
practical clothes _____
rain jacket _____
raincoat _____
shirt _____
shorts _____
short-sleeved _____
silk tie _____
smart _____
snow boots _____
striped _____
stylish _____
suit _____
sweatshirt _____
top _____
trainers _____
trendy _____
trousers _____
underwear _____
unisex _____

intage sunglasses _____
waistcoat _____
wear _____
woollen _____
ip _____

Skills and interests

be) passionate (about) _____

chieve _____
chievement _____
dmire _____
arry on _____
ocus on _____
et into _____
ive (something) up _____

o in for _____
nspiration _____
each for _____
ole model _____
it around _____

Sense of identity

n memory of _____
ribal people _____
ribe _____
way of life _____

Personal values

chievable _____
sk for nothing in return _____

ttitude _____
eat yourself up _____

elieve in _____
ritical of _____
eserve something _____

isapprove of _____
o a good deed _____

xpress your disapproval of _____

xpress your support for _____

ollow trends _____
enerosity _____
ive a sense of purpose _____

o with the flow _____

onesty _____
ope _____
opefully _____
oint of view _____
opelessly _____
favour of _____
earn from your mistakes _____

ok up to _____

---

make a difference _____

mess up _____
offer a reward _____

opposed to _____
profound _____
small gestures _____
take advantage of _____
take time to _____
want something in return _____

Home

Location

capital city _____
hometown _____
megacity _____
neighbourhood _____
security firm _____
security lights _____

urban _____

Rooms, furniture and equipment

blinds _____
burglar alarm _____

creak _____
curtains _____
dustbin _____
lock _____
pillow _____
wardrobe _____

School

Educational system

take a gap year _____

uni _____

School life

behave badly _____
cognitive _____
distract _____
distraction _____
drop out of _____
educate _____
education _____
educational _____
educationally _____
encourage _____
encouragement _____
engage _____

engagement _____
enhance _____

---

enhance the reading experience _____

enhancement _____
exclude from school _____

explanation _____
express yourself _____

feel distracted by _____

find out about _____
hand over _____
have a short attention span _____

improve literacy rates _____

improvement _____
in silence _____
inform _____
information _____
introduce yourself _____
memorisation _____
memorise _____
on the tip of your tongue _____

pin _____
prepare yourself _____
read in the old-fashioned way _____

repetition _____
repetitive _____
reply _____
revise _____
rustle _____
spine _____
take up _____

thinkable _____

uniform _____

Work

Jobs

carpenter _____
chef _____

curator _____
detective _____
fashion designer _____

gallery owner _____

judge _____
model _____
nutritionist _____
physical therapist _____

politician _____
presenter _____
rescuer _____
rewarding _____

VOCABULARY BANK

Translate the phrases into your own language.

she'd make a great …

surgeon
tailor
tour guide

tour leader
travel journalist

TV director

unpleasant
unrewarding

Career

activate
ask for permission

assist
attend
budget

deal with
decide
decisive moment

effective
execute

informed
keep up-to-date with

offer a job
problem-solve

succeed
success
successfully
suggest improvements

type a note

Working conditions and employment

headquarters
incentive
take part in

Family and social life

Family and friends

close friend
ex
fiancé
online friend

Relationships

accept
acceptable
acceptably
acceptance

agree to do something

agree with
appreciate
be always there for

blow a kiss
break somebody's heart

call on somebody
cut yourself off from your family/ home

date
defend
detract from
end a relationship

express sympathy

get along/on well with

get to know
give somebody a hand

give somebody peace of mind

go for
hang out with
have a good relationship with

have a lot in common with

have one foot firmly planted at home

have similar interests

let somebody down
look after
lose touch with
make contact with

make somebody's day

offer a helping hand

opposite sex
owe
pull somebody's leg

reassure your friend

rely on
socialise with
split up with
stop seeing each other

talk somebody into

urge
walk away from

Everyday activities

break from your routine

do the same thing over

repeat a sequence

turn up
wait for

Conflicts and problems

be met with suspicion

belittle
challenge beliefs

criticised for
fall out with
have an argument
impossible
put somebody off

refuse
reject
tell somebody off

trick
unavoidable
uninformed
unthinkable

Food

Food and drinks

apple pie
apricot
aubergine
avocado
bacon
beef
beetroot
bitter
black pepper
bland
brown rice
butter
cabbage
cake
carrot
cauliflower
cayenne pepper
cheeseburger
cherry
chicken
chilli pepper
chips
chocolate mousse
chocolate syrup
coconut
coffee
crisps
crispy

runchy biscuits
ark chocolate
elicious
isgusting
ried
ry biscuits
atty
g
rm
zzy drink
esh
uit salad
arlic
rape
rapefruit
reen beans

reen salad
round pepper
ome-made pizza
ome-made soup
ot, spicy
ce cream
uice
ean
ttuce
ong-grain rice
aple syrup
ild
ilk
ilk chocolate
ixed salad
ushroom
ushroom soup

live
live oil
melette
nion
range
asta sauce
eanut butter
ineapple
otato
rawn sauce
udding
umpkin
adish
aw
d meat
d pepper
pe
tten
almon
alt
ardines
de salad
iced bread
oda water
our
our milk
parkling water
pinach

stale biscuits
still water
strong
sugar syrup
sushi
sweet
sweetcorn
tinned soup
unripe
vegetable soup
white bread
white rice
wholemeal bread

Meals and their preparation
add
animal products

boil
chop (up)
cook
cooked
cookery course
cookery lessons
cuisine

curry
cut off
expiry date
feed
fry
go off
heat
ingredient
jar
leftovers
local produce
low-calorie meal

main course
menu
mix
mixture
oven
pan
pancake
peel
plate
pour
protein
recipe
roast
sell-by date

serve
sharp knife
slice
spoon
starter
store food
throw away
warm

Eating habits
balanced diet
cold snack
dietary needs
fast food
fattening diet
fattening food
fussy
gorge yourself
healthy diet
healthy food
healthy lifestyle
healthy meal
healthy snack
heavy meal
hot meal
human consumption

light snack
meat consumption
nutritious
organic food
quick snack
take a sip
vegan
vegetarian diet
vitamin

Eating out
bill
order
three-course meal

Shopping and services

Buying and selling
affordable
get
organise a sale

queue
second-hand clothes

try on

Advertising
advertising
claim
point out
promote
suggest
suggestion

Money
due date
save up for
withdraw money from a cashpoint

VOCABULARY BANK

Translate the phrases into your own language.

Travelling and tourism

Sightseeing, trips and excursions

adventure _____
arrive _____
avoidable _____
backpack _____
backpacker _____
beach holiday _____
business trip _____
carry on _____
come across _____
come face to face with _____
_____
connected _____
crash through _____
cross a river/valley _____
_____
destination _____
dip _____
disconnected _____
familiar _____
flashlight _____
for pleasure _____
go away _____
go backpacking _____
_____
holidaymaker _____
immerse yourself in a foreign culture _____
_____
insect repellent _____
_____
location _____
overland tour _____
_____
overnight journey _____
_____
package holiday _____
_____
penknife _____
pepper spray _____
pleasant _____
put up a tent _____
rope _____
round-the-world trip _____
_____
search through _____
set off (on a journey) _____
_____
short cut _____
skiing holiday _____
sleeping bag _____
solitary _____
stroll _____
sunscreen _____
suntan lotion _____
temple _____
tour _____
travel abroad _____
travel agent _____

travel company _____
travel insurance _____
traveller _____
trekking _____
unfamiliar _____

Forms of transport

airport _____
baggage reclaim _____
_____
boat _____
book plane tickets _____
_____
bus journey _____
cable car _____
car hire _____
catch a bus _____
catch a train _____
crossing _____
cruise _____
cycle downhill _____
_____
cycle uphill _____
_____
drive _____
_____
emerge _____
fasten a seatbelt _____
_____
ferry _____
flight _____
get off _____
go through security _____
_____
helicopter _____
journey _____
land _____
miss a bus _____
miss a train _____
on foot _____
passenger _____
plane _____
public transport _____
return journey _____
rickshaw _____
ride _____
_____
_____
sail _____
school bus _____
security check _____
_____
sledge _____
terminal _____
ticket _____
train _____
travel by bus _____
_____
travel by train _____
_____
voyage _____
walk barefoot _____

Traffic

break down _____
get a lift _____
get stuck in traffic _____
GPS _____
head for _____
hold somebody up _____
keep on _____
keep up with _____
_____
pick somebody up _____
_____
pull over _____
run out of _____
rush hour _____
traffic jam _____
traffic pollution _____
_____
travel on the left _____
_____
travel on the right _____

Accommodation

budget hotel _____
campsite _____
double room _____
put somebody up _____
_____
seaside resort _____
single room _____
ski resort _____
three-star hotel _____
_____
twin room _____
_____
youth hostel _____
_____

Culture

Art

local handicrafts _____
_____
recreate _____

Film, theatre, books

adapt _____
adaptation _____
art critic _____
_____
audience _____
based on _____
be nominated for an Oscar _____
_____
box office _____
cast _____
deeply engaging _____
_____
direct _____
entertain _____

entertainment _____
fictional character _____
film _____
find something easy to follow _____

have a good chance of winning _____

have great reviews _____

inspiration _____
inspire _____
interview _____

leave something to your imagination _____

movie business _____
play the part of _____
present _____
presentation _____

produce _____
production _____
publish _____
put on _____
review positively _____
scene _____
screenplay _____
sword _____
tell a story _____

Media

appear in a TV series _____

hidden camera _____
press conference _____

reality TV _____
TV channel _____

Music

accompaniment _____
accompany _____

band _____
be in the charts _____

come out _____
create _____
creation _____
do a live gig _____
drummer _____
festival-goer _____
have a hit single _____

hit _____
lead guitarist _____
musician _____
perform _____
performer _____

play a venue _____
release an album _____
sign a recording contract _____

sign up for _____
singer-songwriter _____

start out _____

talent competition _____

vocalist _____
winner _____

Description

banned _____
brilliant _____
cheesy _____
contain an element of surprise _____

cut somebody off from reality _____

ecstatic _____
engage emotions _____

fabulous _____
fascinating _____
fortunately _____
frightening _____
hilarious _____
I couldn't believe my eyes _____

iconic _____
interestingly _____
laugh your head off _____

make somebody laugh _____

naturally _____
originate _____
popular with _____
random _____

ridiculous _____
sense _____
sensuous _____
shocking _____
stir up emotions _____
surprisingly _____
sympathetic _____
take by surprise _____
trivial _____
violent _____

Sport

Types of sport

(table) tennis _____
athletics _____
boxing _____
competitive sport _____
extreme sport _____
hockey _____

individual sport _____
indoor sport _____
jogging _____

judo _____
marathon _____
motor racing _____
outdoor sport _____

sailing _____
skating _____
snowboarding _____
squash _____
swimming _____
team sport _____
volleyball _____
walking race _____

wrestling _____

People in sport

athlete _____
coach _____
runner _____
trainer _____

Doing sport

(long-distance) race _____

action _____
beat an opponent _____

beat the champion _____
blow a whistle _____
bounce the ball _____
break a world record _____

challenge _____
chase after _____
cheer somebody on _____

come first _____
come last _____
come second _____
compete _____
competitor _____
cycle _____

cycle race _____
defeat an opponent _____

defeat the champion _____

determination _____
dive for the ball _____
do sport _____
enter a competition _____

fall over _____
fan _____
final _____
get on (your bike) _____
goalkeeper _____
gold medal _____
join a club _____
kick a ball _____
lead _____

VOCABULARY BANK

Translate the phrases into your own language.

lose a game/a match _____

lose a point _____
match _____
miss a goal _____

opponent _____
opposing team _____
overtake _____
pick up _____
player _____
poke _____
position _____
power _____
red card _____
referee _____
report on _____
rival _____
row _____
score a goal _____
score points _____
spectator _____
speed _____
speed up _____
splash your body with water _____

sponsor _____
sports event _____
supporter _____
swing your arms _____
take on (a challenge) _____

take the lift up the mountain _____

teammate _____

tournament _____
train for _____
training _____
trophy _____
try out _____
turn professional _____

win a game/a match _____
win a point _____
win a prize _____
work out _____
yellow card _____

Sports equipment

(hockey) stick _____
(snow)board _____
bicycle rack _____
boots _____

goggles _____
helmet _____
racket _____

Sports facilities

(ski) slope _____
athletics track _____

badminton court _____

basketball court _____

boxing ring _____
cricket pitch _____
football pitch _____
golf course _____
handball court _____

hockey pitch _____

locker room _____
motor racing track _____
netball court _____
rink _____
rugby pitch _____
sailing club _____
sauna _____
squash court _____
stadium _____
sumo ring _____
tennis court _____
volleyball court _____
wrestling ring _____

Negative effects of doing sports

break your neck _____
get injured _____
hurt yourself _____

Health

Lifestyle

active _____
body clock _____
burn something off _____

caffeine _____
feel alert _____
keep fit _____
keep in shape _____

on a diet _____
powerful _____
put on weight _____
sleep through _____
starving _____

Illnesses, symptoms and treatment

be allergic to _____
bitten by a dog _____
bitten by a rat _____

bitten by a snake _____

bitten by an insect _____

bleed _____

blocked nose _____
break _____
break your arm _____
break your leg _____
break your thumb _____
break your toe _____
burn _____
burn your fingers _____

burn your hair _____
burn your hand _____
burn your tongue _____

catch (a disease) _____

children's ward _____
cholera epidemic _____
count sheep _____
cut your finger _____

deep cut _____
die _____
die from _____
die of (a disease) _____

dislocate your hip _____
dislocate your knee _____
dislocate your shoulder _____

dislocate your thumb _____
doctor's surgery _____
eye drops _____
fall asleep _____
feel dizzy _____
feel sick _____
feel well _____
fever _____
flu _____
flu epidemic _____
food allergy _____
gain weight _____
get dizzy _____
have a black eye _____
have a bruise _____
have a cut _____
have a pain in your forehead _____

have a panic attack _____
have a sore finger (somebody has a sore finger) _____
have a temperature _____

hay fever _____
hospital _____
hurt _____
illness _____
infection _____
injury _____
insomnia _____
local surgery _____
make a complete recovery _____
maternity ward _____

medicine _____
muscle pain _____
nosebleed _____
nut allergy _____
operation _____
recover from _____

see a doctor _____
serious condition _____
seriously ill _____
having cut _____
sneeze _____
snore _____
sprain your ankle _____
sprain your foot _____
sprain your knee _____
sprain your wrist _____
stable condition _____
sting _____
stitch _____
stomach pain _____
sunburn _____
swollen _____
symptoms _____
tissue _____
treat patients _____
unconscious _____
wear off _____
weight problems _____

write a prescription _____

First aid

bandage a knee _____

bandage _____
deliver a baby _____
drown _____
emergency team _____

give an injection _____
give somebody first aid _____

heart attack _____
look down _____
look up _____
off-duty _____
paramedic _____
patient _____
put a plaster on _____

put ice on _____
rescue team _____
safety _____
save lives _____
stop the blood flowing _____

take (antihistamine) tablets _____

trap _____

Science and technology

The internet and modern technology

(be) made up of _____
anti-virus software _____

broadband connection _____

connect _____
connected to _____
connection _____
gadget _____
get access to _____
go viral _____

have access to _____
imitate _____
instant communication _____

link _____
online purchase _____
outside world _____
password _____
post _____

provide _____
set the alarm on your phone _____

set up a webpage _____

share a webpage _____

social networking site _____

streamed _____
turn into _____
upload a video _____

vertical _____
video camera _____
view _____
view a video _____
viewer _____
viral _____
viral video _____

Scientific discoveries

cutting-edge _____
electricity _____
genius _____
innovation _____
multi-purpose _____
predict _____

The natural world

Landscape

bay _____
branch _____
breadth _____
broad _____
broaden _____
calm sea _____
clearing _____
coast _____
come in _____

continent _____
country _____
dangerous current _____

deep _____
deepen _____
depth _____
desert _____
desert island _____
dirt track _____
fast-flowing river _____

flow _____
giant wave _____
go out _____
heavy sea _____
height _____
heighten _____
high tide _____
huge wave _____
in the bushes _____
length _____
lengthen _____
locate _____
long _____
low tide _____
mountain _____
mountain peak _____
mountain range _____
mountain ridge _____
ocean current _____
path _____
pitch black _____
pond _____
rainforest _____
remote _____
remote island _____
rising tide _____
river bank _____
rough sea _____
route _____
seabed _____
slow-moving river _____

spring _____
strength _____
strengthen _____
strong current _____

VOCABULARY BANK

Translate the phrases into your own language.

surround _____
suspension bridge _____
tidal wave _____
trail _____
tropical island _____
valley _____
wide _____
widen _____
width _____
winding path _____
winding river _____

Animals and plants

bear _____
bear encounter _____

bee _____
bite _____
cage _____
cheetah _____
crops _____
cub _____
dolphin _____
domestic animal _____
donkey _____
female bear _____
female elephant _____
female gorilla _____
fox _____
hedgehog _____
herd _____
leaf/leaves _____
lion _____
on the loose _____
pet _____
predator _____
prey _____
puma _____
roar _____
root _____
sea lion _____
shark _____
skunk _____
squirrel _____
tiger _____
trunk _____
whale _____
zoo _____

The weather

climate _____
look as if/as though _____

strong _____
the elements _____
wind _____

Environmental protection

air quality _____
climate change _____
endangered species _____

environment _____

environmental issues _____

global warming _____
gradually disappear _____

inhabitant _____
low-energy light bulb _____

organic _____
pollution _____
recycle _____

recycling bin _____

renewable energy _____

running water _____
save electricity _____

solar panels _____

Natural disasters

collapse _____
earthquake _____
erupt _____
evacuate _____
evacuation _____
get help from _____
heat up _____
hurricane _____
survive _____
survivor _____
tsunami _____
volcanic eruption _____
volcano _____

Environmental disasters

affect _____
alarming statistics _____

die out _____
discarded _____
energy consumption _____
food waste _____
global statistics _____
government standards _____

household waste _____

industrial waste _____

international standards _____

manufacturing industry _____

minimum level _____
official statistics _____

record level _____
safety standards _____

waste _____

State and society

Social events and phenomena

average _____
donate money to _____

donation _____

foundation _____
get out of _____
happen to _____
on average _____
participant _____
prevent somebody from _____

raise money for _____
rebellion _____
voluntary work _____
vulnerable people _____

The problems of the modern world

anonymous _____
arson _____
arsonist _____
be arrested _____
be charged with a crime _____

be fortunate _____
be found guilty _____

be found not guilty _____

be less fortunate _____

be released _____

be sentenced _____
beggar _____
break the law _____
burglar _____
burglary _____
burgle a house _____

case _____
cell _____
charge _____
collect evidence _____
commit a crime _____

consider _____
criminal _____
criminal damage _____
cyberbullying _____

deal drugs _____
death penalty _____

dig a tunnel _____
digital footprint _____
drug dealer _____
drug dealing _____
elderly people _____
escape _____
escape attempt/attempted escape _____

evidence _____
expand _____
fake _____
give a snapshot of _____
go to court _____
have a criminal record _____

homeless _____
identity theft _____
imprison _____
innocent _____
interview victims _____
interview witnesses _____

intrude on _____
investigate _____

kill _____
knock over _____
lack of _____
lock somebody (up) _____

major _____
majority _____
make (prisons) harder _____

make an example of _____

miscalculate _____
mug _____
mugger _____
mugging _____
murder _____
murderer _____
phone-addicted people _____

piracy _____
pirate _____
pirate software _____

population _____
poverty _____
prison guard _____

prisoner _____
protect yourself _____
punish somebody severely _____

question _____
release from prison _____

report a crime _____
rob a place _____
rob somebody _____
robber _____
robbery _____
sadly _____
sentence _____
serve a sentence _____
set fire to _____
shoplift _____
shoplifter _____
shoplifting _____
shortage of food and water _____

steal _____
suspect _____

the accused _____
the point of no return _____

theft _____
thief _____
trial _____
unemployment _____
vandal _____
vandalise _____
vandalism _____
victim _____
violence _____
witness _____
young offender _____

Politics and economy

abolish _____
agricultural sector _____
benefit from _____
catering industry _____

city council _____
collect taxes _____
developing countries _____

economic growth _____

elections _____
facilities _____
financial sector _____
local level _____
production _____
statistics _____
tourism income _____
tourist industry _____
voluntary sector _____

Authorities

citizen _____
elect _____

Culture of English-Speaking Countries

Alcatraz Island   a small island in San Francisco Bay which is famous for its military and federal prison, where hardened prisoners used to be kept (1934-1963)

Barack Obama   an American politician; he was the 44th US president in 2009-2017; in 2009 he was awarded the Nobel Peace Prize for his efforts to strengthen international diplomacy and cooperation between people

Beyoncé   an American R&B and pop singer, songwriter, actress and dancer as well as pop culture icon

Bill Bryson   an Anglo-American writer of books about travel, the English language, science and other non-fiction topics

Brookfield Zoo   a zoological park in the Brookfield suburb of Chicago

California Gold Rush   a period when hundreds of thousands of gold seekers came to California (1848-1855); it was then that the jeans were first created as hard-wearing trousers for those looking for gold

Charlotte Johnstone   a British journalist working for *Telegraph Travel* who specialises in travel stories

Christina Aguilera   an American singer, songwriter, actress and TV personality

Coachella   (the Coachella Valley Music and Arts Festival) is one of the largest and most famous music and arts festivals in the world; it takes place every year in California

Constitutional monarchy   a system of governing a country in which the power of the king or queen is regulated by the constitution and shared with the parliament; Great Britain, Belgium, Denmark, Japan, Monaco and Spain are contemporary constitutional monarchies

Doctors without Borders   an international non-profit humanitarian medical organisation; it was founded in France in 1971 and its aim is to help those living in areas affected by wars, natural disasters, etc. where people have no access to healthcare

Ed Sheeran   a British singer, songwriter, guitarist and record producer; his music mixes pop, rock and folk

Essex   a county situated in south-eastern England and to the north of London

Fisherman's Wharf   a district of San Francisco, California and the place where fishermen keep their boats; it has many popular attractions including Pier 39, where tourists can see giant sea lions lying on the docks

Foo Fighters   an American rock and grunge band founded by Dave Grohl, the former drummer of the legendary group from Seattle, Nirvana

GBBO   (Great British Bake Off) is a British TV baking competition in which amateur bakers compete to impress the judges with their baking skills to become Britain's best amateur baker

Great Barrier Reef   the world's largest complex of coral reefs situated in the Pacific Ocean along the north-eastern coast of Australia

Glastonbury Festival   one of the biggest music and performing arts festivals in the world; it is held near the village of Pilton, in Somerset, England

Gwyneth Paltrow   an American actress, singer and businesswoman; she won an Oscar for her role in *Shakespeare in Love*

Hawaii   a group of islands in the Pacific Ocean; it is the newest of the fifty states of the USA and its capital is Honolulu

James Dean   an American film and theatre actor, pop culture icon and symbol of non-conformist attitudes; he died in a car accident in 1955 at the age of 24

Jennifer Aniston   an American actress and film producer; she is best known for her role as Rachel Green in the comedy television series *Friends*

Jennifer Hudson   an African-American singer and actress; she won an Oscar for her role in the musical *Dreamgirls*

Kings of Leon   an American rock group playing a blend of indie rock, pop and alternative rock

Laura Kenny   a British track cyclist; she has won four gold medals in the Olympics and has been a winner of numerous international track cycling championships

Little Mix   a British all-girl band which was formed during the eighth series of the British edition of *The X Factor*; it was the first band ever to win the contest

Lord George Byron   one of the greatest British poets of the Romantic movement in Britain and Europe

Marla Olmstead   a young American artist who specialises in abstract painting

Marlon Brando   one of the greatest American actors in history; he is best-known for his role of Vito Corleone in the film *The Godfather*

Masterchef   an American cooking television show in which amateur cooks compete for the title of Masterchef, which is now produced in more than 40 countries around the world

millennial   a person who was born between 1980 and 2000

Millie Bobby Brown   a British actress and model; she played the role of Eleven in the science fiction drama series *Stranger Things*

Red Nose Day   a British charity event which is organised by the Comic Relief foundation to raise money for people living in poverty in the UK and Africa; it is held every two years and is symbolised by an artificial red nose – a prop which shows the event is meant to make people laugh as well as raise money

Reese Witherspoon   an American actress and film producer; she won an Oscar for her role in *Walk the Line*

San Francisco   a city and county in the state of California, US; it is famous for the Golden Gate Bridge, the former prison on Alcatraz, cable cars and its hilly landscape

School of Rock   an American comedy starring Jack Black in the leading role; it is also a rock musical created by Andrew Lloyd Webber and based on the film; it has been on Broadway in New York City and in the West End in London

Seattle   a city in the state of Washington in the north-western part of the USA; one of its landmarks is the Space Needle – an observation tower with a rotating restaurant at the top

Serena Williams   an American tennis player; she has won many prestigious awards and titles (Grand Slam singles and doubles, the Olympics and WTA); she has an older sister, Venus Williams, who has been a multiple tennis champion as well

Stephanie Rice   an Australian swimmer; she won three gold medals in the Olympics in Beijing in 2008 and has also won five medals in the world championships

Stranger Things   an American science fiction drama series created by Netflix

The Beatles   a British rock group from Liverpool; it was one of the greatest bands in the history of music

The Chemical Brothers   a British band which plays electronic music

The FA Cup   (The Football Association Challenge Cup) is the oldest annually held football competition in the world

The London Marathon   one of the most popular marathons in the world; it has been organised on the streets of London since 1981

The London to Brighton Bike Ride   a fundraising event that takes place every year during which participants compete in a bike race from London to Brighton and raise money for charity

The Adventure of the Speckled Band   a crime story about one of Sherlock Holmes' cases written by Sir Arthur Conan Doyle

The Ramones   an American band which is considered to be the first true punk rock group

The Shard   a 72-storey pyramid-shaped building whose walls are covered with glass; it is located in Southwark in London

The United Nations   an international organisation with 193 member states whose aim is to secure global peace and safety, develop friendly relations among countries and ensure human rights are respected across the world

Vampire Weekend   an American band playing indie rock; it was founded in New York City in 2006

Veganism   a philosophy and lifestyle in which someone excludes products of animal origin from their diet and other common everyday activities

William Sutcliffe   a contemporary novelist writing young adult fiction

PEOPLE

1 Complete the text with the words from the box.

> beanie   cotton   faded jeans   hair straightener
> fleece   leather   scruffy   unisex   ~~vintage~~

BE TRENDY THIS SUMMER

IN ...

The new season will surely bring new trends: _vintage_ sunglasses are always in fashion, so wear them proudly.

1 The natural look is very in, so let your curly hair down and forget about a _____ .
2 To get your hair under control, invest in a colourful _____ – it may seem like a garment for a snowboarder but trust me, it's very stylish.
3 For everyday wear, try plain _____ of good quality, just make sure they are blue.
4 As for tops and T-shirts, no synthetic fabrics, only pure _____ .

OUT ...

5 A casual style does not mean you can be _____ , so forget about your old baggy trousers and washed-out sweaters.
6 No matter what big fashion houses say, it's never OK to cause suffering to animals, so if you're thinking about buying a _____ jacket – think again!
7 This season in women's clothing is going to be about girly patterned dresses and maxi skirts, so forget about shopping for _____ clothes.
8 And whatever you do, remember that a _____ is only an option if you go trekking in the mountains – it's sports equipment, not a fashionable piece of clothing!

2 Choose the correct answer A–D.

She must be very ___ living in that huge house all by herself.
A busy   (B) lonely   C lazy   D single

1 Helen finally feels ___ : she's got her own company and a lovely family – all she's ever wanted.
A honest   B vain
C easy-going   D fulfilled

2 Why are you always so ___ about my plans? Why don't you ever believe in me?
A sceptical   B down-to-earth
C hopeless   D disobedient

3 My brother's best friend is really ___ – all he cares about is other people's appearance and not what they have to say.
A resilient   B shallow   C rude   D sceptical

4 Mrs Branson's grandson is extremely ___ – he's only five and always says 'Good evening', 'Thank you very much' and 'Excuse me'.
A courageous   B honest
C well-mannered   D hard-working

5 I think she's too ___ – she didn't say anything when she won a prestigious science competition because she didn't want to seem too important. Can you believe it?
A modest   B honest   C rude   D decisive

6 Blake is very ___ and practical, that's why he's always responsible for the money.
A hopeful   B cynical
C rebellious   D down-to-earth

HOME

1 Complete the text with the words from the box.

> blinds   burglar alarm   creak   curtains   locks
> neighbourhood   security firm   ~~urban~~   wardrobes

I'm sure you're going to love this house. It's located outside the city, but the area offers all the _urban_ attractions like a cinema, a shopping centre and a gym. Look around: this house is in the middle of a quiet and friendly [1]_____ , where mostly families with children live. There is no furniture in the house, except large wooden [2]_____ in the bedrooms. Some of them are from the 1960s, so they [3]_____ when you open the doors, but this sound gives them a vintage quality. What's more, there are [4]_____ in the windows, because the living room gets lots of sun in the afternoons, but you could choose to hang colourful [5]_____ , if you prefer a cosier, romantic look. Also, you will be safe here. The [6]_____ on the doors are Swiss and the best you can get. There is also a [7]_____ installed – it's really loud. When it is activated, the [8]_____ sends a car to check what is happening in just five minutes. So, I believe this is the perfect house for you and your children.

SCHOOL

1 Choose the correct answers A–D.

Most people read __ when they want to really concentrate on a text.

A cognitive   B educationally

C in silence   D literacy rates

1 She was excluded __ school for her behaviour.

A of   B out   C for   D from

2 When literacy rates improve, it means that

A students have to pay more for education.

B students have better reading and writing skills.

C there are more tests in Literature.

D students have trouble writing essays.

3 If something is on the tip of your tongue

A you want to say something unpleasant to a person.

B you have an infection in your mouth.

C there is so much to say that you don't know where to start.

D you know something but you cannot remember it immediately.

4 During the first class of the year, each student should __ themselves.

A impress   B explore   C introduce   D encourage

5 When you do not understand a subject at school, a teacher is supposed to offer you a clear __

A explanation.   B discouragement.

C memorisation.   D improvement.

2 Complete the text with the words from the box.

> distract   drop out of   express   hand in
> prepare   ~~taught~~   uniform

Mathew is into music. He _taught_ himself to play the guitar and the trumpet. He loves it because it lets him [1] _____ himself and communicate his private emotions through music. That's why he decided to try to join the school band. His parents agreed as long as it didn't [2] _____ him from his schoolwork. Before he went to the audition, he had to [3] _____ all the papers and projects for school that week. He practised every evening to [4] _____ himself as well as possible. And … he got in! He was so happy! He played at two school events and a local Family Day. After a month, however, he decided to [5] _____ the band. Why? He says the band [6] _____ made him look like a complete idiot, and that was impossible to ignore.

WORK

1 Complete the text with the names of jobs.

My class

They all used to be in the same class and I used to be their class tutor. However, each of them had totally different ambitions. For example, Fiona always liked dressing up. No wonder she became a f_ashion_ d_esigner_. Gabi was also into clothes and fashion, but she became a [1]t_____ and now makes clothes for designers. Sophie was called the most beautiful girl in school and, since she became a [2]m_____, you can now see her face on the covers of magazines. Tom was very good at Geography and always wanted to travel – now he's a [3]t_____ l_____ in Africa! Liz, on the other hand, preferred Biology and Chemistry and always wanted to be a doctor. She studied hard and she's a well-known [4]s_____ in one of the best hospitals in the country. Then there's Pete, who would often read crime stories under his desk and who loved solving puzzles. Now I hear he's a great [5]d_____ and he sometimes helps the police in the town! His best school friend, Tim, works as a [6]j_____, and I hear they often meet in court. David, who claimed he was not interested in current affairs, studied politics at university and is now a [7]p_____. As for Robert, he always loved eating, so it's no surprise he became a [8]c_____ in a local French restaurant. Julia, who was always careful about what she ate, has become a [9]n_____ and now advises others how to eat healthily, while Henry, with his love of television, is a [10]p_____ and appears on the TV news. Only Chris, who had a dream of becoming a famous photographer, does something completely different today – he's a [11]c_____ and makes furniture. That's life.

2 Match the words with the definitions.

to execute   [g]

1 to budget

2 to assist

3 to problem-solve

4 to attend

5 to succeed

6 to keep up-to-date

a to find answers to difficult situations

b to achieve something that you wanted

c to make sure you have the latest information

d to plan how much money will be spent

e to help

f to take part in an event

g to do or perform something which was planned

FAMILY AND SOCIAL LIFE

1 Choose the correct answers A–D.

He cut himself __ his family completely and has not contacted them for years.

(A) off from   B away from   C away to   D out from

1 When you split up with somebody, you __ .
A fall in love   B end a relationship
C start having a relationship
D get to know someone

2 The news about his promotion really __ my day!
A created   B did
C made   D cheered up

3 They used to be close friends, but they lost __ after college.
A communication   B interests
C friendship   D touch

4 We have a lot __ common.
A in   B on   C with   D –

5 If you want to be loved, you should always look __ other people.
A for   B at   C about   D after

2 Complete the sentences with the correct form of the phrasal verbs from the box.

> ~~agree with~~   call on   fall out   get on
> hang out   let down   rely on

I'm sorry but I don't _agree with_ you – I think we should do exactly the opposite.

1 You look depressed. Have you _____ with your parents again?

2 Why don't you _____ Ann this afternoon and see if she needs any help with the decorations?

3 Do you want to _____ this evening? We could go to the cinema or a café.

4 I heard they are really _____ well with each other – they are great friends.

5 Many students _____ their parents for money – they still need their help.

6 She never wanted _____ her parents – she just found studying at university too difficult.

FOOD

1 Complete the adverts with one word in each gap.

If you want to stay fit, drink our **j**_uices_! Try the grapefruit juice, a great source of vitamin C.

. . . .

Forgotten your school lunch? Don't worry! Buy our freshly made [1]**s**_____s. We have dozens of them on offer. Cheese, ham, egg. You name it, we have it! They are [2]**d**_____ too!

. . . .

We know you live in a hurry and have no time to cook. That's why we take care of your [3]**d**_____ needs. If you're a sportsperson, we can provide rich, nutritious [4]**m**_____ with meat. If you're on a diet, we have a selection of healthy, [5]**l**_____-**c**_____ snacks. On our menu we also have [6]**v**_____ soup, Indian [7]**c**_____ and different pasta [8]**s**_____ ! Order and enjoy!

2 Choose the correct answers A–D.

I always eat __ vegetables – I never cook them.
A unripe   (B) raw   C crispy   D cold

1 I usually put some butter in a pan, add garlic and __ a piece of meat in it – it's delicious and juicy.
A boil   B cook   C bake   D fry

2 If you don't cover your bread, it will go __ .
A stale   B rotten   C ripe   D salty

3 White __ with butter and honey is good for breakfast but don't eat too much of it.
A lettuce   B mango   C bread   D chocolate

4 Before our main course we had a __ .
A supper   B starter   C breakfast   D snack

5 Mild food doesn't have any __ spices in it.
A ripe   B sour   C sweet   D hot

6 We shouldn't waste food and we should minimise the amount of __ we produce.
A ingredients B mixture   C leftovers   D snacks

7 Products such as meat, eggs and cheese contain a lot of __ , which we need to grow.
A sugar   B cuisine   C ingredients D protein

8 Jam is usually sold in __ .
A jars   B boxes   C tins   D bottles

SHOPPING AND SERVICES

1 Complete the text with one word in each gap.

I hate shopping, especially for clothes. I like looking good but going to a clothes shop is an absolute nightmare for me. If I need to _get_ something to wear, I start online. There is a lot of [1]**a**_____**g** showing perfect models wearing nice clothes. They [2]**c**_____**m** that if I buy their clothes, I will look and feel as wonderful as they do. But I know that's not true. I look at a website for about an hour and decide to go to a shopping centre. It's frustrating because there are always crowds of people and long [3]**q**_____**s**. But at least I can [4]**t**_____ **o**_____ some of the clothes to see how I look. I usually look ridiculous – the latest trends are not for me. But I see they are organising a [5]**s**_____ , so maybe I'll buy something inexpensive with the money I managed to [6]**s**_____**e** up. Unfortunately, there's nothing for me. So, as usual, I go to my favourite [7]**s**_____-**h**_____ shop, where they have a great selection of vintage clothes which look as good as new. The clothes there are [8]**a**_____**e** – they don't cost a lot – and they fit me. I still hate shopping but I've learnt to love vintage fashion.

VOCABULARY BANK

TRAVELLING AND TOURISM

1 Complete the sentences with the words from the box.

> flight   journey   passengers   seatbelt
> security   ~~the river~~   the tent

There was no bridge, so we had to cross _the river_ on foot.

1 I fastened my _____ .
2 After some transportation problems we carried on our _____ .
3 Tom's taxi to the airport was late and he missed his _____ to Turkey.
4 We arrived late, so we had to put up _____ in the dark.
5 I went through the _____ check at the airport.
6 When I travel by bus, I'm shocked how rude people are to other _____ .

2 Are the statements true (T) or false (F)?

If you want to go trekking, you go on a cruise. ⬡ F
1 Pepper spray may be used for preparing food. ⬡
2 When you take a shortcut, you get home faster. ⬡
3 Cable cars travel on the streets. ⬡
4 A return journey takes you away from home. ⬡
5 Barefoot trekking means wearing special boots. ⬡
6 Ferries travel on water. ⬡
7 You wait for your bags at baggage reclaim. ⬡
8 A familiar place is a place you don't know. ⬡
9 Cycle rickshaws produce a lot of pollution. ⬡
10 If you go on a solitary holiday, you are alone. ⬡
11 A destination is a place you want to get to. ⬡
12 If there are a lot of mosquitoes, use an insect repellent. ⬡

CULTURE

1 Choose the correct answers A–D.

Which person is not a musician:
A a drummer   B a festival-goer
C a lead guitarist   D a vocalist
1 They played their first __ and they got money for it!
A review   B gig   C screenplay   D cast
2 Go to the __ and buy three tickets for the latest Ryan Reynolds movie and I'll get the popcorn.
A ticket box   B cinema shop
C ticket store   D box office
3 The film received horrible __ – I think it will be the worst film of the year.
A critics   B reviews   C grades   D opinions
4 At the press __ , the director told the reporters about his vision of the story.
A interview   B showing   C conference   D event
5 They dream that one day their single will be in the US __ and maybe even get to number one.
A charts   B statistics   C reports   D reviews
6 Wow, Maria met all the __ of the How I Met Your Mother comedy series! All the main actors and actresses – I'm so jealous!
A screenplay   B band
C performance   D cast

2 Complete the sentences with the correct form of the words in capitals.

Film _production_ started only yesterday and already there are problems. **PRODUCE**
1 He's an incredible live _____ – the audience loves him! **PERFORM**
2 The _____ took place in London. The winner got a job on TV. **COMPETE**
3 She's an excellent _____ . I watch all her shows, even the ones about politics! **PRESENT**
4 He works in _____ – you know, singing, dancing, telling jokes on stage. **ENTERTAIN**
5 Everything that goes on in this house is filmed by _____ cameras, but it's not really a secret – all the people know about it. **HIDE**
6 Tim and his friends are so excited – they're going to New York to sign a _____ contract for their band! **RECORD**
7 The film is an _____ of a Jane Austen novel. **ADAPT**
8 The diva sings to the _____ of a symphony orchestra. **ACCOMPANY**
9 They play very calming, _____ music – perfect for relaxation. **SENSE**
10 The film doesn't show you everything – it leaves a lot to the _____ . **IMAGINE**

SPORT

1 Choose the correct answers A–D.

Which word is <u>not</u> used with sport?
A competitive   B extreme
C single   D outdoor
1 Which is <u>not</u> a team sport?
A volleyball   B cricket   C hockey   D judo
2 Which sport is <u>not</u> done indoors?
A sailing   B basketball
C wrestling   D table tennis
3 All the __ shouted happily when he scored the last goal.
A opponents   B goalkeepers
C fans   D coaches
4 She skied down the __ .
A ice rink   B slope   C pitch   D court
5 What does a footballer <u>not</u> do?
A kick a ball   B chase after a rival
C blow a whistle   D miss a goal
6 Basketball matches are played on __ .
A a pitch   B a court   C a course   D a track

2 Complete the text with the words from the box.

> coach extreme golf helmet kicking
> motor racing opponent pitch ~~wrestling~~

My grandson is keen on sports and that's OK. What worries me is that whenever he talks about the sports, I feel as if he's speaking to me in a foreign language. For example, he says he prefers _wrestling_ to judo because it's more spectacular when you beat your ¹_____ . He's now packing for a sports camp where he's going to try ²_____ . Of course I mustn't tell his parents about that! He's trying on his new ³_____ for biking. He says it will protect his head whatever happens! You know what? This very moment he's ⁴_____ a ball in my living room. But my flat is not a rugby ⁵_____ ! Well, I'm proud of my grandson but I wish he would take up ⁶_____ and play it on my nicely trimmed lawn. It would be a lot safer than all these ⁷_____ sports. I know a fantastic ⁸_____ for this sport – maybe he'll agree to teach my Benny.

HEALTH

1 Complete the text with the words from the box.

> count sheep eye drops fall feel dizzy
> feel sick injured insomnia nosebleed
> pain ~~sore~~ symptoms

Doctor, I'm lucky to be still alive. When I watch YouTube videos on my phone for just four hours, my eyes get _sore_. Surfing the Internet for ten hours gives me a terrible ¹_____ in my back. When I watch TV series for only two or three hours, I start to ²_____ and have to lie down. What's more, I've started to get allergy ³_____ to the crisps I munch on when watching TV. My eyes are burning and I need to use ⁴_____ to feel better.
Sometimes I even ⁵_____ and can't drink any fizzy drinks. When I have PE lessons, I sweat doing even the simplest exercise, and ⁶_____ over a lot, especially when we play team sports. Last week I had a ⁷_____ , which was so embarrassing because it caused so much fuss. But nights are even worse. After a good supper, I can't get to sleep. I ⁸_____ for hours and nothing. Could it be the beginning of ⁹_____ ? I'm already very tired.
As I am obviously seriously ill, please exempt me from my PE lessons. I am afraid I will get ¹⁰_____ otherwise.

2 Complete the definitions.

> You probably have it when you sneeze and cough when certain plants bloom. **h**_ay_ **f**_eve_**r**

1 You do it when you make a loud noise while sleeping.
   s _ _ _ _
2 It's a disease that affects a particular part of your body and is caused by a virus or bacteria.
   i _ _ _ _ _ _ _ **n**
3 You stick it on your skin when you have a small wound.
   p _ _ _ _ _ _
4 It's like a finger but on your foot.
   t _ _
5 You get this if you spend too much time in the sun.
   s _ _ _ _ _ _
6 You wear your watch on it.
   w _ _ _ _
7 You do this, e.g. with your knee, when the bones in your knee move out of their usual position.
   d _ _ _ _ _ _ _ **e**
8 When you get heavier, it means you've gained it.
   w _ _ _ _ **t**

SCIENCE AND TECHNOLOGY

1 Complete the definitions.

> a piece of equipment used to record films
> **v**_ideo_ **c**_amera_

1 a word you use to, e.g. access your computer
   p_____**d**
2 the action you do to put a video online
   u_____**d** a video
3 a website where you can connect with your friends or people with similar interests
   s_____ **n**_____ **s**_____
4 a smart, useful and cleverly-designed piece of equipment
   g_____**t**
5 all the things you bought on the Internet
   o_____ **p**_____
6 publish a message or picture on a website
   p_____**t**
7 a set of programs that look for and remove viruses in programs and documents on your computer
   a_____-**v**_____ **s**_____**e**
8 a special word or picture on the Internet that you click on to move quickly to another part of this document or to another document
   l_____
9 you do this with sound or video if you play it on your computer while it is being downloaded from the Internet, rather than saving it onto your computer and playing it later
   s_____**m**
10 this happens when a picture or video spreads quickly to many people, especially on the Internet or mobile phones
   g_____ **v**_____

2 Complete the sentences.

The Internet is an invention which connects even the most remote places with the **o** _u_ _t_ _s_ _i_ _d_ **e w** _o_ _r_ **d**.

1 Today's smartphones use the most **c** _ _ _ _ _ _ - **e** _ _ _ technology to provide the best possible experience to their users.

2 Due to the fire, the city's energy generators have been shut down and over 200,000 people are without **e** _ _ _ _ _ _ _ _ **y**.

3 Albert Einstein is by far one of the greatest physics **g** _ _ _ **u** _ **s** in history – his logical thinking skills were exceptional.

4 Dubai is a country full of original concepts and technological **i** _ _ _ _ _ _ _ _ **n** – one of them is drones spying on people who leave rubbish in the streets.

5 I love this **m** _ _ _ _ - **p** _ _ _ _ **e** tool – it's a corkscrew, a screwdriver, a torch and a laser pointer in one.

6 Scientists **p** _ _ _ _ _ **t** that in the future we will be able to print 3D copies of transplantable organs.

7 The author of the documentary did not **p** _ _ **v** _ _ **e** any scientific proof for his theories – it's just assumptions.

8 If hackers get **a** _ _ _ _ **s** to your personal information, they may, for example, take out a bank loan that you will have to pay back.

THE NATURAL WORLD

1 Complete the sentences with the correct form of the words in capitals.

The river is over 400 metres _wide_, so it's hard to see what's happening on the other bank. **WIDTH**

1 Pompei was destroyed by a _____ eruption. **VOLCANO**

2 Air _____ in Asian cities is horrible; that's why so many people wear face masks. **POLLUTE**

3 Remember to put all the tins and cans in the _____ bin. **RECYCLE**

4 She lives in a 19th century house with no _____ water and no heating. **RUN**

5 The hurricane was coming and they had to _____ the old floodwall to stop the water from destroying the town. **STRONG**

6 Solar power is just one example of ecological, _____ energy. **NEW**

7 If people don't address the important _____ issues now, they will soon have no place to live. **ENVIRONMENT**

8 The obligation to change shoes inside the school building is one of the _____ standards all students must follow. **SAFE**

9 Canoeing down a _____ mountain stream was extremely difficult and tiring. **WIND**

10 World energy _____ is the total amount of energy all the people in the world use every year. **CONSUME**

2 Complete the text with one word in each gap.

IT'S A MUST-SEE!

The long-awaited sequel of the famous 1998 disaster movie stars the brilliant Brian Hurrey and Lilian Dress. Hurrey plays Professor Killian, whose aim is to save humanity. The stunning Lilian Dress helps the professor to save the world. And the world has to face not one disaster but many. First, the air **q**_uality_ on Earth is so bad that it causes climate [1]**c**_____ . Meteorologists predict strong winds leading to disastrous [2]**h**_____**s**. People have been [3]**ev**_____ from all major cities. Heavy rains and melting Arctic ice will make water levels rise, which means the destruction of towns on the [4]**c**_____**t** and disappearance of many [5]**is**_____**s**. This also means that many animal [6]**sp**_____**s** may become [7]**en**_____**d**.

Is this all a result of global [8]**w**_____? Will Professor Killian save the planet and all its [9]**in**_____**s**? Will he find a new source of renewable [10]**e**_____ ? You simply must see for yourselves. Animal lovers won't be disappointed either: the ocean scenes include [11]**w**_____**s** and [12]**d**_____**s**!

Tonight – only on Channel 7!

STATE AND SOCIETY

1 Complete the definitions.

the state of not having a job
u _n_ _e_ _m_ _p_ _l_ _o_ _y_ **e d**

1 action against the rules, accepted ways of behaving or the authority of a country
r _ _ _ _ _ _ _ **n**

2 the number of people living in a particular area
p _ _ _ _ _ _ _ _ _ **n**

3 most people
m _ _ _ _ _ _ **y**

4 give money to, e.g. a charity
d _ _ _ _ _

5 somebody who takes part in something
p _ _ _ _ _ _ _ _ _ **t**

6 unpaid work, e.g. for a charity
v _ _ _ _ _ _ _ _ **w** _ _ _

7 someone who legally lives in a particular town, country or state
c _ _ _ _ _ **n**

8 somebody who pretends to be somebody else
f _ _ _

9 somebody who asks other people for money or food
b _ _ _ _ _

10 choose a leader (e.g. the president)
e _ _ _ _

2 Choose the correct answers A–D.

We don't need security __ outside the building, there's a street lamp right in front of the door.
(A) lights B firm
C lock D alarm

1 He committed __ and was sent to prison.
A death B escape
C murder D kill

2 The __ said he was not guilty and had not left home on the night of the crime.
A police officer B judge
C suspect D prison guard

3 In general, I think criminals should be __ .
A punished B released
C burgled D collected

4 Abraham Lincoln __ slavery in the 19th century.
A abolished B punished
C released D broke

5 She's been __ with identity theft – she stole other people's private information.
A accused B questioned
C sentenced D charged

6 There was no clear __ that Mr Gunheim was at the bank on the night of the robbery, so the police had to release him.
A court B judge
C sentence D evidence

3 Complete the gaps with words from the box. There are three extra words.

> arrest beggar burglary burgled
> citizens criminal escape foundation
> offender stole thief

ORCHARD LOCAL NEWS

The police are looking for a person who _stole_ twenty packages of anti-aging cream from The Beauty Shop in Oak Avenue last Friday. The shop's personnel are looking for the ¹_____ who ran away at 15:30. They say it was a medium-height, plump woman, wearing a pink dress and an orange hat.

A florist's in Skylark Street has been ²_____ by an unknown man who is still at large. The ³_____ occurred last night. The burglar was seen leaving the shop by a witness, who called the police, but the ⁴_____ managed to ⁵_____ , taking all the roses that were in the shop.

The teenager who attacked two elderly ladies in Rose Street and stole their handbags is already under ⁶_____ . The young ⁷_____ claimed he desperately needed money to buy his grandmother some medicine.

CULTURE OF ENGLISH-SPEAKING COUNTRIES

1 Choose the correct answers A–D.

Which of these women is not a singer?
A Jennifer Hudson
B Beyoncé
(C) Jennifer Aniston
D Christina Aguilera

1 Blue jeans were first made during
A the Second World War.
B the California Gold Rush.
C the 18th century.
D World War I.

2 The political system of the United Kingdom is a
A republic.
B constitutional monarchy.
C dictatorship.
D democracy.

3 The Shard is a famous landmark in
A New York.
B London.
C Seattle.
D Sydney.

4 Which of these does Bill Bryson not write?
A travel books
B popular science books
C books on the English language
D sci-fi stories

5 The Doctors without Borders organisation was set up in
A France.
B Belgium.
C the United States.
D the United Kingdom.

2 What are the speakers talking about? Match the words from the box with the sentences below.

> Coachella Fisherman's Wharf Lord Byron
> Masterchef The Beatles
> The Great Barrier Reef

They're one of the most important rock bands in the history of music, and they made Liverpool famous too! _The Beatles_

1 The festival takes place in California, usually in the spring. It's very popular. _____

2 I'd love to go there one day. First of all, it's in San Francisco, and secondly – I'd love to see those sea lions. _____

3 I really admire those amateurs – they are able to prepare an exotic and delicious dish in just 40 minutes! _____

4 I've never been a fan of the Romantic poets, but his poetry speaks to me. _____

5 The colours, the animals, the plants underwater – it's really amazing. _____

1 **In pairs, ask and answer the questions.**

Talk about looks and personality.

1 Do you enjoy being the centre of attention when you're in a group? Why?/Why not?
2 How much do you care about your appearance? Why?
3 When was the last time you didn't want to go with the flow? What happened?
4 Have you ever fallen out with a friend? What happened?
5 Do you like wearing cutting-edge fashions? Why?/Why not?

2 Look at the photo of the young people wearing fashionable clothes. Take turns to talk about what you can see in your photos. Talk about the people, the clothes and the other things in the photo.

3 You and your friend want to buy a birthday present for a fashionable female friend. Here are some of the presents you could choose. Talk together about the different presents and say which would be best.

4 **Talk about buying presents.**

- Do you enjoy buying presents for people? Why?/Why not?
- Where do you usually go to buy presents?
- What sort of presents do you like receiving? Why?
- Do you think it's easy or hard to buy fashionable presents for friends? Why?
- Who is the hardest person you know to buy a present for? Why?

1 In pairs, ask and answer the questions.

Talk about sport.
1 How do you feel if you are defeated in a sport? Why?
2 Have you ever seen someone break a world record? Give details.
3 When was the last time you took on a sporting challenge? Give details.

4 Why do you think so many people look up to sportsmen and sportswomen? Do you?
5 How important is it to earn a lot of money in professional sports?

2 Discuss this question together. 'Is winning more important than taking part in a sport?' What do you think?

For winning:

Winning a sport ...
- is the whole point of playing a competitive game.
- (or the idea of winning) makes sportspeople work hard and push themselves to achieve great things.
- is important to sportspeople because they earn more prize money.
- makes sportspeople more motivated to succeed again in the future.

3 Look at the two photos showing people who work in sports. What can you see in the photos? Which job would you prefer to do? Why?

4 Read the instructions on your card and role-play the conversation.

Student B:

You and your friend (Student A) are discussing a suggestion that sports should be removed from the curriculum.
- When asked, give your opinion: say that it's a good idea because it would give students more time to spend on their exam subjects.
- Agree with Student A's opinion. But say that students can organise their own sports in their free time.
- Disagree strongly with Student A's opinion by saying that students have lots of free time.
- Agree and end the conversation.

1 **In pairs, ask and answer the questions.**

Talk about travel.
1 Tell me about the most dangerous journey you've ever made.
2 What's the best form of transport when you're on holiday in a foreign country? Why?
3 Have you ever tried immersing yourself in a foreign culture? Why?
4 Would you like to go on a package holiday or would you prefer to organise it yourself? Why?
5 How can travel challenge your beliefs about yourself and the place you live?

2 **Look at the photo of an interesting journey. Take turns to talk about what you can see in your photos. Talk about the people, the place and the other things in the photo.**

3 **You and your friend are planning to take a gap year. Here are some of the places where you could work when you travel. Talk together about the places and say which would be the most interesting.**

4 **Talk about a gap year.**
- What are the advantages of having a gap year before you go to university?
- What are the disadvantages of having a gap year before you go to university?
- What would you like to do most during your gap year and how would you organise this?
- Which places would you include on your itinerary? Why?
- Would you rather take a gap year on your own or with a friend? Why?

1   In pairs, ask and answer the questions.

Talk about food.
1   Describe a healthy, balanced diet including food products and other ingredients you like.
2   What three-course meal would you make for your best friend on his/her birthday?
3   When was the last time you ate tinned food instead of a home-made meal? Why?
4   What are the benefits of eating organic food?
5   Have you ever eaten food past its sell-by date? Why?/Why not?

2   Discuss this question together. 'Should we all be vegetarian?' What do you think?

> **For eating meat:**
>
> **Eating meat ...**
> *   is natural for humans – our bodies are designed to eat meat.
> *   is a good way to eat a balanced diet, e.g. protein is important for our bones, muscles, skin and blood.
> *   doesn't necessarily mean being cruel to animals if we treat them well while they are alive.
> *   is delicious!

3   Look at these two meals. What can you see in the photos? Which would you prefer to eat? Why?

A

B

4   Read the instructions on your card and role-play the conversation.

> **Student B:**
>
> **You are the waiter in a restaurant. Take Student A's order.**
> *   Respond to Student A and ask what you can get him/her.
> *   Say it's chicken and pumpkin soup.
> *   Say that you have a salad with beetroot, cauliflower and avocado.
> *   Say no, it's quite mild.
> *   Say yes, it comes with fresh, home-made wholemeal bread.
> *   Say yes and end the conversation.

1 In pairs, ask and answer the questions.

Talk about the environment.
1 What do you think is the most serious environmental issue the world is facing? Why?
2 How can teenagers influence politicians on the subject of climate change?
3 What forms of renewable energy are the most popular in your country?
4 Have you ever been in danger because of a rough sea, a strong current or a rising tide? What happened?
5 What natural disasters do you think will become more common in the future? Why?

2 Look at the photo of a natural landscape. Take turns to talk about what you can see in your photos. Talk about the people, the place and the other things in the photo.

3 You and your friend are discussing ways you can help to stop climate change in your school. Here are some ideas. Talk together about the different ideas and say which would be most useful and why.

4 Talk about climate change.
- Are you worried about climate change? Why?/Why not?
- What do you do at home to help stop climate change?
- Is it easy to recycle things where you live? Why?/Why not?
- What sources of renewable energy are used in your country?
- What are the dangers to animals from climate change?

1 In pairs, ask and answer the questions.

Talk about health.
1 Have you ever been bitten by an animal or an insect?
2 Do you have any food allergies?
3 Have you ever burnt any part of your body?
4 Has anyone ever helped you when you had health problems? What happened?
5 When was the last time you laughed your head off? What happened?

2 Discuss this question together. Take different sides of the argument during your discussion. 'Is it acceptable to test new medicines on animals?' Decide who is going to take each side. Then share your ideas.

3 Look at the two photos showing people who have been injured. What can you see in the photos? Which injury do you think is worse? Why?

4 Read the instructions on your card and role-play the conversation.

Student B:

The situation:

You are a patient at a doctor's surgery. Student A is the doctor. You have hurt your leg. Think about how it happened and what symptoms you have. Tell the doctor. Listen to his/her advice. Ask if you need to go to hospital. Ask if you need to have an operation. Ask if you need any medicine.

Your goal:

To get treatment from the doctor for your leg.

1 In pairs, ask and answer the questions.

Talk about entertainment.

1 Have you ever been to a live gig? Would you like to? Why?/Why not?

2 Do great reviews make you want to buy a song or watch a film? Why?/Why not?

3 What was the last video you watched?

4 Do you think you have a short or long attention span? Why?

5 Do you prefer to read e-books or to read books the old-fashioned way?

2 Look at the photo of the musicians. Take turns to talk about what you can see in your photos. Talk about the people, the place and the other things in the photo.

3 You and your friend want to start doing a hobby related to music. Here are some of the things you could choose. Talk together about the different ideas and say which you would enjoy most.

4 Talk about making music.

- Would you rather play music or make music? Why?
- If you were a musician, would you prefer to make music by yourself or with friends? Why?
- Who is your favourite musician or songwriter of all time? Why?
- If you could play any venue, where would you play? Why?
- If you released an album, what would it be like? Why?

1 In pairs, ask and answer the questions.

Talk about crime and criminals.

1 Which crimes are the biggest problem in your town or in your country?

2 If you were a judge, would you release criminals from prison earlier if they behaved well in prison? Why?

3 At what age do you think people are old enough to take responsibility for criminal actions?

4 Do you know anyone who has been a victim of identity theft? What happened?

5 When did you last see something vandalised? What happened?

2 Discuss this question together. 'Is the main purpose of a prison to punish a criminal or to help him/her not to break the law again when he/she is released?' What do you think?

3 Look at the two photos showing two stages of the justice system. Which of the jobs in the justice system would you prefer to do? Why?

4 Read the instructions on your card and role-play the conversation.

Student B:

The situation:

You and Student A are discussing placements for voluntary work. There are two places available: one is at a youth centre helping young people with their Maths and one is at an old people's home, keeping elderly people company. Discuss the advantages and disadvantages of both placements, talk about your skills and interests and decide which you will do.

Your goal:

You want to work at the youth centre.

Present tenses – review

We use the **Present Simple** to talk about:

- states and permanent situations:
  We **live** in the centre of Sydney.
  I **love** shopping.
- actions which are repeated regularly:
  I **make** my bed every morning.

Affirmative		Negative		
I You We They	play.	I You We They	don't (do not)	play.
He She It	plays.	He She It	doesn't (does not)	play.

Yes/No questions			Short answers
Do	I you we they	play?	Yes, I/you/we/they **do**. No, I/you/we/they **don't**.
Does	he she it		Yes, he/she/it **does**. No, he/she/it **doesn't**.

Wh- questions			
Where	do	I you we they	live?
	does	he she it	

Subject questions
Who	lives here?

Common time phrases in the Present Simple:
always, regularly, usually, often, sometimes, never, every day/week/month, three times a year.

Spelling rules – third person singular:

- general rule: infinitive + -s, e.g. *run – runs*
- verbs ending in a consonant and -y: *y + -ies*, e.g. *carry – carries*
- verbs *do* and *go* and verbs ending in -ss, -x, -ch, -sh: + es, e.g. *do – does, go – goes, push – pushes*
- *have: has*

We use the **Present Continuous** to talk about actions, events and changes happening at the moment of speaking: *My dad is painting the kitchen right now.*

Affirmative			Negative		
I	am		I	'm not (am not)	
You We They	are	cleaning.	You We They	aren't (are not)	cleaning.
He She It	is		He She It	isn't (is not)	

Yes/No questions			Short answers
Am	I		Yes, I am. No, I'm not.
Are	you we they	cleaning?	Yes, you/we/they are. Not, you/we/they aren't.
Is	he she it		Yes, he/she/it is. No, he/she/it isn't.

Wh- questions			
What	am	I	cleaning?
	are	you we they	
	is	he she it	

Subject questions
Who	is cleaning the windows?

Common time phrases in the Present Continuous:
at the moment, now, today, this morning/afternoon, this year, these days, at present.

Spelling rules – the *-ing* form:

- general rule: infinitive + -ing: e.g. *cook – cooking*
- verbs ending in a consonant + -e: *e + -ing*, e.g. *make – making*
- one-syllable verbs ending in a single vowel + a consonant: the consonant is doubled + -ing, e.g. *swim – swimming*

Present tenses – review

We use the **Present Perfect** to talk about actions and events which started in the past and continue up to now:
We've had this TV for three years.

When describing actions which started in the past and continue into the present, we often use *since* and *for*:

* *since* describes when the action or state began:
since 2012/Sunday/last month/my birthday/I moved here

* *for* describes how long the action or state has continued:
for five minutes/a week/a long time/ages/most of my life

Affirmative			Negative		
I/You We They	've (have)	finished.	I/You/ We/ They	haven't (have not)	finished.
He/ She/ It	's (has)		He/ She/ It	hasn't (has not)	

Yes/No questions			Short answers	
Have	I/you/ we/they	finished?	Yes, I/you/we/they **have**. No, I/you/we/they **haven't**.	
Has	he/she/ it		Yes, he/she/it **has**. No, he/she/it **hasn't**.	

Wh- questions			
What	have	I/you/we/they	learnt?
	has	he/she/it	

Subject questions	
Who	**has studied** French before?

Spelling rules – the past participle form
Regular verbs

* general rule: infinitive + *-ed*, e.g. *work – worked*
* verbs ending in *-e*: + *-d*, e.g. *like – liked*
* verbs ending in a consonant + *-y*: ~~y~~ + *-ied*, e.g. *cry – cried*
* one-syllable verbs ending in a single vowel + consonant*: the consonant is doubled + *-ed*, e.g. *stop – stopped*

   *except *-x* and *-w*, e.g. *boxed, flowed*

* two-syllable verbs ending in a vowel + consonant: the consonant is doubled when the stress is on the second syllable, e.g. *refer – referred*
* *travel*: although the stress is on the first syllable, *-l* is doubled, e.g. *travel – travelled*

Irregular verbs

Many verbs have an irregular past participle form (e.g. *write, go, lose*). A list of irregular verbs can be found in the Student's Book on page 159.

Pay attention to how we use the past participle for *go*, i.e. *been* and *gone*:
*Monica **has been** to the USA. (Sometime in the past, she is not there now.)*
*Monica **has gone** to the USA. (She is there right now.)*

---

1 Complete the sentences and questions with the correct forms of the verbs in brackets. Use the Present Simple, the Present Continuous or the Present Perfect.

   Hi Clara, I *'m driving* (drive). Can I call you back later?

1 Graham _____ (not/clean) the bathroom for two weeks now, so he really needs to do it this weekend.
2 Every September, Helen _____ (order) all the stuff she needs for school online.
3 What _____ (wait) for? The washing-up isn't going to do itself, you know.
4 I _____ (never/live) in a house with a balcony.
5 _____ (you/really enjoy) tidying up? If so, you can do my room any time you like!

2 Complete the text with the correct forms of the verbs from the box.

(go   hate   have   make   meet   ~~move~~   pack)

Hi Vicky,
How are you? Guess what! We *'re moving* house again! I know, I know! It's ridiculous, right? I really
¹_____ it! We ²_____ three different flats in two years. I ³_____ some really wonderful people here and suddenly it's time to leave again. Mum and Dad ⁴_____ up things upstairs right now – I should be helping, but the thought of putting all my stuff in boxes again ⁵_____ me want to cry. It would be so much better if Dad had a normal job. I just want to stay in one place for a few years!
I ⁶_____ crazy with all this constant change.
Miss you,
C.

3 Write sentences and questions from the prompts. Do not change the order of the words.

   Bill / not go / to the gym / every day
   Bill doesn't go to the gym every day.

1 At the moment / Kate / look for / a part-time job.
   _____
2 How often / you / update / your profile?
   _____
3 Why / Paul / look after / his friend's dog / today?
   _____
4 Who / see / this thriller / before?
   _____
5 Martha / not do / any sports / since January.
   _____

4 Complete the questions with the correct forms of the verbs in brackets. Then ask and answer the questions in pairs.

   Where *do your parents come from* (your parents/ come from)?

1 Who _____ (live) in your house, apart from you?
2 Who usually _____ (do) the cooking in your family?
3 How long _____ (you/be) at your current address?
4 _____ (your family/ever/move) house?
5 How long _____ (it/usually/take) to get to school?
6 Why _____ (you/learn) English?

Quantifiers

Nouns can be *countable* or *uncountable*.

Countable nouns:

- have both singular and plural forms:
  *This **apple** is very sweet.*
  *These **apples** are very sweet.*

- can be used with *a/an/the* or a number:
  an egg, the egg, the eggs, two eggs

Uncountable nouns:

- have no plural form:
  ***Milk** is very healthy.*

- can be used with *the*, but not with *a/an* or a number:
  water, the water, a water, one water

We often use the following quantifiers with countable and uncountable nouns:

Countable nouns	Uncountable nouns
How many?	How much?
How many eggs are there?	*How much sugar is there?*
many	much
*Are there **many** eggs?*	*Is there **much** sugar?*
*We haven't got **many** eggs.*	*We haven't got **much** sugar.*
a lot of / lots of	
There are **a lot of/lots of** eggs in the fridge.	There is **a lot of/lots of** sugar in the cupboard.
a few	a little
*I need **a few** eggs.*	*I need **a little** sugar.*
some	
There are **some** eggs in the fridge.	There is **some** sugar in the cupboard.
few	little
There are **few** eggs in the fridge.	There is **little** sugar in the cupboard.
any (?)	
Are there **any** eggs in the fridge?	Is there **any** sugar in the cupboard?
any (–)	
There aren't **any** eggs in the fridge.	There isn't **any** sugar in the cupboard.

1 Complete the text with the words from the box. There are two extra words.

> a little a lot of any few little
> many much some

There are *a lot of* cooking programmes on television these days. They seem to be on day and night. In fact, ¹_____ channels are nothing but cooking. How ²_____ TV chefs do we need? I actually think that very ³_____ people make ⁴_____ of the dishes they see on these programmes. Perhaps people spend so ⁵_____ time watching cooking shows that they don't actually have time to cook or eat!

2 Complete the sentences with the correct quantifiers. Use one word in each gap.

How *much* time do you need to clean the flat?

1 Don't put so _____ salt on your food. It's not good for you.
2 I would like _____ chilli sauce with my burger, but not too much, please.
3 They have a _____ of different pizza toppings to choose from. Which do you fancy?
4 I have a _____ time to help you.
5 _____ people have actually tasted the world's most expensive coffee – almost nobody can afford it.
6 I have to get another job. At the end of the month I have very _____ money left.
7 How _____ cups of oil do you need for this cake?
8 Is there _____ butter in the fridge? I really need a sandwich.

3 Complete the sentences to make them true for you. Use quantifiers.

I've got *a lot of/very few* after-school classes.

1 I spend _____ time watching TV series.
2 I have _____ second-hand clothes in my wardrobe.
3 I send _____ text messages every day.
4 I don't put _____ sugar in my tea.
5 I do _____ sport at the weekend.
6 I have read _____ really good books.
7 I don't know _____ people who never shop online.
8 I need _____ money to have a good time with friends.

Complete the sentences with a one-word quantifier in each gap.

Lots of people find it difficult to eat healthily.

1 I'm sure there was _____ chicken in the freezer.
2 Have you got _____ friends in London?
3 How _____ days off school do we get for Christmas?
4 There aren't _____ cakes left – just three – help yourself!
5 I've read a _____ positive reviews for that new sushi restaurant in the High Street.

Use one of the words in brackets to write sentences with the opposite meaning.

He drinks a lot of fizzy drinks. (much / many)
He doesn't drink many fizzy drinks.

1 I eat lots of meat. (many / much)
_____

2 There are some good restaurants near my house. (some / any)
_____

3 I drink lots of cola. (very little / very few)
_____

4 My mother bakes a lot of cakes. (much / many)
_____

5 I had some cereal for breakfast. (any / many)
_____

6 I used to eat lots of vegetables. (very little / very few)
_____

7 I do lots of cooking at home. (much / many)
_____

Complete the text with *much, many, a lot of, lots of, (a) few, (a) little, some* or *any*.

Although we meet *a lot of* different people every day, finding a person we get on well with and trust is not so easy. That might be the reason I don't have ¹_____ close friends, just ²_____ . We're all really busy so, unfortunately, we have ³_____ opportunities to hang out together as often as we would like to. However, every month we try to find ⁴_____ time to meet and catch up on what's going on in our lives. We don't need ⁵_____ to enjoy ourselves – good company is enough. I can't imagine not having ⁶_____ friends at all. Even if I have very ⁷_____ free time on my hands, I can always find an hour to get together with my mates.

Present Perfect and Past Simple

We use the **Present Perfect** to talk about actions and events which:

- finished in the past, but either we don't know when they happened, or this information is not important:
  *My dad **has been** to many concerts.*

Common time expressions used with the Present Perfect:

- **ever** – used in questions:
  *Have you **ever** danced in a shopping centre?*

- **never** – used in negative sentences:
  *My grandparents have **never** watched a film online.*

- **already** and **just** – used in affirmative sentences, between *have* and the past participle form of the main verb:
  *I have **already** read this book. They have **just** arrived.*

- **yet** – used in negative sentences or questions, at the end of the sentence:
  *She hasn't called **yet**. Has she called **yet**?*

We use the **Past Simple** to talk about actions and events which started and finished in the past. We often say when they happened:
*My dad **went** to a concert yesterday.*

Affirmative		Negative		
I/You/He/She/It We/They	danced.	I/You He/She It/We They	didn't (did not)	dance.

Yes/No questions			Short answers	
Did	I/you he/she it/we they	dance?	Yes, I/you/he/she/it/we/they **did**. No, I/you/he/she/it/we/they **didn't**.	

Wh- questions			
Where	did	I/you/he/she/it/we/they	dance?

Subject questions		
Who	danced	in the shopping centre?

Common time phrases in the Past Simple:
yesterday, last (year), (three days) ago, when, in the past, then.

Spelling rules – the Past Simple form

Regular verbs

The rules for forming the Past Simple form of regular verbs are the same as those for the past participle form of regular verbs.

Irregular verbs

Many verbs have an irregular Past Simple form (e.g. *write, go, lose*). There is a list of irregular verbs in the Student's Book on page 159.

FOCUS 2 GRAMMAR REVIEW

1 Complete the questions and answers with the correct forms of the verbs in brackets and auxiliary verbs (be, do or have).

1 What's the most you _have ever paid_ (ever/pay) for a pair of sunglasses?
Well, I _____ (never/pay) more than 25 pounds because I always lose them or sit on them.

2 _____ (you/look) at the sales yesterday?
Yes, I _____ but the bargains had already gone.

3 _____ (you/decide) what you're going to wear yet?
No, I _____ . I think either the black dress or the blue skirt and top.

4 Where _____ (she/be) on Sunday evening?
I don't know. I _____ (not/see) her that day.

2 Complete the conversation with the words in brackets. Use the Present Perfect or the Past Simple.

R: Hi Simon. How are you doing?
S: Really well?! I _'ve just finished_ (just/finish) my last exam.
R: Oh great. Lucky you. I ¹_____ (not/finish/yet) – three more to go.
S: Oh, well, good luck. Listen, ²_____ (you/ever/see) a flashmob?
R: Yes, I ³_____ (see) one on YouTube yesterday. It ⁴_____ (be) fantastic. But I ⁵_____ (not/see) a real one.
S: No, neither have I, but I ⁶_____ (watch) a few online. Yesterday, I ⁷_____ (watch) a surprise flashmob for a girl's 18th birthday.
R: Oh, right!
S: So, I want to organise one for my sister's birthday. Will you help me? You have to learn a dance.
R: Dance? Are you sure? ⁸_____ (you/ask) anybody else yet?
S: Yes, I ⁹_____ (already/ask) lots of people. I ¹⁰_____ (speak) to Sally five minutes ago and she said yes.
R: But she's a good dancer!
S: Don't worry, we have plenty of time. I ¹¹_____ (not/choose) the music yet!

3 Put the words in the correct order to make sentences and questions. Use the verbs in the correct tense.

on / post / Sally / video / just / YouTube / a / .
Sally has just posted a video on YouTube.

1 the / guitar / ago / I / play / three / learn / years / to / .
_____

2 you / yet / suit / buy / a / new / ?
_____

3 driving / Rob / yesterday / first / have / lesson / his / .
_____

4 Helen / song / this / write / when / ?
_____

5 account / open / yet / Tom / not / a / bank / .
_____

4 Complete the conversation in a shop with the Past Simple or the Present Perfect forms of the verbs from the box. Use short forms where possible.

be (x2) contact just / enter meet
need never / hear offer see work

SA: Good afternoon. Can I help you with anything?
S: Er, yes actually ... Oh! Lilly, it's you! It _'s been_ a long time! How are you?
L: I'm good, thanks. I'm earning a bit of extra money here, you know.
S: That's great! How long have you been working here?
L: Well, I'm still going to college, so I only work here on Saturdays. I ¹_____ an advert online a few weeks ago. They ²_____ someone to work, so I ³_____ the manager, we had a chat and he ⁴_____ me the job. It ⁵_____ two weeks since I started, but I already love it! The clothes are really cool and we get to choose the music. And of course loads of celebrities come in!
S: Seriously?! ⁶_____ you _____ anyone famous here?
L: Sure. That guy who presents the weather forecast. And Tanya something, I don't remember her name but she's in the latest crime series on Channel Z. And ... Sarah, don't turn around! Simon Bellevue ⁷_____ the shop! He's so gorgeous!
S: Simon who?
L: Simon Bellevue! The talk show host! Everybody knows him!
S: Well, I don't. I ⁸_____ of him.
L: Oh, Sarah ... turn on your TV from time to time! OK, wait here. I'm going to ask for his autograph!

5 Complete the second sentence so that it means the same as the first. Use the correct forms of the verbs in capitals.

I've lived here since 2012. **MOVE**
I _moved here in_ 2012.

1 Jack became the owner of this vintage cupboard in 2015. **OWN**
Jack _____ 2015.

2 My parents have been married for twenty years. **GET**
My parents _____ .

3 They last went to the seaside six months ago. **BE**
They _____ six months.

4 Kate has been on a diet for two weeks. **GO**
Kate _____ .

5 Mary first met Greg in 2009. **KNOW**
Mary _____ 2009.

6 Tom has been unemployed for a few months. **LOSE**
Tom _____ .

7 Adam started reading that book three days ago and is now on page 230. **READ**
Adam _____ 230 pages of that book.

Comparative and superlative adjectives
• too and enough

- We use the comparative form of adjectives and the word *than* when we want to compare two people or things:
  *This shirt is **cheaper than** the sweater.*

- We use the superlative form of adjectives to show that a person or thing has the highest degree of a certain quality (compared to at least two other people or things):
  *This is **the most expensive** ring in the shop.*

- To compare two people or things, we can also use *(not)* as + adjective + as:
  *This jacket is **not as comfortable as** that coat.*

Adjectives		Comparative	Superlative
one-syllable adjectives	young nice hot	younger nicer hotter	the youngest the nicest the hottest
one- and two-syllable adjectives ending in -y	pretty dry	prettier drier	the prettiest the driest
two-syllable or longer adjectives	modern expensive dangerous	**more** modern **more** expensive **more** dangerous	the most modern the most expensive the most dangerous
irregular adjectives	good bad far	better worse further	the best the worst the furthest

We often use **too** (= more than you need or want) and **not enough** (= less than you need or want) with adjectives.
The patterns are: *too + adjective* and *not + adjective + enough*:
*The designer was **too busy** to talk to the press.*
*The horse **wasn't fast enough** to win the race.*

Complete the sentences with *too* or *enough* and the adjectives in brackets.

I was planning to give something to charity, but nothing I have is *valuable enough* (valuable).

1 I'd like to buy designer clothes but they are _____ (expensive).
2 I want to learn to drive but I'm _____ (scared).
3 I'd like a larger bed but my room is _____ (big).
4 My brother never lends me money because he is _____ (mean).
5 My parents won't let me have a motorbike. They say it is _____ (dangerous).

2 Complete the sentences and questions with one word in each gap.

This bed isn't big *enough* for two people.

1 Are you _____ careful with money than your friends?
2 I'm bad at football, but I'm even _____ at tennis.
3 Black skinny jeans are the _____ fashionable trousers this season.
4 Shopping with friends is better _____ shopping alone.
5 This is _____ biggest shopping centre in our town.
6 Denim jackets are as popular _____ leather jackets this season.

3 Complete the texts with the words from the box.

> as (x2)   enough   more (x2)   most
> richer   than (x3)   the (x2)   too

TEEN ATTITUDES TO MONEY

We ask brother and sister Tom and Zoey about their attitudes to money and shopping:

Zoey, 16

I think I'm very good with money. I don't have much money though because I'm still at school, but I'm *more* careful than my brother. For example, he spends his birthday money as soon as he gets it. Also, he's older [1]_____ me and has a weekend job, so he's [2]_____ than I am. To be honest, I think he's stupid with his money. The [3]_____ expensive thing I've ever bought is a leather jacket, and that was second-hand, so it wasn't [4]_____ expensive as a new one. I don't go out much – Tom says I'm not sociable [5]_____ , but I just like staying at home.

Tom, 17

I'm [6]_____ generous than Zoey. In fact, I'm probably [7]_____ generous! If I have money, I spend it. I'm richer than Zoey because I work at the weekend but she's more careful [8]_____ me, so she always has money and I never have any. Actually, I think Zoey's [9]_____ meanest person I know! My clothes are more expensive [10]_____ Zoey's but I buy expensive clothes because the people who make cheap clothes have [11]_____ worst working conditions in the world. I spend a lot of money on going out. Zoey isn't [12]_____ popular as I am, so she stays at home more!

4 Complete the second sentence so that it means the same as the first. Use the opposites of the adjectives in bold.

Bobby isn't **hard-working** enough to continue learning Russian.
Bobby is _too lazy_ to continue learning Russian.

1 Jenna is too **short** to ride on the rollercoaster.
Jenna is _____ to ride on the rollercoaster.

2 These blue socks are **wetter** than the black ones.
The black socks are _____ than the blue ones.

3 Tony's arms are **stronger** than Kyle's arms.
Kyle's arms are _____ than Tony's arms.

4 The weather here is usually **better** in the afternoon than in the morning.
The weather here is usually _____ in the morning than in the afternoon.

5 This ring is not **big** enough to fit on my finger.
This ring is _____ to fit on my finger.

6 Dean is too **impatient** to enjoy fishing.
Dean is _____ to enjoy fishing.

5 Complete the text with the correct comparative or superlative forms of the adjectives in brackets.

Lego is one of the _simplest_ (simple) toys available, but according to many people it is also one of the ¹_____ (good) in the world. Most teens and adults remember Lego from their childhood. Lego allows children to be ²_____ (creative) than many other toys – there are 915 million ways to combine just six Lego bricks! The word Lego comes from the phrase '_leg godt_' which means 'play well' in Danish. Check out
³_____ (amazing) Lego facts:

- A pile of 50,000,000,000 Lego bricks would reach ⁴_____ (far) than the moon.

- In 2003, the yellow skin colour of some Lego mini-figures was changed to a ⁵_____ (authentic) skin colour.

- On average, there are 62 Lego bricks for everyone on Earth!

- Approximately seven Lego sets are sold every second, and Lego films and computer games have made the product even ⁶_____ (popular) than in the past.

Future forms

We use the **Present Continuous** for future plans and arrangements, usually with a time reference:
I'm **leaving** tomorrow, so I can't go to the cinema with you.

We use **be going to** + infinitive for:
- intentions and future plans which may change:
  What **are you going to prepare** for lunch?
- predictions about the future based on what we know and can see now:
  We're **not going to get** to the station on time.

We use **will** + infinitive for:
- decisions made at the time of speaking:
  Wait for me! I'**ll help** you with the shopping.
- predictions about the future based on opinions, intuition or experience:
  You can borrow my dictionary, but I'**ll probably need** it back next week.

1 Complete the sentences with the verb forms in the box. There are three extra verb forms.

> isn't going to rain   isn't raining   'll be   'll laugh
> 'm going to laugh   're announcing   're taking
> 's having   's going to have   ~~won't be~~

It's possible that in 2100 there _won't be_ any official school exams.

1 The clouds have gone and the sky is clear.
It _____ soon.

2 He _____ a look at those magazines after lunch.

3 We _____ a taxi to get to the airport. I've already phoned for one.

4 I'm sure Tom _____ disappointed that we didn't win the dancing competition.

5 We _____ the winners of the competition on Friday.

6 I promise I _____ at all your jokes.

2 Complete the sentences with the future forms of the verbs in brackets.

I'_m going_ (go) to the cinema on Saturday.

1 Joe needs new trainers because they _____ (play) a match next weekend.

2 It's very cold. It looks like it _____ (snow).

3 I haven't got any plans this evening.
I _____ (probably/watch) TV.

4 My friend _____ (have) a big eighteenth birthday party next month.

5 I don't think England _____ (win) the next World Cup.

6 I've decided that I _____ (not/get) married).

3 Put the words in the correct order to make sentences and questions.

you / cinema / a / ticket / are / to / going / online / buy / ?
Are you going to buy a cinema ticket online?

1 will / problem / I / you / this / help / solve /.
_____

2 our / Saturday / not / we / doing / on / are / homework /.
_____

3 the / when / to / going / are / do / you / shopping / ?
_____

4 is / week / my / house / friend / next / not / best / moving /.
_____

5 probably / a / my / off / will / few / take / days / mum /.
_____

6 tomorrow / driving / to / the / are / mountains / the Smiths / morning / ?
_____

4 Complete the sentences with one word in each gap.

Mr Richter *is* flying to Amsterdam this Thursday.

1 Me and my classmates are _____ to collect more specimens for our Biology project.

2 I have a headache and a runny nose. I _____ going to be ill.

3 I think this year, we _____ probably organise a fancy dress party for our local kindergarten.

4 Next week my parents _____ meeting their old friends from university. They've already booked a table for Friday at their favourite restaurant.

5 I promise I _____ start revising for my final test tomorrow.

5 Complete the dialogues with the most appropriate future forms of the words in brackets. Use short forms.

Conversation 1: Shop assistant and Jake

SA: Which phone colour would you like, sir? We have black, white and beige.

J: Hmm, good question. I think I'*ll have* (have) the black.

SA: Very good, sir. I ¹_____ (just/check) that we have that particular model here in the shop … Yes, we do. How would you like to pay?

J: Erm … I guess I ²_____ (pay) in cash.

Conversation 2: Molly and Scott

M: Have you decided what you ³_____ (do) this afternoon?

S: Yeah, I ⁴_____ (meet) Paul at 2 and we ⁵_____ (play) Frisbee if the weather is fine.

M: Well, it's clear and blue at the moment, so I don't think it ⁶_____ (rain).

6 Read the situations and write your reactions. Use future forms.

It's started raining and you're outside without an umbrella. You say: *I'm going to get wet.*

1 Your friend suggests you meet up at the weekend. You've already arranged to visit your grandma. You say: I'm sorry I can't meet you. I _____
_____

2 Your brother starts school at 8 a.m. It's 7.50 and he is still at home. You say: Hurry up! _____
_____

3 Your best friend tells you something that no one else should know. You say: I promise I _____
_____

4 Your neighbour is worried he has lost his smartphone. You want to offer help. You say: Don't worry, I _____
_____

5 Your little cousin is running around the house with a glass plate in his hands. You say: Be careful! _____
_____

7 Find and correct the mistakes in the sentences. Use future forms.

I think I'm not living with my parents when I'm twenty.
I don't think I'll live with my parents when I'm twenty.

1 The phone is ringing. Are you answering it, please?
_____

2 The students will sit their final exam tomorrow at 9 a.m.
_____

3 I'm going to order some new books online tonight if I have time.
_____

4 I can't come over this evening. Jane and I will meet at 7 p.m. to talk about our Science project.
_____

5 Look at all this traffic! We are being late for the appointment, I'm afraid.
_____

8 Complete the sentences to make them true for you.

I think in 2025, *there will be very few printed newspapers.*

1 I hope next week I _____
_____

2 Next Monday at 9 a.m. I _____
_____

3 I believe that in 2030 people on Earth _____
_____

4 My plans for the weekend? I _____
_____

5 I think that in five years there _____
_____

First and Second Conditionals

We use **First Conditional** sentences to talk about things which may happen in the future under certain conditions: If you **don't switch on** the printer, it **won't work**.

We use the Present Simple in the *if*-clause (describing the condition) and *will/won't* in the main clause (describing the effect). Either of the two clauses can come first in the sentence. If the *if*-clause comes first, we use a comma after it.

If + Present Simple, (condition)	will/won't + infinitive (effect)
If he **starts** a blog,	I'll **read** it.
will/won't + infinitive (effect)	if + Present Simple (condition)
I'**ll read** his blog	if he **starts** one.

We use **Second Conditional** sentences to talk about present situations or states which are impossible or very unlikely, or about something that could happen in the future but is rather improbable: If I **had** more time, I **would learn** programming.

We use the Past Simple in the *if*-clause (describing the condition) and *would/wouldn't* or *could/couldn't* in the main clause (describing the effect). Either of the two clauses can come first in the sentence. If the *if*-clause comes first, we use a comma after it.

If + Past Simple, (condition)	would/wouldn't/could/ couldn't + infinitive (effect)
If your laptop **crashed**,	who **would** you **ask** for help?
would/wouldn't/could/ couldn't + infinitive (effect)	if + Past Simple (condition)
Who **would** you **ask** for help	if your laptop **crashed**?

1 Complete the conditional sentences and questions with one word in each gap.

If you play video games all the time, you <u>won't</u> be a happy, healthy person.

1 _____ you move to Asia if you got a job there?
2 I think I would go back to 1970 if I _____ .
3 You'll get bad marks at school if you _____ stop playing on the computer.
4 What _____ you write a blog about if you had the time?
5 If I had £500 to spend, I _____ buy new speakers.
6 What will you say if he _____ you for your phone number?
7 If you use social-networking, you _____ lose your privacy.

2 Put the words in the correct order to make conditional sentences. Add commas where necessary.

the same phone / know / won't / as your sister / you / you / buy
If <u>you buy the same phone as your sister, you won't</u> know which is yours.

1 go crazy / if / would / he / wasn't able to
Liam _____
check his email at least once every hour.
2 charges / last all day / she / if
Will Lucy's phone battery _____
_____ it fully?
3 late again / we'll / is / get stuck
If Mum _____
in the rush hour traffic.
4 she / would / had more time / talk to her friends
If Jasmine _____
rather than text them.
5 able / be / if / to / online / wouldn't / go
He _____
he had to give up his phone.

3 Complete the sentences and questions with the correct forms of the verbs in brackets.

1 If your family <u>had</u> (have) a pet dog, who _____ (take) it for a walk every morning?
2 If my parents _____ (know) more about computers, they _____ (understand) why I need a new laptop.
3 Hank _____ (not/become) an IT specialist if he _____ (not/go) to university.
4 We _____ (wear) T-shirts and shorts in winter if we _____ (live) in a hot country.
5 If he _____ (not/hurry) up, he _____ (miss) the beginning of the film.
6 What's wrong with you? If you _____ (not/eat) your lunch, you _____ (be) hungry soon.
7 OK, OK you can borrow my bike, but if I _____ (lend) it to you, _____ (you/ride) safely?
8 If everybody _____ (look) the same, we _____ (get tired) of looking at each other.

4 Complete the conditional sentences with your own ideas.

What will you do if <u>there is no electricity tonight</u>?
1 If he gets a pay rise, _____
_____
2 If I weren't so busy, _____
_____
3 What would you tell your parents if _____
_____
4 Will Rebecca be angry if _____
_____
5 If we were in London today, _____
_____
6 If you were my true friend, _____
_____

5 Complete the sentences with the correct forms of the verbs in brackets. Then finish the sentences to make them true for you.

If I _get_ (get) some money for my next birthday, _I'll save it._

1 If I _____ (find) £1000 in the street, _____

2 If I _____ (not/have) any homework this evening, _____

3 If it _____ (be) nice weather tomorrow, _____

4 If I _____ (can/drive), _____

5 If my parents _____ (win) the lottery, _____

6 If I _____ (live) to be 150, _____

7 If everybody _____ (think) the same as me, _____

6 Rewrite the sentences using the First or Second Conditional.

You want to visit your friend but you're waiting for an invitation.
If my friend invites me, I'll visit her.

1 You want to go to a concert but the tickets shouldn't be too expensive.

2 Your little sister wants to play with you but you're really tired today.

3 You want to go for a jog but it has to stop raining.

4 Your parents need to buy a bigger car but they cannot afford it this year.

5 You're thinking of going for a walk. You have a lot of work.

6 You would like to get a part-time job, but you need to study for your exams.

Modal verbs for obligation and permission

To express obligation or necessity, we use:
- **must**, especially when we refer to something the speaker feels is necessary or important:
  I **must** phone Mum.
- **have to**, especially when we refer to something that is necessary because of a rule or law, or because someone else says so:
  We **have to** wear a uniform at school.
  She **has to** be home at 10 p.m.
- **need to**: need to is similar to have to
  I **need to** sleep eight hours every night.
  Ann often **needs to** look after her younger sister.

To express lack of obligation or necessity, we use:
- **don't have to**:
  You **don't have to** vacuum every day – once a week is enough.
  My dad **doesn't have to** wake up early. He starts work at twelve.
- **don't need to/needn't**:
  You **don't need to** go to university this year.
  You **needn't do** the washing up. We've got a dishwasher.

To express permission, we use:
- **can**:
  You **can** invite some friends if you want.
- **be allowed to**:
  Students **are allowed to** work part-time.

To express lack of permission or prohibition, we use:
- **can't**:
  You **can't** leave the classroom without permission from your teacher.
- **mustn't**: (a strong prohibition)
  You **mustn't** play loud music after 10 p.m.
- **not be allowed to**: (a strong prohibition)
  You **aren't allowed to** speak during the exam.

1 Complete the sentences with the correct forms of must or have to.

We _have to_ go to school this Saturday – we're having a rehearsal for a new play.

1 I've heard it's a great novel. I _____ read it!
2 All students _____ wear uniforms in my school.
3 Does Amy _____ work in the café three times a week?
4 I'm really tired. I _____ go to bed early.
5 I don't think Jo has heard about the meeting and she _____ be present – it's important.
6 Visitors _____ switch off their mobiles here.
7 What do we _____ prepare for our next English class?

2 Complete the sentences with the verbs from the box.

> are allowed to   can   can't   doesn't have to
> ~~don't have to~~   must (x2)   needs to

Ally and Mike *don't have to* be at home at 9 p.m. on Saturdays, so they usually stay out until 10 or 11 p.m.

1 Helen _____ stay at home today because she was in the office on Saturday.

2 Richard _____ walk his dog now – his dad has already done it.

3 I'm afraid you _____ use a dictionary during the test. Please put it back on the shelf.

4 I _____ go now. I don't want my friends to wait for me.

5 It was great to meet you, Alex. We _____ do it more often.

6 My sister is a student, but she still _____ phone my parents every day.

7 My younger brothers _____ play video games for an hour a day only, but they would like to do it more often.

3 Complete the sentences with the correct modal verbs. Sometimes more than one answer is possible.

John *can't / mustn't* go on holiday on his own – he's too young.

1 Students _____ / _____ call their teachers by their first name.

2 You _____ wait for me at the school gate at 3 o'clock. Don't be late! It's the teacher's order.

3 We _____ / _____ / _____ stand up every time someone enters. We can sit.

4 Teenagers _____ / _____ forget that their parents are responsible for them.

5 You _____ / _____ / _____ eat everything if you aren't hungry.

6 _____ you _____ / _____ you use your mobile phone at school?

7 _____ Tina _____ / _____ Tina _____ play tennis with her sister at weekends? Can't her sister find someone else?

4 Complete the text with the correct forms of modal verbs. Use <u>one</u> word in each gap.

THE STRICT TEACHER: She stands at the front of the class and you *have* to listen to her. When she asks a question, you're not [1]_____ to call out the answer, you have to put your hand in the air. You [2]_____ talk in class and you have to do your homework on time, no excuses.

THE RELAXED TEACHER: The opposite of the strict teacher. You are allowed [3]_____ call out answers and sometimes, you [4]_____ call him by his first name. You have [5]_____ do your homework but you [6]_____ need to do it exactly on time. But there are rules. You [7]_____ use your phone in class, and when you talk to your classmates, it [8]_____ to be about the subject of the lesson.

5 Rewrite the sports centre rules. Use modal verbs for permission and obligation. Sometimes more than one answer is possible.

Pets are not permitted in the sports centre.
You *can't / aren't allowed to* bring pets into the sports centre.

1 It is necessary to have the correct change for the lockers in the changing rooms.
You _____ have the correct change for the lockers in the changing rooms.

2 It is not necessary to wear a swimming cap in the pool.
You _____ wear a swimming cap in the pool.

3 Parents are permitted to enter the baby pool with their child.
Parents _____ enter the baby pool with their child.

4 It is not permitted to eat in the gym.
You _____ eat in the gym.

5 It is necessary to wear comfortable shoes in the gym.
You _____ comfortable shoes in the gym.

6 Complete the gaps with the correct forms of modal verbs. Sometimes more than one answer is possible.

21st CENTURY PARENTING
What kinds of parents are there?

Tiger parents are strict and say their children …

- *must* / *have to* / *need to* be the No 1 student in every subject except P.E. and Drama.
- [1]_____ play the piano or violin only and [2]_____ play any other instrument.
- [3]_____ always show respect for them.
- [4]_____ play video games or watch TV – they must focus on school and extra activities.

Hipster parents are non-traditional and easy-going and say their children …

- [5]_____ do more or less whatever they want.
- [6]_____ be top of the class – they can have poor grades as long as they enjoy learning.
- [7]_____ follow many rules – they can usually make their own decisions.
- [8]_____ call them by their first names instead of 'Mum' and 'Dad'.

Defining relative clauses

We use defining relative clauses to give important information about a person, thing, place, etc., so that it's clear which one we are talking about. We use the following relative pronouns:

- **who** and **that** to refer to people:
  *I have a friend **who/that** works as a video game teacher.*
- **which** and **that** to refer to objects:
  *The computer **which/that** I use at work is very slow.*
- **where** to refer to places:
  *This is the office **where** I work.*

We can leave out the relative pronouns *who, which* and *that* when they are followed by a noun or pronoun:
*Are you reading the report (**which/that**) I have written?*

1 Rewrite the sentences using the relative pronouns in brackets.

I've got an uncle. He started his own business. (who)
I've got an uncle who started his own business.

1 My father drives a car. The car belongs to his company. (that)
_____

2 There's a college in my city. You can do business studies there. (where)
_____

3 I've got a sister. She works in a shop. (that)
_____

4 One day I'd like to get a job. The job includes foreign travel. (which)
_____

5 I've got a part-time job. I don't enjoy it. (that)
_____

2 Complete the sentences with defining relative pronouns. Sometimes more than one answer is possible. If a relative pronoun is not necessary, write (x).

This is the type of business _x_ I think people will be keen to invest in.

1 Do you have an idea for a product or service _____ you think people will love?
2 This is the university department _____ economics, finance and banking are taught.
3 Nobody wants a career _____ they find boring or unrewarding.
4 Welcome to the house _____ Steve Jobs lived when he first had the idea for Apple computers.
5 I'm not the sort of person _____ likes to take risks.
6 We are now on the boat _____ Coco Chanel bought after she made her millions as a fashion designer.
7 If you have an idea for a product _____ is more environmentally friendly, please tell us about it.

3 Write sentences with defining relative pronouns from the prompts. Sometimes more than one answer is possible.

Sochi / the Russian city / the 2014 Winter Olympics were held
Sochi is the Russian city where the 2014 Winter Olympics were held.

1 An igloo / a traditional type of Inuit house / made of snow
_____

2 A puck / a small flat disk / is used instead of a ball in ice hockey
_____

3 An ice dancer / a performer / skates to music
_____

4 Ski jumping and cross-country skiing / winter sports / are becoming more and more popular.
_____

5 This amazing speed skating track / the place / three world records were broken yesterday
_____

4 Complete the sentences with relative pronouns. Sometimes more than one answer is possible.

During my gap year I stayed in a village _where_ there are no doctors.

1 Do you know anyone _____ doesn't like chocolate?
2 This is the company car _____ I told you about.
3 Is there a shop in your town or city _____ you can buy organic food?
4 The woman _____ is talking to the receptionist is the manager's wife.
5 Do you know anyone _____ works in the food industry?
6 I'd like to buy a printer _____ is quick and quiet.
7 How important is it to eat food _____ doesn't damage the environment?

5 Complete the sentences. Use *who, which, that, where* or no pronoun (x).

All the information _which/that/x you need is on the Internet._

1 This is the professor _____
_____

2 Most of the products _____

3 This is a clothes shop _____

4 This letter comes from a person _____

5 I know a lot of people _____

6 This is the website _____
_____

1.2 Dynamic and state verbs

1 Choose the correct forms.

1 I *think / am thinking* it's a good idea.
2 I *am thinking / think* about the project.
3 We *have / are having* two dogs.
4 Janet *has / is having* a shower.
5 Those trousers *look / are looking* nice on you.
6 What *are you looking / do you look* for?
7 I *am liking / like* shopping.
8 Look, Jane *is having / has* such a good time at the party!
9 I'm afraid, I *need / I'm needing* the answer right now.
10 *Are they looking / Do they look* OK now?

1.5 Present Perfect Continuous

2 Choose the correct forms.

1 He *has promised / has been promising* to come.
2 The cost of living in that country
   has risen / has been rising for some time.
3 He *hasn't heard / hasn't been hearing*
   from them recently.
4 Tom *has known / has been knowing* Helen
   since they were children.
5 Oh, I *have cut / have been cutting* my finger!
6 I'm sorry, I know I'm late. How long
   have you *been waiting / waited*?
7 Well, believe it or not, we haven't *met / been
   meeting* Luke since that day.
8 'Pinky' is my favourite place for a good coffee.
   I've *gone / been going* there on and off
   for the last two years.
9 I love your matchbox car collection! How many cars
   have you *collected / been collecting* so far?
10 Just look at this white tree! Isn't it beautiful?
   How long has it *snowed / been snowing*?

**3 Complete the sentences with the correct form of the
verbs in brackets. Use the Present Perfect Continuous
when possible.**

1 '_____ (you/be) to the National Gallery?'
   'No, I haven't.'
2 What _____ (you/do) since you graduated?
3 Oh, you _____ (have) a haircut!
   You look fantastic!
4 'How long _____ (you/look) for a job?'
   'For a month now.'
5 'How long _____ (you/have) this dress?'
   'For ten years, I think.'
6 The company _____ (produce) the two new
   engines since the beginning of this year.
7 How come you _____ (never/visit) a single
   foreign country in your life?
8 This picture? I have no idea who painted it though it
   _____ (hang) here for ages.
9 The future looks bright. They _____ (sell)
   more and more gardening tools through their
   website since May.
10 _____ (you/ever/work) abroad?

Summative Practice   Unit 1

4 Find the mistakes and correct the sentences.

1 I can't talk now. I have dinner at the moment.
   _____
2 I am looking for my glasses for two hours!
   _____
3 Laura has been knowing her for ages.
   _____
4 I have always been preferring surfing to skiing.
   _____

**5 Complete the sentences with the correct form of
the verbs in brackets. Use the Present Simple or
Continuous, the Past Simple or Continuous, the
Present Perfect Simple or Continuous.**

1 He _____ (wait) for us when we arrived.
2 He _____ (meet) Martha three years ago, so
   he _____ (know) her since 2016.
3 How long _____ (you/have) that hat?
   It _____ (look) quite old-fashioned!
4 I _____ (be) to France, but
   I _____ (never/be) to Germany.
5 Sam _____ (think) it's important to study hard.
6 '_____ (Tim/think) about a new job at the
   moment?' 'He _____ (think) about it for the
   last few weeks but he _____ (not/make) up
   his mind yet.'
7 'You _____ (look) worried.' 'I am. I _____
   (lose) my passport. I _____ (look) for it since
   yesterday and I _____ (leave) tomorrow!'

**6 Complete the dialogue with the correct form of the
verbs in brackets.**

C: Helen Simpson? I ¹_____ (not/see) you for ages!
H: Clare? It's great to see you again! Where
    ²_____ (you/be) all this time?
C: I ³_____ (just/come) back from London! You
    really ⁴_____ (change) since we last saw each
    other. You ⁵_____ (look) wonderful!
H: Well, I ⁶_____ (put) on some weight, I'm afraid.
    And my hair is shorter than before. When ⁷_____
    (we/last/see) each other? I can't remember.
C: Let me think. I ⁸_____ (believe) the last time
    was when we graduated, four years ago.
H: What ⁹_____ (you/do) since then?
C: I ¹⁰_____ (study) in London. What about you?
H: I ¹¹_____ (be) very busy lately. I ¹²_____
    (work) as a fashion designer for half a year now.
C: Do you still live with your parents?
H: No, I ¹³_____ (live) in a flat in the town centre.
    It's nice.
C: How long ¹⁴_____ (you/have) it?
H: Since last year. It's a large flat, with three bedrooms.
    I ¹⁵_____ (try) to rent the two extra rooms,
    but no one has turned up yet.
C: Well, I ¹⁶_____ (look) for a room since I
    arrived! I'd really like to have a look at them.

2.2 Narrative tenses

1 Complete the story with the correct form of the verbs in brackets.

One evening I ¹_____ (sit) in my room doing my homework. The clock ²_____ (just/strike) seven when I heard steps coming from the ground floor. The steps ³_____ (keep) going up and down the living room. At first I ⁴_____ (think) it was my mum. She ⁵_____ (go) to the supermarket and I ⁶_____ (expect) her to come any time; next I suspected it might be a burglar, so I ⁷_____ (not/make) any noise. Then I made a decision to call out but nobody ⁸_____ (answer). At that time I used to live in a large, isolated house on the outskirts of the town, and all of a sudden I felt really scared. At last, I ⁹_____ (decide) to go and see. I ¹⁰_____ (go) down the stairs when all of a sudden the front door slammed – someone ¹¹_____ (just/go) out! The problem was that we continued to hear the steps day after day but we never saw anyone.
Now we live in a flat in the town centre. We have lived here since we ¹²_____ (moved) five months ago.

2.5 Verb patterns

2 Choose the correct forms.

1 I don't mind *doing* / *to do* homework every day.
2 Pete can't afford *to buy* / *buying* a new camera.
3 My parents don't allow me *going* / *to go* out in the evenings.
4 Yes, it's true, my brother can spend hours *to play* / *playing* computer games.
5 We were going to the beach when John finally finished *to tell* / *telling* us the story.

3 Complete the dialogue with the correct form of the verbs in brackets.

A: What was your school trip like, Martha? Did you enjoy ¹_____ (visit) London?
B: It was great! On the first day we ²_____ (go) to Trafalgar Square because we wanted ³_____ (visit) the National Gallery …
A: Did everything go well?
B: Well … actually not everything, I must ⁴_____ (say). While we ⁵_____ (visit) the Gallery, Pete and Joe suddenly ⁶_____ (disappear). We ⁷_____ (wait) for them at the gallery exit but they ⁸_____ (not/turn) up. Before entering the gallery the teacher ⁹_____ (warn) us ¹⁰_____ (not/get) lost, but apparently they did. After a while we decided ¹¹_____ (go) back to the hotel without them.
A: What happened next? Did you manage ¹²_____ (find) them?
B: Oh, yes, we did. When we got to the hotel, we discovered that they ¹³_____ (already/be) there for an hour. When we went into their room, they ¹⁴_____ (watch) a football match on TV. The teacher ¹⁵_____ (get) really angry!

Summative Practice   Units 1–2

4 Choose the correct forms. In one sentence both answers are correct.

1 I *have had* / *have been having* this house since 2012.
2 I think I *have seen* / *have been seeing* her before.
3 She *has read* / *has been reading* for hours.
4 Laura *has become* / *has been becoming* a doctor.
5 Laura *has worked* / *has been working* at the hospital since she became a doctor.

5 Find the mistakes and correct the sentences.

1 I didn't see Aunt Julia for ages.
_____
2 She drove along the highway when she had the accident.
_____
3 We studied Maths for two hours, but we haven't solved the problems yet.
_____
4 I usually enjoy to ski, but today I'm having a break.
_____
5 The teacher made them to learn the poem by heart.
_____

6 Complete the sentences with the correct form of the verbs in brackets. Use the Past Simple, the Past Continuous, the Past Perfect, the Present Perfect Simple and the Present Perfect Continuous.

1 I _____ (consider) whether to go or stay when the man asked me to sit down.
2 When I met Phil in 2015, he _____ (be) a basketball player for over 10 years.
3 The police offered money to anyone who could tell them who _____ (commit) the crime.
4 'I _____ (not/know) he worked here. How long _____ (he/work) for you?' 'Since 2015.'
5 'He's my best friend.' 'How long _____ (you/know) him?' 'For 15 years.'
6 She _____ (never/be) abroad before and that's why she made a mistake.
7 I asked him whether anything _____ (happen) while I was abroad.
8 Before the match he discovered that he _____ (lose) his tennis racket.
9 We _____ (play) football when I _____ (slip) and _____ (break) my leg.
10 When I got up, he _____ (have) breakfast, so I joined him.
11 _____ (wait) long? The table is now ready for you. Please follow me.
12 The bus _____ (arrive) 15 minutes late because there _____ (be) an accident on the crossroads in the town centre.
13 I _____ (attend) Mr Brainy's classes for a month now, since I _____ (sign) up for the course in September.
14 _____ (you/meet)? Alan _____ (join) the company in 2016 and _____ (work) as chief coordinating engineer since then. And Chris _____ (decide) to work for us right after graduating from university.

3.2 Present and past speculation

1 **Choose the correct forms.**

 1 Tom is late. He *must have missed* / *can't have missed* the bus.

 2 I don't know why Tom's late. He *must have missed* / *might have missed* the bus.

 3 'Where's Sue?' 'I don't know. She *may be* / *must be* in the garden.'

 4 'Is Sue in the garden?' 'She *can't be* / *might not be* in the garden. She's always at work at this time of the day.'

 5 'Who is that man at the door?' 'Oh, it *must be* / *can be* the courier with my beautiful new shoes. Just a minute!'

 6 We don't really know who burgled their house. It *might have been* / *can have been* a complete stranger or one of their neighbours.

 7 I have absolutely no idea. The photo is not clear. It looks like a snake, a python, but it *could be* / *could have been* a piece of thick rope.

 8 That *can't be* / *mustn't be* true. Felicity was here with me when it all happened, so she *might not have done* / *can't have done* it.

3.5 *Used to* and *would*

2 **Find and correct the mistakes.**

 1 He would be overweight, but he's been on a diet and he's slimmer now.
  _____

 2 I used to travel by train to Manchester last week.
  _____

 3 When we were kids, we would be so happy just playing in the garden in front of our house.
  _____

 4 Did you used to study Latin in secondary school?
  _____

 5 I wouldn't like spinach when I was a child but now I do, though only uncooked, in salads.
  _____
  _____

 6 Drivers would to use mainly this street to get to the bridge, but now they tend to choose the ring road.
  _____
  _____

3 **Complete with a modal, *would* or *used to* (when either *used to* or *would* are correct, write *would*).**

 1 The guests _____ arrive any time now.

 2 When I was young, I _____ play in a band with my school friends.

 3 'Isn't that Tom?' 'It _____ be Tom. He's in Scotland.'

 4 Gill _____ have long hair but now she wears it short.

 5 'Isn't that Sue?' 'I'm not sure, but it _____ be Sue after all. She's just come back from Australia.'

 6 'Yesterday I saw Sandra at the concert.'
  'It _____ Sandra. She's in India at the moment.'

 7 When I lived in the country, I _____ go for a run every day.

 8 She _____ be happy when she lived in Paris.

Summative Practice   Units 1–3

4 **Choose the correct forms.**

 1 'How long *have you been working* / *are you working* on this project?' 'We *have been working* / *are working* on this project since September, but we *might not* / *must not* finish it in time.'

 2 'I *have seen* / *have been seeing* Leonardo's Last Supper twice.' 'When *did you last see* / *have you last seen* it ?'

 3 I *was sitting* / *sat* on top of a hill when I *heard* / *was hearing* the sound of dogs and horses approaching.

 4 Francis was sure he *has met* / *had met* the man before.

 5 He wanted *to know* / *know* what *had provoked* / *provoked* my bad temper.

 6 I encouraged her *to talk* / *talk* about the episode but she decided *to keep* / *keeping* it to herself.

 7 So she didn't call you again? That's a pity because I *might have helped* / *may help* her then.

 8 I can't help *feeling* / *to feel* nervous before an exam.

 9 Believe or not, once Tim *would break* / *broke* his leg near this lake.

 10 It *was* / *has been* a surprise. I *haven't* / *hadn't* expected to win anything at that moment.

 11 What *was he thinking* / *had he thought* about when he *painted* / *was painting* the picture?

 12 'Where *is* / *was* Don?' 'Check the kitchen. He *can* / *could* be there.'

5 **Choose the correct forms.**

 A group of athletes are at the station, ready to leave for Paris …

 A: I can't **¹***see* / *to see* Susan anywhere. I'm afraid she won't turn up. The train's about to leave.

 B: Well, that's strange. She's never late. Surely something **²***may have* / *must have* happened.

 A: She **³***might have* / *must have* missed the bus.

 B: Or she **⁴***may have* / *can't have* overslept. Let's call her. Hello, is that you, Sue? Where are you? We **⁵***are waiting* / *have been waiting* for you for half an hour and the train is about to leave!

 C: Oh, I'm so sorry, Ian! I was about to call you. I'm afraid you'll have to go without me. I **⁶***went* / *was going* to the bus stop when I **⁷***was meeting* / *met* Julie. Julie and I **⁸***would* / *used to be* close friends when we were at school. We **⁹***would go* / *were going* camping together. I **¹⁰***hadn't* / *haven't* seen her for ages before today, so I wanted **¹¹***know* / *to know* all her gossip. I just couldn't help **¹²***to go* / *going* for a coffee with her and I completely forgot about the time!

 A: Well, that's a pity! But I suppose you may just as well join us later. You know our team can't do without you.

 C: Yes, I'll join you tomorrow. And Julie **¹³***might come* / *might have come* with me. She's thinking about it.

 B: All right. See you tomorrow … and try **¹⁴***not to miss* / *not missing* the train!

4.2 Future forms

Complete the dialogue with the correct forms of the verbs in brackets. Use the Present Simple, Present Continuous, *be going to*, *will/won't* and *shall*.

A: Oh, no. I completely forgot. James and Mary ¹_____ (come) to dinner tonight and I haven't prepared anything.

B: Is that really tonight? I completely forgot too!

A: Are you busy at the moment, Ewa?

B: Not at all. How can I help? ²_____ (I/go) to the shops and pick something up?

A: Would you mind? The little shop on Baker Street ³_____ (close) at 7:00 and I ⁴_____ (not/able to) go there, come back and cook something before they arrive.

B: OK, don't worry. Besides, I've never known James to be on time for anything, so I'm pretty sure they ⁵_____ (be) late!

A: Yeah, I know. But today could be the day he's on time for the first time ever! I ⁶_____ (cook) lasagne – it's their favourite. I've got tomatoes and garlic but there isn't any pasta or cheese. I can start preparing the sauce right now and heat the oven. When you get back I can put everything in the oven and we can quickly prepare a salad together.

B: That sounds like a good plan. I ⁷_____ (leave) right now. Oh, wait a minute. Is that your phone ringing?

A: Yes, it is. Hang on, I ⁸_____ (answer) that and then tell you exactly what pasta to buy ... Hmm. Guess what? That was James. They aren't coming.

B: Really? What a shame. So why don't we just order a pizza and watch a film on TV together?

A: Perfect! Let's do that!

4.5 Future Continuous and Future Perfect

Choose the correct forms.

1 What *will you be doing* / *will you have done* at this time in five years?

2 By the end of the year I *will have changed* / *will be changing* my job.

3 By the end of November, she *will have finished* / *will finish* university.

4 Now, listen to this. This time next month, I'*ll be travelling* / '*ll have travelled* in Nicaragua. I'll send you a postcard!

5 They *will be watching* / *will have watched* a film from nine to eleven.

6 We *will be having* / *will have had* dinner at eight o'clock.

7 We *will be having* / *will have had* dinner by eight o'clock.

8 I could call you at 6 p.m. *Will you have checked* / *Will you be checking* it by then?

9 'Are you going to the exhibition on Saturday?' 'I'm afraid I *will be working* / *will work* all day on Saturday.'

10 'What *are you doing* / *will you be doing* at this time tomorrow?' 'I *will have had* / *will be having* lunch at the Ritz.'

Summative Practice   Units 1–4

3 Choose the correct forms.

1 How many books *have you borrowed* / *have you been borrowing* from the library this year?

2 How long *have you been reading* / *have you read* this novel?

3 I *met* / *was meeting* him when I *was working* / *worked* abroad.

4 When I *got* / *had got* home, I discovered I *had lost* / *lost* my keys.

5 By the time he was thirty, he *had already become* / *already became* the manager of the company.

6 The teacher asked the students to finish *to write* / *writing*.

7 I can't find my glasses. I *might have left* / *might leave* them in the library.

8 We *used to be* / *would be* friends, but we quarrelled two years ago. I *haven't seen* / *haven't been seeing* him *since* / *for* then.

4 Complete the sentences with the correct form of the verbs in brackets.

1 The fire engine arrived a few minutes after I _____ (phone) for help.

2 I _____ (never/be) to Spain. If Carmen _____ (invite) me to stay, I _____ (travel) to Madrid next summer.

3 'How long _____ (queue)?' 'I _____ (queue) for half an hour. I think I _____ (give) up now and come back tomorrow.'

4 As soon as the film _____ (finish), I _____ (do) my homework, I promise.

5 I hope that by the end of the year I _____ (save) enough money to go abroad.

6 I _____ (revise) for my exams at this time tomorrow.

7 It _____ (rain) while we _____ (leave) home.

5 Complete the dialogue with the correct form of the verbs in brackets.

A: I met Julia yesterday. She gave me two tickets for Expo. She didn't need them any more because she ¹_____ (already/be) to the exhibition. Would you like to go next Saturday?

B: I'd love to, but unfortunately I ²_____ (work) all day on Saturday.

A: Oh, that's a shame. What about Sunday?

B: It all depends on what time you're going. I can join you as long as you ³_____ (go) in the afternoon.

A: All right, we ⁴_____ (go) in the afternoon. What about 4 o'clock?

B: Great! I'm pretty sure I ⁵_____ (finish) by then.

A: You're working too much. How long ⁶_____ (you/work) in that restaurant?

B: I ⁷_____ (work) there for six months. It's hard but I like it. It's a vegetarian restaurant and we invent all sorts of healthy recipes. Yesterday I ⁸_____ (make) twenty vegetable soups, fifty pumpkin pies ... And I ⁹_____ (write) a book about healthy food since September!

5.2 Articles: no article, *a/an* or *the*

1 Complete the sentences with *a/an*, *the*, Ø (no article).

1 What would ___ men do without ___ women?
2 ___ red-haired woman was sitting at ___ table by ___ window looking sadly at ___ street.
3 Earth orbits ___ sun. ___ first is ___ planet, ___ other ___ star.
4 There's ___ student at ___ door over there. I think he's ___ student I studied with in ___ Netherlands. ___ world is really small.
5 ___ best movie I've ever seen is *Modern Times*. ___ film describes ___ adventures of ___ factory worker and I think it's really worth watching mainly because of Charlie Chaplin's unforgettable performance.

5.5 Non-defining relative clauses

2 Find the mistakes and correct the sentences. Sometimes there is more than one mistake in a sentence.

1 Barrie, that lives next door, is having a party tonight.
_____

2 'What does she do?' 'She's teacher.'
_____

3 Atlantic Ocean, who is second largest ocean in world, lies between the Europe and the America.
_____
_____

4 Lewis Carroll who wrote *Alice's Adventures in Wonderland*, was professor at Oxford University.
_____
_____

5 Lots of people visit British Museum, which parts of the Parthenon are displayed.
_____
_____

6 That's a film I'd like us to see at weekend.
_____

7 Food we ate at a restaurant by sea was awesome!
_____

8 You will definitely need the pair of jeans and the warm sweater.
_____

3 Write D (*defining*) or ND (*non-defining*) next to each sentence; insert the proper punctuation where necessary and add an article when missing.

1 A person who steals things is thief. ☐
2 The new film by Polański which was well-reviewed by critics was great success. ☐
3 The BBC which had begun sound broadcasting in 1922 launched world's first public television service in 1936. ☐
4 I need person who can speak English fluently. ☐
5 The new London guidebook published in January this year which contains lots of useful information will appear in bookshops next month. ☐

Summative Practice — Units 1–5

4 Choose the correct forms.

1 We *were going / went* to school when it *started / was starting* snowing.
2 We *have forgotten / had forgotten* our umbrellas, so we had to go into a shop until the rain *stopped / would stop*.
3 'I *was walking / walked* to my caravan when suddenly I *saw / was seeing* an elephant crossing the road.' 'It *can't have been / can't be* an elephant! Elephants don't live in Scotland.'
4 It *didn't always use to be / wouldn't always be* like that.
5 Lea *is having / has* a good relationship with all her friends.
6 Dad *has bought / has been buying* a new car.
7 I *don't believe / am not believing* it will work.
8 Dad *has driven / has been driving* his new car for one week.

5 Find and correct the mistakes. There is sometimes more than one mistake in a sentence.

1 As soon as you eat vegetables every day, you'll get all the minerals you need.
_____

2 If my friends will be online, I'll chat with them.
_____

3 Will you be finishing by eight o'clock?
_____

4 This time tomorrow we will ski in the Alps.
_____

5 By the end of the day we will be eating our three portions of vegetables.
_____

6 I saw a shark swimming close to the boat. A shark, that was 2 metres long, followed us for about three miles.
_____
_____

6 Fill in the gaps with:
- an article where needed,
- a relative pronoun where needed,
- *used to* where possible,
- the correct form of the verbs in brackets.

Notes on Britain's Geography

[1]_____ Scotland, [2]_____ Wales and [3]_____ northwestern England are mountainous. [4]_____ Ben Nevis, in [5]_____ southwestern Scotland, is [6]_____ UK's highest peak. [7]_____ highest peak in England is [8]_____ Scafell Pike. It is situated in the famous Lake District, which [9]_____ (be) the home of the poets in [10]_____ 19th century. The area is like a miniature Switzerland. When you visit it, you [11]_____ (soon/find out) it offers an astonishing variety of landscapes. Even if the area is small, it [12]_____ (take) you quite a long time to see it all. Most of the time you will be climbing up and down the peaks, or you will be walking along the Lake District's narrow valleys and lakesides. By the end of the day, you [13]_____ (see) a lot, but at the same time, very little when compared with what you might [14]_____ (still/see). Windermere, [15]_____ is England's largest lake, offers hundreds of interesting possibilities. The main agricultural activity in the Lake District is sheep farming, which [16]_____ (be) the major industry in the region since Roman times.

6.2   Second Conditional, *wish/if only*

Choose the correct forms.

1 I wish I *lived / would live* in London.
2 If only you *would give up / give up* smoking.
3 I wish I *had / would have* a friend like Julie.
4 I would do the housework if I *had / had had* time.
5 I *would have gone / would go* to the cinema if
   I *didn't have / hadn't had* to do the housework. Sorry!

Complete the sentences with the correct forms of the verbs in brackets.

1 If I _____ (be) you, I _____ (put) ice
   on the burn on your arm – it's the best thing to do.
2 I wish you _____ (think) about others for
   a change.
3 If you _____ (can/choose) a superpower,
   which one _____ (you/have)?
4 I wish I _____ (be able to/heal) people.
5 If only I _____ (not/need) to work all
   summer in this horrible office.
6 I wish you _____ (not/play) computer games
   every evening.

6.5   Third Conditional

Complete the sentences with the correct forms of the verbs in brackets. Use Third Conditional.

1 If Tom _____ (see) the advert,
   he _____ (apply) for the job.
2 If he _____ (get) the job, he _____
   (become) the best employee in no time.
3 If his boss _____ (promote) him,
   he _____ (earn) a lot of money.
4 If he _____ (make) a fortune,
   he _____ (gamble) in a casino.
5 If he _____ (keep) going to the casino,
   eventually he _____ (lose) all his money.
6 If he _____ (not/think) so much about his
   problems, he _____ (not/be) fired.
7 If I _____ (show) Tom that job advert, he
   _____ (repeat) the same mistakes again.

Match 1–8 with a–h.

1 If I made a promise,
2 I wouldn't trust him
3 What time would we get there
4 If you hadn't driven so fast,
5 We'd go to the beach
6 If I hadn't won the lottery,
7 What would you have done
8 I wish you

a I wouldn't have bought that luxury flat.
b if it wasn't so cold today.
c I'd keep it.
d wouldn't drive so fast.
e if I hadn't given you the money?
f we wouldn't have crashed.
g if we took the 10.45 train?
h if I were you.

Summative Practice   Units 1–6

5 Complete the sentences with the First, Second or Third Conditional.

1 _____ (you/stop) Liz if you had seen her?
2 _____ (you/tell) Mike if you saw him?
3 _____ (you/invite) your friends if you see
   them?
4 I'm sure he would have phoned him if he
   _____ (know) his telephone number.
5 I'm sure he would phone them if he
   _____ (know) their telephone number.
6 I'm sure he will phone Jane if he
   _____ (know) her telephone number.

**6 Find and correct the mistakes. There is sometimes
more than one mistake in a sentence.**

1 We travelled a lot since we started working for
   a travel agency.
   _____

2 We'll have worked at that time, but by six o'clock
   we'll finish.
   _____

3 I would love reading comics when I was a child.
   _____

4 The accident would have been much worse if the
   driver drove faster.
   _____

5 They walked to the station when it was beginning
   to rain. It was then that they had realised they have
   forgotten their umbrellas. _____
   _____

7 Choose the correct forms.

A: Where did you go for the Christmas holidays?
B: I went to [1]*the / –* USA. I wanted to leave London's
    cold winter behind, so I chose [2] *the /–* California,
    [3]*where / which* the average temperature is never
    below 21°C.
A: Did you have a good time?
B: Not in [4]*the / –* Los Angeles. Surprisingly, the weather
    wasn't warm enough. If it [5]*had been / was* warmer,
    I wouldn't have caught a cold.
A: What a pity! Did you have a fever as well?
B: Yes, and I also had a sore throat. I had to call
    [6]*a / the* doctor. [7]*The / A* doctor told me to stay in
    bed, so I did as he said. If I hadn't stayed in bed, I
    [8]*wouldn't have recovered / wouldn't recover* in time
    to go to San Francisco. Luckily, I [9]*had / have* already
    visited [10]*the / –* LA before. So [11]*as soon as / as long
    as* I got better, I went to San Francisco.
A: What's San Francisco like?
B: Oh, I think it's fantastic. I wish I [12]*lived / live* there! But
    I [13]*will go / go* back as soon as I can. I might [14]*to go /
    go* during the summer holidays. Surely it [15]*will be /
    will have been* warmer at that time. I've got some
    friends there [16]*who / which* like surfing, so I [17]*will
    be surfing / will have surfed* with them all day long
    during the summer.
A: I didn't know you could surf.
B: I [18]*have been surfing / surfed* all my life. I really enjoy
    it! I've always enjoyed [19]*to do / doing* all kinds of
    water sports.

7.2   Reported Speech – statements

1   Change the direct statements into reported statements.

1   'I don't like this picture,' she said.
_____

2   'We saw her yesterday,' he replied.
_____

3   'I am late because I missed the train,' she explained.
_____

4   'I don't want to see this man again,' he added.
_____

5   'We can't come because we are doing our homework now,' they told us.
_____

6   'It was hot yesterday,' he pointed out.
_____

7.5   Reported Speech – questions and imperatives

2   Change the direct questions or imperatives into reported speech.

1   'Did you see the film yesterday?' he asked me.
_____

2   'How's your grandmother?' he asked me.
_____

3   'What's your name?' he asked her.
_____

4   'Where did you find the key?' she asked me.
_____

5   'Are you writing a new book?' I asked her.
_____

6   'Stop talking!' the teacher told us.
_____

7   'Don't eat at your desks!' the boss told us.
_____

3   Change the direct speech into reported speech.

1   'You will have to tell me the whole story once again, John' the woman added.
_____

2   'The children have already finished the game,' the girl said.
_____

3   'Do you understand this message?' the officer asked us.
_____

4   'Play it again!' the boy asked the man.
_____

5   'It's raining,' the policeman noticed.
_____

6   'Why didn't they talk to the shop assistant?' the manager wanted to know.
_____

7   'Where have they been?' the little girl asked the woman.
_____

Summative Practice   Units 1–7

4   Choose the correct forms.

1   How long *have you had / have you been having* that car?

2   How long *have you read / have you been reading* that novel?

3   When we *arrived / were arriving*, a policeman was *waiting / waited* for us. He told us he *had been / has been* there since long before we arrived.

4   When we were younger, we *used to like / would like* dancing.

5   Find and correct the mistakes. There is sometimes more than one mistake in a sentence.

1   You don't get a cat unless you promise to look after it
_____

2   Pat will have cooked all day tomorrow. She's having guests for dinner.
_____

3   They will be finishing dinner by nine o'clock.
_____

4   Mount Vesuvius, that is active volcano, overlooks the Bay of Naples.
_____

5   If I have enough money, I'd go to Australia.
_____

6   If I had known the answer, I wouldn't ask you to help me
_____

7   She asked me was I good at Maths.
_____

6   Choose the correct forms.

Oldacre laughed, but he was clearly afraid of Lestrade, [1]*who / that was* visibly upset.
'I [2]*haven't hurt / hadn't hurt* anybody,' he said. 'You [3]*can't / mightn't* really mean it!' Lestrade replied angrily. 'Because of you McFarlane is in prison. We thought he [4]*had / has* killed you. He was in danger of being hanged,' he added.
'I only did it for a joke,' said Oldacre.
'You won't [5]*be playing / have played* any more jokes from now on!' said Lestrade.
He [6]*told / said* the policemen to take Oldacre away. When they [7]*had gone / have gone*, Lestrade [8]*said / told* 'I must thank you, Mr Holmes. I was rude to you earlier today and I am sorry. I really thought that the case was finished. It would [9]*have been / be* very bad indeed if Mr McFarlane had been hanged for something he didn't do.'
'Don't worry,' Holmes told him. 'Nobody will know what happened. It isn't necessary to say that I did anything to help,' he added.
'But don't you want people to know how clever [10]*you have been / have you been*?' asked Lestrade.
'No', said Holmes. 'I am happy with my work and that is enough for me.'

From Sir Arthur Conan Doyle, *The Return of Sherlock Holmes*

8.2 The Passive

Turn the following sentences into the passive. Add the agent when necessary.

1 Alfred Hitchcock directed the film.
   _____

2 They are building a new house.
   _____

3 They were helping the students.
   _____

4 People will always remember him.
   _____

5 We make cheese from milk.
   _____

6 Peter has painted the picture.
   _____

7 You must hand in the keys before leaving.
   _____

8 The children opened all the windows.
   _____

9 The police are going to arrest the two criminals.
   _____

10 Scientists have found a new species of butterfly in the Amazon rainforest.
   _____
   _____

8.5 *Have something done*

Change the sentences using the structure *have something done*.

1 My teeth were checked.
   _____

2 My camera is being repaired at the moment.
   _____

3 Their house will be painted soon.
   _____

4 My bank account is checked every month.
   _____

5 My eyes were tested.
   _____

6 The car has just been serviced.
   _____

7 Our computer has just been repaired.
   _____

Find and correct the mistakes.

1 I think I'll have my car repair.
   _____

2 The house was built in 1850 by someone.
   _____

3 Mr Smith is been interviewed at the moment.
   _____

4 I had the meal send up to my room.
   _____

5 Where do you usually have mended your shoes?
   _____

6 How often the cat is fed?
   _____

7 Can be sports equipment hired?
   _____

4 Choose the correct forms.

1 Should young offenders *be / been* sentenced to a longer time in prison?
2 My watch is slow. I'll have *mended it / it mended*.
3 She *said / told* me I was wrong.
4 They told me *stay / to stay* at home.
5 He asked me where *was my book / my book was*.
6 He asked me whether *was I / I was* tired.
7 I saw a */ the* man at the station. *The / A* man reminded me of someone I *have met / had met* long ago.
8 *Unless / As soon as* you eat less junk food, you won't be able to lose weight.

5 Complete the sentences with the correct form of the verbs in brackets.

1 I wish my brother _____ (think) about others for a change.
2 If an election was held now, he _____ (be) elected.
3 If I _____ (see) Sue, I would have told her about the concert.
4 I can't find my umbrella. I must _____ (leave) it in the train.
5 '_____ (you/work) when they arrive tomorrow?' 'No, I think I _____ (finish) by that time.'
6 Yesterday I _____ (read) when I _____ (hear) a loud ring on the doorbell.
7 After we _____ (walk) for an hour, we _____ (stop) for a rest.
8 How many times _____ (you/visit) the National Gallery this year?
9 How long _____ (you/study) English?

6 Complete the text with the words from the box.

> by   described   granted   had changed
> have gained   led   the   were arrested
> were employed   were given   were willing   who

Emmeline Pankhurst

Emmeline Pankhurst, [1]_____ was born in Manchester in 1858, was a passionate campaigner for women's right to vote. In 1903 she founded the Women's Social and Political Union and [2]_____ a group of women who [3]_____ to take part in drastic actions such as smashing windows and organising demonstrations to attract public attention. [4]_____ government and the establishment were shocked [5]_____ the tactics of these women and many [6]_____ . Militant suffragettes were often [7]_____ as fanatics.

During World War I women [8]_____ in factories and took on many of the jobs traditionally assigned to men, such as drivers and postmen. Because of these social changes, by the end of the war most people [9]_____ their views about women and the vote, and in 1918, women over 30 [10]_____ the right to vote. But it was only in 1928 that women were [11]_____ equal voting rights with men. In the same year, Emmeline Pankhurst died. The question is: would women [12]_____ the right to vote if Emmeline Pankhurst hadn't campaigned for it?

Accepting suggestions

That sounds fantastic!

I'd love to go.

Well, it's worth a try.

I suppose it'll work.

That's fine with me.

Agreeing with an opinion

I (completely) agree that/with …

I couldn't agree more that/with …

I think so too.

It is true that …
I am of the same/a similar opinion because …

Apologising

Informal phrases

I'm really sorry (that) …

Sorry for bothering you.

Sorry to bother you.

Sorry for any trouble.

Sorry I didn't write earlier, but I …

Sorry I haven't written for so long./Sorry for not writing for so long.

I'm writing to tell you how sorry I am to … (about) …

It will never happen again.

Formal phrases

I apologise for …

Please accept my apology …

Asking for information

Could you tell me when the course starts?

Can you tell me how much it costs?

Could you tell me if there are any discounts?

I would like to know/ask if …

I would like to know more details about …

I would like to ask for further information about/ concerning …

I would be (very) grateful if you could …

I wonder if you could …

I would like to ask if/when/where/why …

Closing formulas: emails and letters

Informal phrases

Best wishes,

Bye for now/See you!

Love,/Take care!/All the best,

Neutral phrases

Yours sincerely,

Regards,

Formal Phrases

(with Dear Sir or Madam/Editor) Yours faithfully,

Contacting people

Ways to contact people

If you have any information, please contact/call/leave a message for Alison on (0961224466).

If you are interested in …, call (John/Ms White) on (0961224466).

To join us, call …

If you have seen it, please …

Call me/us on … for more details.

Maintaining contact

Drop me a line sometime.

I hope to hear from you soon.

Give me a call later.

Let me know if you can make it or not.

I was glad to hear about …

Let me know as soon as possible.

Declining suggestions

It doesn't sound very good.

I don't think I fancy it.

I'm sorry, but I can't join you.

I'm not really into …

I've got some doubts about it.

I don't see how it could work.

Actually, I would prefer not to.

Describing an event

I'll never forget …

It was an unforgettable (day/occasion/event).

The celebration takes place/took place on/in …

The event is celebrated annually.

The festival originated …

Describing lost property

I lost (my bag/passport/coat/dog).

Describing features

It is/was …

Size   huge/tiny/35cm x 25cm

Shape   round/rectangular/square/narrow

Colour   white/red and brown/light/dark green

Material   made of leather/plastic/linen

Age   new/young/old/six years old/modern/ancient

It has/had (two handles/a leather strap/a blue cover/two pockets/short sleeves/a black tail).

Reasons for search

I keep (all my files there).

It was something I borrowed/got as a birthday present.

It is of great value./ It's a really precious thing.

I can't do without it.

It means a lot to me.

Describing a person

The first thing you notice about (him/her) is …

(He/She) is special for a number of reasons.

He/She is the kind of person who …

The most unusual/interesting person I've ever met …

She dresses casually/smartly/well/in black/fashionably.

He always wears scruffy/stylish clothes.

Height   of medium height/tall/fairly short/long-legged

Build   muscular/well-built/overweight/skinny/slim/thin

Age   in his teens/middle-aged/in her late forties/elderly

Facial features   round/oval/freckles/dimples/scar/mole/ wrinkled/almond-shaped eyes/ pale/tanned/a crooked nose/moustache/beard

Hair   balding/short/shoulder-length/long/wavy/curly/ thick

WRITING BANK

Describing a place

The most fascinating/interesting/lively part of the city is …

The most famous attraction is …

The town is well known for its …

It is the kind of place that/where …

The place I like best is …

It is situated in a quiet residential area.

The place is surrounded by …

It lies in the north/south/east/west of Spain.

It is the most thrilling/picturesque/fabulous place.

The sights are worth seeing.

Disagreeing with an opinion

I disagree that/with …/I don't agree that/with …

I am totally against …

I see what you mean but …

I see your point of view but …

I'm afraid I can't agree with …

I'm not convinced about …

I don't think it's the best solution …

I must say I do not agree/strongly disagree with …

I am of a different/the opposite opinion because …

Contrary to popular belief …

Encouraging participation

Come on, don't be afraid/it's not difficult/it's easy!

Why don't you come and meet some interesting people/
see some great things?

Come and tell us what you think.

Come and have fun!

Don't miss it!

Ending emails and letters

Informal phrases

It was good to hear from you.

Email me soon.

I'd better get going./I must go now./Got to go now./
I must be going now.

Bye for now.

Looking forward to your news/to hearing from you again

Say hello to …

Give my love/my regards to (everyone at home).

Have a nice (trip).

See you (soon/in the summer).

Write soon.

Keep in touch!

Neutral phrases

I look forward to hearing from you/your reply.

I hope to hear from you soon.

Formal phrases

I wonder what other readers think about …

I hope you will publish more articles about this problem.

I would be grateful if you could publish my letter.

Expressing contrast

<u>However,</u> many people say that action should be taken straight away.

<u>Even though/Although</u> many residents support the mayor and his policy, he also has many enemies.

<u>In spite of/Despite</u> winning in the local election, his real ambition was to work for one of the EU institutions.

It can be argued that …

Expressing doubt

I have read the advert/about your services and/but I am not quite sure if …

I cannot understand if …

It is not clear to me if …

Expressing interest

I am interested in …/I have been looking for …

I am planning to … and that is why I found this advertisement/offer/text interesting/important. I would like to thank you for/congratulate you on …

I was very interested in your … (article/editorial/ presentation).

I was surprised/fascinated/shocked to …

Expressing opinion

I believe/think/feel (that) …

I really believe …

In my opinion/view,

The way I see it,

It seems/appears to me (that) …

To my mind,

My opinion is that …

As far as I am concerned,

People often claim that …

Some people argue that …

Expressing preferences

I really enjoy/like/love … because …

I prefer … to …

I'd like to …/I hope to …

… is great because …

I find … boring/dull.

I don't like/I can't stand/I really hate …

It's not really my thing.

Expressing purpose / result / reason

He worked as a volunteer in the Philippines <u>to/in order to/so as to</u> help local people organise their lives anew after the tsunami.

The man committed the crime and <u>therefore/ consequently</u> was sentenced to life imprisonment.

The team missed their deadline <u>because of/as a result of</u> numerous mistakes they had made right at the start.

Giving advice

You should/ought to …

You'd better …

If I were you, I would …

It might be a good idea (for you) to …

Why don't you …?

Have you thought of/about …?

Giving examples

for example,/for instance,

like …/such as …

especially/in particular/particularly

Giving reasons for opinions

I think so because …

In fact/Actually, …

The reason why I believe so is …

Introducing points in a 'for and against' essay

What are the arguments for and against this idea?

What are the benefits and drawbacks of such a step?

This approach has both advantages and disadvantages.

Inviting

I'd like to invite you to …

I'd like you to come …

Would you come to …?

I'm writing to invite you to (Warsaw/my party).

I'm having (a party).

I hope you'll be able to join us/to make it.

If you want, you can bring a friend.

You are welcome to …

Join us today!

Come and meet me …

Why don't you come …?

Listing arguments

First argument

First of all,

First/Firstly,

To begin with,

One (dis)advantage is that …

The main/major argument in support of … is that …

On the one hand,/On the other hand,

One argument in favour is that …

Successive arguments

Secondly,

Thirdly,

Another (dis)advantage is that …

It is also important/vital to consider …

In addition/Additionally,

Apart from this/that,

Moreover/What is more,

Last argument

Finally,

Last but not least,

Making recommendations

Positive opinion

You'll love it!

I recommend it to everyone.

If you like modern art, you should definitely see it.

It's a must!

I think it's worth seeing because …

I was impressed by …

I couldn't put it down.

It's a classic./It's a masterpiece of its kind.

The plot is believable/entertaining/thought-provoking.

It will change the way you see …

If I were you, I wouldn't hesitate to take part in …

I highly recommend (joining) …

Negative opinion

One weakness (of the book/film/workshops) is that …

It is rather long/boring/confusing/slow.

The cast is awful/unconvincing.

The script is dull.

It is poorly/badly written.

Adjectives

Positive   brilliant/spectacular/striking/impressive/
           powerful/convincing

Negative   violent/predictable/unconvincing/far-fetched/
           dull/bland/disappointing

Neutral   slow/sentimental/serious

Making requests

Informal phrases

Can you …, please?/Could you …?

Do you think you could …?

Let me know if you can (come).

Could you tell me …?

Formal phrases

Would it be possible for you to …?

I'd be grateful if you could …

I wonder if I could ask you to/for …

I'm writing to ask for your help/advice …

Making suggestions

I think I/you/we should …

Perhaps I/you/we could …

What do you think about …?

What about …?/How about …?

How do you feel about …?

Would you like me to …?

Why don't we (go) …?

Let's (go to) …

Shall we (go) …?

Do you fancy (going to the cinema)?

WRITING BANK

Opening formulas: emails and letters

Informal phrases

Dear Margaret,

Hi Anne,

Neutral phrases

Dear Mr and Mrs Edwards,

Dear Ms Brennon,

Formal phrases

Dear Sir or Madam,

Dear Editor,

Starting an email/a letter

Informal phrases

It was good to hear from you.

I hope you're doing well/you're fine/you're OK.

How are you (doing)?

I'm writing to tell you …

Thanks for your letter.

I wonder if you remember/have heard …

I wanted to tell you about …

I just wanted to ask/remind/thank you …

Just a quick email to tell you …

Formal phrases

I am writing to thank you for …

I would like to express my …

I am writing in connection with … (the article/editorial/ report) …

I have just read … (the article) entitled … in Saturday's paper/last month's edition of …

I am writing to ask/enquire about …

I read/found your advertisement in … and would like to …

Suggesting solutions

Steps must/should be taken to solve the problem of …

One (possible) way to solve/overcome this problem is to …

An alternative solution to this issue is …

Summing up

All in all/On balance/On the whole/To sum up/In conclusion,

All things considered/Taking everything into account,

Telling a story

It all happened some time ago.

It was three years ago.

While I (was playing),

First,

Then,

Finally,

Suddenly,

Unfortunately,

Fortunately,

It was the best/worst time ever.

We had a great/awful time when we were …

Thanking

Informal phrases

I'm writing to thank you for … .

Thank you so much.

It was so/really/very kind of you to …

Formal phrases

I really appreciate your help.

Thank you for sending it back to me.

I am really grateful for your help.

It's very kind of you.

I hope it's not too much trouble for you.

Thank you for doing me a favour.

Writing about books/films

Introduction

The film/book tells the story of …

The film/story is set in …

The book/novel was written by …

The film is directed by …

It is a comedy/horror film/love story.

This well-written/informative/fascinating book …

It is based on real events/on a true story/on a book.

It has been made into a film.

Plot description

The story concerns/begins/is about …

The plot is (rather) boring/thrilling.

The plot has an unexpected twist.

The plot focuses on …

The film reaches a dramatic climax …

Writing about future plans

I might …

It is my dream to …

My ambition/goal is to …

I hope that …/I hope to …

I am thinking of …

Present tenses – review

Exercise 1
1 hasn't cleaned
2 orders
3 are you waiting
4 've never lived
5 Do you really enjoy

Exercise 2
1 hate
2 've had
3 've met
4 are packing
5 makes
6 'm going

Exercise 3
1 At the moment Kate is looking for a part-time job.
2 How often do you update your profile?
3 Why is Paul looking after his friend's dog today?
4 Who has seen this thriller before?
5 Martha hasn't done any sports since January.

Exercise 4
1 lives
2 does
3 have you been
4 Has/Have your family ever moved
5 does it usually take
6 are you learning

Quantifiers

Exercise 1
1 some 2 many 3 few 4 any 5 much

Exercise 2
1 much 2 some 3 lot 4 little
5 Few 6 little 7 many 8 any

Exercise 3
Example answers:
1 a lot of / a little / little / some
2 a lot of / some / few / a few
3 a lot of / a few / some
4 any / much
5 a lot of / a little / little / some
6 a lot of / a few / few / some
7 any / many / a lot of
8 a lot of / a little / little / some

Exercise 4
1 some 2 any 3 many
4 many 5 few

Exercise 5
1 I don't eat much meat.
2 There aren't any good restaurants near my house.
3 I drink very little cola.
4 My mother doesn't bake many cakes.
5 I didn't have any cereal for breakfast.
6 I used to eat very few vegetables.
7 I don't do much cooking at home.

Exercise 6
1 many 2 a few 3 few 4 a little/some
5 much 6 any 7 little

Present Perfect and Past Simple

Exercise 1
1 have never paid
2 Did you look, did
3 Have you decided, haven't
4 was she, didn't see

Exercise 2
1 haven't finished yet
2 have you ever seen
3 saw
4 was
5 haven't seen
6 've watched
7 watched
8 Have you asked
9 've already asked
10 spoke
11 haven't chosen

Exercise 3
1 I learnt to play the guitar three years ago.
2 Have you bought a new suit yet?
3 Rob had his first driving lesson yesterday.
4 When did Helen write this song?
5 Tom hasn't opened a bank account yet.

Exercise 4
1 saw
2 needed
3 contacted
4 offered
5 's been
6 Have (you) met
7 has just entered
8 've never heard

Exercise 5
1 has owned this vintage cupboard since
2 got married twenty years ago
3 haven't been to the seaside for
4 went on a diet two weeks ago
5 has known Greg since
6 lost his job a few months ago
7 has (already) read

Comparative and superlative adjectives (too and enough)

Exercise 1
1 too expensive
2 too scared
3 not big enough
4 too mean
5 too dangerous

Exercise 2
1 more 2 worse 3 most 4 than
5 the 6 as

Exercise 3
1 than 2 richer 3 most 4 as
5 enough 6 more 7 too 8 than
9 the 10 than 11 the 12 as

Exercise 4
1 not tall enough
2 drier
3 weaker
4 worse
5 too small
6 not patient enough

Exercise 5
1 best
2 more creative
3 the most amazing
4 further
5 more authentic
6 more popular

Future forms

Exercise 1
1 isn't going to rain
2 's going to have
3 're taking
4 'll be
5 're announcing
6 'll laugh

Exercise 2
1 are playing
2 's going to snow
3 'll probably watch
4 is having
5 will win
6 'm not going to get married

Exercise 3
1 I will help you solve this problem.
2 We are not doing our homework on Saturday.
3 When are you going to do the shopping?
4 My best friend is not moving house next week.
5 My mum will probably take a few days off.
6 Are the Smiths driving to the mountains tomorrow morning?

Exercise 4
1 going
2 'm
3 'll
4 are
5 'll

Exercise 5
1 'll just check
2 'll pay
3 'm going to do
4 'm meeting
5 're going to play
6 'll rain

Exercise 6
Example answers:
1 I'm visiting my grandma.
2 You're going to be late.
3 I won't tell anyone.
4 I'll help you look for it.
5 You're going to break it.

Exercise 7
1 Will you answer it, please?
2 The students are sitting their final exam tomorrow at 9 a.m.
3 I'll order some new books online tonight if I have time.
4 Jane and I are meeting at 7 p.m. to talk about our Science project.
5 We're going to be late for the appointment, I'm afraid.

Exercise 8
Example answers:
1 will know my exam results
2 am having my first job interview
3 will have trouble getting food
4 am going to visit my grandparents in the countryside
5 won't be any wars in Europe

First and Second Conditionals

Exercise 1
1 Would 2 could 3 don't 4 would
5 would 6 asks 7 will

Exercise 2
1 would go crazy if he wasn't able to
2 last all day if she charges
3 is late again, we'll get stuck
4 had more time, she would talk to her friends
5 wouldn't be able to go online if

Exercise 3
1 would take
2 knew, would understand
3 won't become, doesn't go
4 would wear, lived
5 doesn't hurry, will miss
6 don't eat, will be
7 lend, will you ride
8 looked, would get tired

Exercise 4
Example answers:
1 he'll start saving up for a new car
2 I would read more books
3 you failed an important test
4 we call the meeting off
5 we would see the new exhibition
6 you wouldn't lie to me

Exercise 5
1 found
2 don't have/didn't have
3 is
4 could drive
5 won
6 lived
7 thought
Students' own answers

Exercise 6
Example answers:
1 If the tickets are not too expensive, I will go to a concert.
2 If I weren't so tired, I would play with my little sister.
3 If it stops raining, I will go for a jog.
4 My parents would buy a bigger car if they could afford it.
5 If I didn't have so much work, I would go for a walk.
6 If I didn't need to study for my exams, I would get a part-time job.

Modal verbs for obligation and permission

Exercise 1
1 must 2 have to 3 have to 4 must
5 has to 6 have to 7 have to

Exercise 2
1 can 2 doesn't have to 3 can't
4 must 5 must 6 needs to
7 are allowed to

Exercise 3
1 can/are allowed to
2 have to
3 don't have to/don't need to/needn't
4 mustn't/can't
5 don't have to/don't need to/needn't
6 Are you allowed to/Can you
7 Does Tina have to/Does Tina need to

Exercise 4
1 allowed 2 mustn't/can't 3 to 4 can
5 to 6 don't 7 mustn't/can't 8 has

Exercise 5
1 have to/need to
2 don't have to/don't need to/needn't
3 can/are allowed to
4 can't/aren't allowed to/mustn't
5 have to/need to

Exercise 6
1 must/have to/need to
2 can't/aren't allowed to
3 have to/need to
4 can't/mustn't/aren't allowed to
5 can/are allowed to
6 don't have to/don't need to/needn't
7 don't have to/don't need to/needn't
8 can/are allowed to

Defining relative clauses

Exercise 1
1 My father drives a car that belongs to his company.
2 There's a college in my city where you can do business studies.
3 I've got a sister that works in a shop.
4 One day I'd like to get a job which includes foreign travel.
5 I've got a part-time job that I don't enjoy.

Exercise 2
1 x
2 where
3 x
4 where
5 who/that
6 x
7 which/that

Exercise 3
1 An igloo is a traditional type of Inuit house which/that is made of snow.
2 A puck is a small flat disc which/that is used instead of a ball in ice hockey.
3 An ice dancer is a performer who/that skates to music.
4 Ski jumping and cross-country skiing are winter sports which/that are becoming more and more popular.
5 This amazing speed skating track is the place where three world records were broken yesterday.

Exercise 4
1 who/that
2 which/that/x
3 where
4 who/that
5 who/that
6 which/that
7 which/that

Exercise 5
1 who/that/x
2 which/that/x
3 which/where/that/x
4 who/that/x
5 who/that
6 which/where/that/x
Students' own answers

Unit 1

Exercise 1
1 think 2 am thinking 3 have
4 is having 5 look 6 are you looking
7 like 8 is having 9 need
10 Do they look

Exercise 2
1 has promised 2 has been rising
3 hasn't heard 4 has known
5 have cut 6 been waiting
7 haven't met 8 been going
9 collected 10 been snowing

Exercise 3
1 Have you been 2 have you been doing
3 have had 4 have you been looking
5 have you had 6 has been producing
7 have never visited 8 's been hanging
9 have been selling
10 have you ever worked

Exercise 4
1 I am having dinner at the moment.
2 I have been looking for my glasses
   for two hours!
3 Laura has known her for ages.
4 I have always preferred surfing to skiing.

Exercise 5
1 was waiting 2 met, has known
3 have you had, looks
4 have been, have never been
5 thinks
6 Is Tim thinking, has been thinking,
   hasn't made
7 look, have lost, have been looking,
   am leaving

Exercise 6
1 haven't seen 2 have you been
3 have just come 4 haven't changed
5 look 6 have put 7 did we last see
8 believe 9 have you been doing
10 have been studying 11 have been
12 have been working/have worked
13 live/am living 14 have you had
15 have been trying
16 have been looking

Unit 2

Exercise 1
1 was sitting 2 had just struck
3 kept 4 thought 5 had gone
6 expected/was expecting 7 didn't make
8 answered 9 decided 10 went
11 had just gone out 12 moved

Exercise 2
1 doing 2 to buy 3 to go
4 playing 5 telling

Exercise 3
1 visiting 2 went 3 to visit 4 say
5 were visiting 6 disappeared
7 waited/were waiting 8 didn't turn
9 had warned 10 not to get 11 to go
12 to find 13 had already been
14 were watching 15 got

Exercise 4
1 have had 2 have seen
3 has been reading 4 has become
5 both answers are correct

Exercise 5
1 haven't seen 2 was driving
3 have been studying 4 skiing
5 made them learn

Exercise 6
1 was considering
2 had been
3 had committed
4 didn't know, has he worked/has he
   been working
5 have you known
6 had never been
7 had happened
8 had lost
9 were playing, slipped, broke
10 was having
11 Have you been waiting
12 arrived, had been
13 have been attending, signed
14 Have you met, joined, has been
   working, decided

Unit 3

Exercise 1
1 must have missed 2 might have missed
3 may be 4 can't be 5 must be
6 might have been 7 could be
8 can't be, can't have done

Exercise 2
1 used to be 2 travelled 3 used to be
4 Did you use to 5 didn't use to like
6 would use

Exercise 3
1 may/might/could 2 would 3 can't
4 used to 5 might/may/could
6 can't have been 7 would 8 used to

Exercise 4
1 have you been working, have been
   working, might not
2 have seen, did you last see
3 was sitting, heard 4 had met
5 to know, had provoked
6 to talk, to keep 7 might have helped
8 feeling 9 broke 10 was, hadn't expected
11 was he thinking, was painting
12 is, could

Exercise 5
1 see 2 must have 3 might have
4 may have 5 have been waiting
6 was going 7 met 8 used to be
9 would go 10 hadn't seen
11 to know 12 going 13 might come
14 not to miss

Unit 4

Exercise 1
1 are coming 2 Shall I go 3 closes
4 won't be able to 5 'll be
6 am going to cook 7 will leave
8 'll answer

Exercise 2
1 will you be doing 2 will have changed
3 will have finished 4 'll be travelling
5 will be watching 6 will be having
7 will have had 8 Will you have checked
9 will be working
10 will you be doing, will be having

Exercise 3
1 have you borrowed
2 have you been reading
3 met, was working
4 got, had lost
5 had already become
6 writing
7 might have left
8 used to be, haven't seen, since

Exercise 4
1 had phoned
2 have never been, invites, will travel
3 have you been queuing, have been
   queuing, will give up
4 finishes/has finished, will do
5 will have saved
6 will be revising
7 was raining, were leaving

Exercise 5
1 had already been
2 am working/will be working
3 go
4 will go
5 will have finished
6 have you been working
7 have been working
8 made
9 've been writing

Unit 5

Exercise 1
1 –, – 2 A, the, the, the
3 the, The, a, the, a 4 a, the, the, the,
The 5 The, The, the, a

Exercise 2
1 Barrie, who lives next door, is having
   a party tonight.
2 She's a teacher.
3 The Atlantic Ocean, which is the
   second largest ocean in the world, lie
   between Europe and America.
4 Lewis Carroll, who wrote *Alice's
   Adventures in Wonderland*, was
   a professor at Oxford University.
5 Lots of people visit the British
   Museum, where parts of the Partheno
   are displayed.
6 That's the film I'd like us to see at the
   weekend.
7 The food we ate at the restaurant by
   the sea was awesome!
8 You will definitely need a pair of jeans
   and a warm sweater.

Exercise 3
1 A person who steals things is a thief. (D
2 The new film by Polański, which was
   well reviewed by the critics, was
   a great success. (ND)
3 The BBC, which had begun sound
   broadcasting in 1922, launched the
   world's first public television service in
   1936. (ND)
4 I need a person who can speak Englis
   fluently. (D)
5 The new London guidebook publishe
   in January this year, which contains lo
   of useful information, will appear in
   bookshops next month. (ND)

Exercise 4
1 were going, started
2 had forgotten, stopped
3 was walking, saw, can't have been
4 didn't always use to be
5 has
6 has bought
7 don't believe
8 has been driving

Exercise 5
1 If you eat vegetables every day, you'll get all the minerals you need.
2 If my friends are online, I'll chat with them.
3 Will you have finished by eight o'clock? / Will you finish by eight o'clock?
4 This time tomorrow we will be skiing in the Alps.
5 By the end of the day, we will have eaten our three portions of vegetables.
6 I saw a shark swimming close to the boat. The shark, which was 2 metres long, followed us for about three miles.

Exercise 6
1 – 2 – 3 – 4 – 5 – 6 the
7 The 8 – 9 used to be 10 the
11 will soon find out 12 will take
13 will have seen 14 still see
15 which 16 has been

Unit 6

Exercise 1
1 lived 2 would give up 3 had 4 had
5 would go, didn't have to

Exercise 2
1 were, would put 2 would think
3 could choose, would you have
4 was/were able to heal 5 didn't need
6 wouldn't play

Exercise 3
1 had seen, would have applied
2 had got, would have become
3 had promoted, would have earned
4 had made, would have gambled
5 had kept, would have lost
6 hadn't thought, wouldn't have been fired
7 had shown, would have repeated

Exercise 4
1 c 2 h 3 g 4 f 5 b 6 a 7 e 8 d

Exercise 5
1 Would you have stopped
2 Would you tell 3 Will you invite
4 had known 5 knew 6 knows

Exercise 6
1 We have travelled a lot since we started working for a travel agency.
2 We'll be working at that time, but by six o'clock we'll have finished.
3 I used to love reading comics when I was a child.
4 The accident would have been much worse if the driver had been driving faster.
5 They were walking to the station when it began to rain. It was then that they realised they had forgotten their umbrellas.

Exercise 7
1 the, 2 –, 3 where 4 –,
5 had been 6 a 7 The
8 wouldn't have recovered 9 had
10 – 11 as soon as 12 lived
13 will go 14 go 15 will be
16 who 17 will be surfing
18 have been surfing 19 doing

Unit 7

Exercise 1
1 She said (that) she didn't like that picture.
2 He replied (that) they had seen her the day before/the previous day.
3 She explained (that) she was late because she had missed the train.
4 He added (that) he didn't want to see that man again.
5 They told us (that) they couldn't come because they were doing their homework then/at that time.
6 He pointed out (that) it had been hot the day before/the previous day.

Exercise 2
1 He asked me if/whether I had seen the film the day before/the previous day.
2 He asked me how my grandmother was.
3 He asked her what her name was.
4 She asked me where I had found the key.
5 I asked her if she was writing a new book.
6 The teacher told us to stop talking.
7 The boss told us not to eat at our desks.

Exercise 3
1 The woman added that John would have to tell her the whole story once again.
2 The girl said the children had already finished the game.
3 The officer asked us if we understood that message.
4 The boy asked the man to play it again.
5 The policeman noticed it was raining.
6 The manager wanted to know why they hadn't talked to the shop assistant.
7 The little girl asked the woman where they had been.

Exercise 4
1 have you had 2 have you been reading
3 arrived, was waiting, had been
4 used to like

Exercise 5
1 You won't get a cat unless you promise to look after it.
2 Pat will be cooking all day tomorrow. She's having guests for dinner.
3 They will have finished dinner by nine o'clock.
4 Mount Vesuvius, which is an active volcano, overlooks the Bay of Naples.
5 If I have enough money, I'll go to Australia. / If I had enough money, I'd go to Australia.
6 If I had known the answer, I wouldn't have asked you to help me. / If I knew the answer, I wouldn't ask you to help me.
7 She asked me if/whether I was good at Maths.

Exercise 6
1 who 2 haven't hurt 3 can't 4 had
5 be playing 6 told 7 had gone
8 said 9 have been 10 you have been

Unit 8

Exercise 1
1 The film was directed by Alfred Hitchcock.
2 A new house is being built.
3 The students were being helped.
4 He will always be remembered.
5 Cheese is made from milk.
6 The picture has been painted by Peter.
7 The keys must be handed in before leaving.
8 All the windows were opened by the children.
9 The two criminals are going to be arrested.
10 A new species of butterfly has been found by scientists in the Amazon rainforest.

Exercise 2
1 I had my teeth checked.
2 I'm having my camera repaired at the moment.
3 They'll have their house painted soon.
4 I have my bank account checked every month.
5 I had my eyes tested.
6 I have just had my car serviced.
7 We've just had our computer repaired

Exercise 3
1 I think I'll have my car repaired.
2 The house was built in 1850.
3 Mr Smith is being interviewed at the moment.
4 I had the meal sent up to my room.
5 Where do you usually have your shoes mended?
6 How often is the cat fed?
7 Can sports equipment be hired?

Exercise 4
1 be 2 it mended 3 told
4 to stay 5 my book was 6 I was
7 a, The, had met 8 Unless

Exercise 5
1 would think
2 would be
3 had seen
4 have left
5 Will you be working, 'll have finished
6 was reading, heard
7 walked/had walked, stopped
8 have you visited
9 have you been studying

Exercise 6
1 who 2 led 3 were willing 4 The
5 by 6 were arrested 7 described
8 were employed 9 had changed
10 were given 11 granted
12 have gained

1.10 Self-check

Vocabulary and Grammar

Exercise 1
1 rebellious
2 down-to-earth
3 fabric
4 hard-wearing
5 brightly-coloured clothes

Exercise 2
1 beanie 2 fleece 3 leggings
4 bangles 5 denim jacket

Exercise 3
1 fashion 2 there 3 fallen
4 underwear 5 waistcoat

Exercise 4
1 don't believe
2 is dancing
3 needs
4 Are you putting
5 doesn't know

Exercise 5
1 has known
2 has been worrying
3 've understood
4 has been singing
5 have been meeting

Exercise 6
1 C 2 B 3 A 4 B 5 A

Use of English

Exercise 7
1 B 2 C 3 B 4 B 5 A

Exercise 8
1 C 2 A 3 C 4 B 5 A

Exercise 9
1 A 2 C 3 A 4 A 5 B

Exercise 10
1 C 2 B 3 A 4 B 5 A

2.10 Self-check

Vocabulary and Grammar

Exercise 1
1 lost 2 teammates 3 pick
4 phase 5 goal

Exercise 2
1 trainer 2 keeps 3 superstitious
4 active 5 repetitive

Exercise 3
1 B
2 C
3 B
4 A
5 B

Exercise 4
1 had trained 2 went 3 ended
4 had surfed 5 hurt

Exercise 5
1 not to get angry 2 jogging
3 join 4 do 5 playing

Exercise 6
1 A 2 B 3 C 4 A 5 A

Use of English

Exercise 7
1 B 2 B 3 C 4 A 5 C

Exercise 8
1 resilience 2 activate 3 supportive
4 powerful 5 decisive

Exercise 9
1 can't stand losing
2 teach me to swim
3 didn't allow me to do
4 had warned me not to climb
5 was telling the team to believe

Exercise 10
1 on 2 off 3 prize 4 went 5 taking

3.10 Self-check

Vocabulary and Grammar

Exercise 1
1 B 2 B 3 A 4 B 5 C

Exercise 2
1 resort 2 business 3 car
4 drive 5 path

Exercise 3
1 downhill
2 jam
3 round-the-world
4 agents
5 cross

Exercise 4
1 must be
2 can't be
3 can't have been
4 could have sprayed
5 must have forgotten

Exercise 5
1 ~~used to be~~ was
2 ~~Would~~ Did
3 ✓
4 ~~wouldn't~~ didn't use to
5 ~~was~~ be

Exercise 6
1 B 2 C 3 B 4 A 5 C

Use of English

Exercise 7
1 A 2 C 3 C 4 A 5 C

Exercise 8
1 didn't use to enjoy flying
2 may be raining / may be rainy
3 can't have got stuck
4 might have moved
5 used to need to have

Exercise 9
1 A 2 A 3 C 4 B 5 A

Exercise 10
1 have been 2 beliefs
3 unfamiliar 4 unthinkable 5 leader

4.10 Self-check

Vocabulary and Grammar

Exercise 1
1 sour 2 balanced 3 stale
4 bland 5 raw

Exercise 2
1 light 2 aubergines 3 long-grain
4 pumpkin 5 wholemeal

Exercise 3
1 consumption 2 sliced 3 standards
4 vegetarian 5 still

Exercise 4
1 I'm going to buy 2 opens
3 Shall 4 will 5 is going

Exercise 5
1 will have gone down
2 you will ('ll) like
3 will have gone
4 won't be working
5 Will you have finished

Exercise 6
1 A 2 B 3 C 4 B 5 C

Use of English

Exercise 7
1 Before the government applies
2 energy consumption will double
3 am going to eat organic food
4 everyone will have already started
5 unless the manufacturing industry does

Exercise 8
1 B
2 A
3 C
4 A
5 C

Exercise 9
1 B 2 A 3 B 4 C 5 C

Exercise 10
1 household 2 voluntary 3 alarming
4 tourist 5 expiry

5.10 Self-check

Vocabulary and Grammar

Exercise 1
1 d light bulbs 2 a panels 3 e river
4 b island 5 c current

Exercise 2
1 broaden 2 gone 3 deepen
4 slept 5 heighten

Exercise 3
1 spring 2 branches 3 pond
4 squirrel 5 hedgehog

Exercise 4
1 a 2 an 3 the 4 The 5 –

Exercise 5

1 Stratford-upon-Avon, where I was brought up, is famous as the birthplace of William Shakespeare.
2 Singapore, which is an island country in south-eastern Asia, is an extremely clean and tidy place.
3 Prince George of Cambridge, whose great grandmother is the Queen of England, was born in 2013.
4 Ganesha, who is a Hindu god, has an elephant's head.
5 Penang, which is an island off the coast of Malaysia, is sometimes called the 'Pearl of the Orient.'

Exercise 6

1 B **2** B **3** B **4** C **5** A

Use of English

Exercise 7

1 came face to face with
2 is made up of
3 dodo died out
4 eventually died from
5 reached for my bag

Exercise 8

1 is there a park near
2 the man who shot a bird
3 is the most polluted
4 a tree with a trunk / which has a trunk
5 the trail (that/which) we followed

Exercise 9

1 renewable 2 rising 3 dying
4 difference 5 environmental

Exercise 10

1 B
2 A
3 B
4 C
5 A

6.10 Self-check

Vocabulary and Grammar

Exercise 1

1 B **2** A **3** C **4** A **5** B

Exercise 2

1 leg **2** heart **3** hand
4 thighs **5** ribs

Exercise 3

1 sore finger
2 shaving cut
3 stomach pain
4 flu epidemic
5 nut allergy

Exercise 4

1 didn't feel **2** had **3** didn't drive
4 would pay **5** was/were

Exercise 5

1 would've hit / hadn't turned
2 wouldn't have offered / had known
3 had hurt / wouldn't have played
4 hadn't eaten / wouldn't have felt sick
5 would've been / hadn't lost

Exercise 6

1 B **2** A **3** B **4** C **5** C

Use of English

Exercise 7

1 C **2** C **3** C **4** B **5** A

Exercise 8

1 if I had known
2 in order not to be
3 my jacket so as to keep
4 wishes she wasn't/weren't allergic
5 didn't have a bruise

Exercise 9

1 not to take part
2 train for the
3 wishes he knew
4 if I were
5 you would not have been

Exercise 10

1 daily **2** sprained **3** obviously
4 surgery **5** operation

7.10 Self-check

Vocabulary and Grammar

Exercise 1

1 played **2** improve **3** enhances
4 released **5** view

Exercise 2

1 beat **2** signed **3** uploaded
4 felt **5** stirred

Exercise 3

1 creation
2 audience
3 entertainment
4 singer-songwriter
5 drummer

Exercise 4

1 ~~I was watching~~ she was watching
2 ~~didn't go~~ hadn't been
3 ~~yesterday~~ the day before
4 ~~we'll meet~~ we'd meet
5 ~~can't be~~ couldn't have been/couldn't be

Exercise 5

1 I was sure
2 I had ever studied drama
3 hadn't
4 I could act
5 to show him

Exercise 6

1 B **2** A **3** C **4** B **5** C

Use of English

Exercise 7

1 memorisation **2** engagement
3 entertainment **4** accompaniment
5 deeply

Exercise 8

1 B **2** A **3** B **4** A **5** C

Exercise 9

1 find it easy to follow
2 plays the part of
3 taken by surprise by
4 is based on
5 reviewed positively

Exercise 10

1 C
2 B
3 A
4 C
5 B

8.10 Self-check

Vocabulary and Grammar

Exercise 1

1 C **2** A **3** B **4** A **5** C

Exercise 2

1 fulfilled **2** anonymous **3** criminal
4 cynical/critical **5** trivial

Exercise 3

1 was severely punished
2 wasn't a shoplifter
3 arsonist was
4 violent muggings
5 committed piracy

Exercise 4

1 was hunted
2 has been burgled
3 is being renovated
4 was being washed
5 will be missed

Exercise 5

1 has had her phone fixed
2 is having his health checked
3 had my headphones replaced
4 Have you (ever) had your phone taken away
5 Has Helen had her make-up done

Exercise 6

1 B **2** B **3** A **4** B **5** C

Use of English

Exercise 7

1 criminals **2** suspect **3** robber
4 mugger **5** burglaries

Exercise 8

1 prepared herself for the trial
2 thieves were charged with stealing
3 promised one another [that] we
4 had broken it themselves
5 How many robberies are committed

Exercise 9

1 C **2** B **3** B **4** A **5** C

Exercise 10

1 was warned to put
2 the latest report sent to
3 hasn't been arranged
4 are often helped by
5 they were being followed by

Pearson Education Limited
KAO Two
KAO Park
Hockham Way,
Harlow, Essex,
CM17 9SR England
and Associated Companies throughout the world.

www.english.com/focus

© Pearson Education Limited 2020

Focus 3 Second Edition Workbook

The right of Daniel Brayshaw, Dean Russell, Anna Osborn and Amanda Davies to be identified as authors of this Work has been asserted by them in accordance with the Copyright, Designs and Patents Act 1988.

First published 2020
Fifteenth impression 2024

ISBN: 978-1-292-23402-1

Set in Avenir LT Pro
Printed in Slovakia by Neografia

Acknowledgements
The publishers and authors would like to thank the following people and institutions for their feedback and comments during the development of the material:

Humberto Santos Duran
Anna Maria Grochowska
Beata Gruszczyńska
Inga Lande
Magdalena Loska
Barbara Madej
Rosa Maria Maldonado
Juliana Queiroz Pereira
Tomasz Siuta
Elżbieta Śliwa
Katarzyna Ślusarczyk
Katarzyna Tobolska
Renata Tomaka-Pasternak
Beata Trapnell
Aleksandra Zakrzewska
Beata Zygadlewicz-Kocuś

The publishers are grateful to the following for permission to reproducecopyright material:

Text
American Library Association: Attributed to Mead in: Robert P. Doyle (1993) Banned Books Week '93: celebrating the freedom to read. American Library Association. p.62 90; **Telegraph Media Group:** From Norwegian-town-places-mirrors-on-hillsides-to-shine-light-into-valley 64, From World News Northern Asia USA Australia Boys basketball dreams becomes a reality 22, From Sam Stern's tips and recipes for student cooks 50, From Student recipes how to survive student catering 50; From The_Shawshank_ Redemption 106; **Villard Books (Random House):** Wake up and Smell the Coffee!: Advice, Wisdom, and Uncommon Good Sense Ann Landers 15 Sep 1996 90.

Images
123RF.com: Andor Bujdoso 48, Andrey Gudkov 69, Andrey Kobylko 33, Anna Ivanova 74, Anna Kucherova 46, Cathy Yeulet 19, denisfilm 5, Dinis Tolipov 55, Diyana Dimitrova 71, 138, dizanna 102, Dmitriy Shironosov 109, dmosreg 71, dolgachov 74, Elnur Amikishiyev 41, Engin Korkmaz 4, Fabio Formaggio 15, famveldman 74, Faysal Farhan 107, foodandmore 53, gitanna 46, indigolotos 46, Jos? Alfonso De Tomas Gargantilla 19, Kostyantine Pankin 111, Kriangsit Pintatib 74, Krissada Chuanyen 46, Lesia Sementsova 74, Lulia Lun 4, Marina Kirezhenkova 74, Michael Pettigrew 74, Michael Simons 74, natika 46, nevarpp 69, Nigel Spooner 13, Olena Danileiko 57, pahham 74, peppers 46, rawpixel 139, rclassenlayouts 46, Ronnachai Limpakdeesavasd 138, Sergey Pivovarov 46, Sommai Larkjit 46, sotnichenko 74, stockbroker 87, szefei 74, Tanat Loungtip 15, 134, Tatiana Krayushkina 71, 138, yasonya 46, Yuliia Kononenko 57; **Alamy Stock Photo:** AF archive 95, Alex Segre 43, 136, Artit Oubkaew 43, 136, David Wall 106, Elizaveta Galitckaia 43, 136, Hemis 35, Hero Images Inc. 85, imagebroker 26, Michael Preston 8, Myron Standret 36, Paul Mayall Italy 43, 136, ZUMA Press, Inc. 106; **DK Images:** Eric Thomas 20, Mockford and Bonetti 32, Steve Gorton 10; **Fotolia.com:** 50, 52, alswart 96, dabldy 60, Frank Boston 49, ikonoklast_hh 14, JackF 32, Neyak 32, nickolae 66, oksix 110, pixarno 76, roza 32, Tom Wang 4, vbaleha 8, Николай Григорьев 62, 62; **Getty Images:** AFP / Stringer 64, 64, Alina555 141, Andrew Aitchison 105, Brendan Hoffman/Stringer 78, Caiaimage/Chris Ryan 85, Francois De Heel 36, Kevin Winter / Fox 22, Lambert 92; **Pearson Education Ltd:** Naki Kouyioumtzis 32; **Shutterstock.com:** 8, 8, 112, ABB Photo 43, 136, Anton Gvozdikov 99, AS Food studio 137, Axel Bueckert 4, Birgit Reitz-Hofmann 99, 140, Blazej Lyjak 43, Blueskynet 88, bokan 99, 140, CartoonMini 97, CC7 71, 138, CosminIftode 135, cunaplus 113, Dave Turner 32, David Fisher 50, Dmitry Morgan 46, Ellya 9, Everett Collection 92, Fifian Iromi 24, Food_Photography 137, G-Stock Studio 27, Gajendra Bhati 15, 134, George Rudy 99, 140, Gordan 131, grynold 128, Hurst Photo 71, 138, Iakov Filimonov 43, 136, Iryna Inshyna 36, Kathy Hutchins 108, Kayo 99, 140, kojihirano 61, kondr.konst 140, Lapina 109, LesPalenik 92, Ljupco Smokovski 83, Lubo Ivanko 103, Magdalena Wielobob 15, 134, Mahmoud Farouk 15, 134, malko 127, Max Lashcheuski 46, muzs 29, nito 15, 134, Oleksandr Fediuk 15, 134, oneinchpunch 134, ostill 115, Paul Prescott 136, Rich Carey 73, sirtravelalot 141, Stas Moroz 40, Stokkete 99, 140, Suphaksorn Thongwongboot 47, Sylverarts 18, 88, Thongchai S 139, Vaclav Mach 71, 138, Viorel Sima 104, Vitalii Petrushenko 113, Vlad1988 29, wavebreakmedia 99, 140, zhangjin_net 135, Zyn Chakrapong 71, 138

Cover images: Back: Shutterstock.com

Illustrations
Illustrated by Ewa Olejnik p. 6, 11, 28, 32, 34, 39, 56, 81, 95, Joanna Balicka p. 63,
Jacek Krajewski (Studio Gardengraf) p. 70.

All other images © Pearson Education Limited.

Every effort has been made to trace the copyright holders and we apologise in advance for any unintentional omissions. We would be pleased to insert the appropriate acknowledgement in any subsequent edition of this publication.